Cesar Millan, star of *Dog Whisperer*, founded the Dog Psychology Center in Los Angeles. In addition to Cesar's educational seminars and work with unstable dogs, he and his wife have founded the Cesar and Ilusion Millan Foundation, a nonprofit organization dedicated to providing financial support and rehabilitation expertise to shelters. A native of Culican, Mexico, Cesar lives in Los Angeles with his wife, Ilusion, and their two sons, Andre and Calvin.

Melissa Jo Peltier, an executive producer and writer of *Dog Whisperer*, has been honoured for her film and television writing and directing with an Emmy, a Peabody, and more than fifty other awards. She lives in Nyack, New York, with her husband, writer-director John Gray, and stepdaughter, Caitlin.

Cesar Millan

WITH MELISSA JO PELTIER

BE THE
PACK LEADER

USE CESAR'S WAY TO TRANSFORM YOUR DOG . . .
AND YOUR LIFE

HODDER

First published in Great Britain in 2008 by Hodder & Stoughton
An Hachette Livre UK company

Offset by arrangement with Harmony Books, an imprint of the Crown Publishing
Group, a division of Random House, Inc., New York.

First published in paperback in 2008

26

A CIP catalogue record for this title is available from the British Library

ISBN 978 0 340 97645 6

Printed and bound in Great Britain by Clays Ltd, Elcograf S.p.A.

Hodder & Stoughton policy is to use papers that are natural, renewable
and recyclable products and made from wood grown in sustainable
forests. The logging and manufacturing processes are expected to
conform to the environmental regulations of the country of origin.

Hodder & Stoughton Ltd
338 Euston Road
London NW1 3BH

www.hodder.co.uk

*Dedicated to my wife, Ilusion, who is the inspiration
and the source of my leadership*

and

*to you, the reader, because I genuinely believe if we can change
our own lives and become better pack leaders to our dogs, to our
families, and to ourselves, then together we can change the world*

ACKNOWLEDGMENTS

n my last book, *Cesar's Way,* I thanked my family, my role models, and all the people who have helped me on my amazing journey to becoming "the Dog Whisperer." Of course, I remember them always, and without them this book would not have been possible. For *Be the Pack Leader,* however, I want to acknowledge all women, and the special power that all women hold—even though they may not realize it yet. I worry about the fact that my kids are growing up in a very unstable world; a world that is going to require some incredible pack leaders if it is going to be made right again. I believe that women hold the key to helping put our world back into balance. But they can't do that until men truly acknowledge and honor the unique wisdom and the leadership women have to offer—and until women can embrace the pack leaders within themselves. More than most men, many women seem to instinctively know that leadership doesn't mean negative energy. It doesn't mean pitting one person against another, one country against another, one religion against another. I also believe that women are more likely than men to act for the good of the pack. And like dogs, we humans need to remember that without the pack we are nothing. I have seen more compassion from women in my life than I have seen from men. Women have taught me true calm-assertive leadership, and because of them I have become a better, more balanced leader in all areas of my life, not just with dogs.

Dogs are all about the pack. They are guided by an instinctual way of being that we humans can have access to if we simply say, "I am here to live every moment to the fullest; to fulfill my own life and to help fulfill everybody else around me." I owe a huge debt of gratitude to dogs for the values they have taught me—such as honesty, integrity, consistency, and loyalty. These are the qualities that make a true pack leader.

IN ADDITION, MY co-author and I wish to thank:
Scott Miller, our literary agent at Trident Media—you are the epitome of class. At Random House, Shaye Areheart, Julia Pastore, Kira Stevens, and Tara Gilbride—we're so blessed to be working with you again. Laureen Ong, John Ford, Michael Cascio, Char Serwa, and Mike Beller at the National Geographic Channel—we're proud to be starting our fourth season on the network. And once again, Nat Geo's crack publicity department under Russell Howard has outdone themselves, especially Chris Albert, who's been with us through all the ups and downs yet always manages to keep smiling. At MPH, thanks to Bonnie Peterson, George Gomez, Nicholas Ellingsworth, Todd Carney, and Christine Lochmann for your help in compiling all the

photos and graphics, and to Heather Mitchell for fact checking and research. Special gratitude to Alice Clearman, Ph.D., and Charles Rinhimer, D.V.M., for your invaluable expertise and input, and to Tom Rubin for your legal assistance. Clint Rowe, it was an honor to work with you and Wilshire, and we are very grateful for your wisdom and insight. Thanks also to producers Kay Sumner and Sheila Emery, and to SueAnn Fincke, who *is* the *Dog Whisperer* show. And of course, endless praise for the hard-working *Dog Whisperer* staff, crew, and editors.

MELISSA JO PELTIER wishes to thank:

Jim Milio and Mark Hufnail—it's been a long, hard road yet here we still are! Yes, you guys truly *are* the two best partners in the known universe.

As always, gratitude for my dad, Ed Peltier, and thanks to my incredible circle of supportive friends (in Manhattan and Nyack), especially Tamara, Gail, Everett, and, most important, Victoria A. My beautiful stepdaughter, Caitlin Gray, never fails to make me smile, even when I'm stressed.

And to my amazing husband, John Gray, thank you for being both my Safe Harbor in every storm as well as my forever partner in our Moveable Feast.

Last but not least, Ilusion Millan, I am so grateful for your generosity of spirit, and, Cesar, bless you for changing my life and helping me to become a much more calm-assertive, stable, and balanced pack leader to the animals and the humans in my life.

CONTENTS

PART TWO

Balancing Ourselves

INTRODUCTION

This past year has been exciting and a little bit overwhelming for me, my family, and the people I work with. There have been television shows to film, seminars to give, and more dogs—and people—to help. We've all been very blessed. But between my first book, *Cesar's Way,* and this one, my canine companions have been continuing to teach me new lessons about dog behavior—and about human behavior as well. Over the past year, I have experienced so many new types of cases and learned so many new things. I have studied more behavioral and scientific research, and joined forces with and studied techniques of those who prefer other methods of helping dogs. All this has deepened and enhanced my perspective. I also took to heart some of the criticisms I received about the last book. Some readers wanted more case studies; others wanted more hands-on, step-by-step instruction. The last request is the hardest to accomplish, since *I am not a dog trainer.* To train your dog to sit, stay, or roll over, there is a very specific progression of steps to go through. To rehabilitate an unbalanced dog, I almost always work from instinct with the dog right in front of me, and my core fulfillment formula of exercise, discipline, and affection, in that order, are still the backbone of my methods. That said, we will be providing easily remembered, practical tips throughout this book, and are adding an entire, easy-to-reference section at the end of the book, with step-by-step suggestions for very specific situations.

We will also be including some amazing true success stories throughout the text—many of which I didn't have access to until my show became more popular. We receive literally thousands of letters each month and the stories are truly amazing, reminding me to give thanks that our work is now accessible to so many more people. These letters were what inspired the promise of this book's subtitle—that you'll be able to use Cesar's way to transform your dog *and* your life. In fact, many people who began using the power of calm-assertive energy to help have better relationships with their dogs are reporting that their human relationships—with their kids, their bosses, and their spouses— are becoming more manageable as well.

The goal of this book is to help you strengthen the bond between you and your dog—but I hope it will also show you how closely linked humans and dogs are—and how much our dogs have to teach us all. The "power of the pack" idea doesn't just apply to dogs. It applies to another species of pack animals whose destinies have been intertwined with those of dogs for tens of thousands of years. That would be our very own species, *Homo sapiens.*

After you read *Be the Pack Leader* I sincerely hope you will feel more strongly the link between you and Mother Nature, and learn to become more in tune with your instinctual self. My goal for you is that you use the power of calm-assertive energy to become the pack leader in every area of your life, and open up to you a new dimension of living that you never before realized was possible.

Now this is the Law of the Jungle—as old and as true
  as the sky;
And the Wolf that shall keep it may prosper, but the Wolf
  that shall break it must die.
As the creeper that girdles the tree-trunk, the Law runneth
  forward and back
For the strength of the Pack is the Wolf, and the strength of
  the Wolf is the Pack.
  —Rudyard Kipling, *The Law of the Jungle*

Mirror, Mirror?

*Money will buy you a pretty good dog, but it won't
buy the wag of his tail.* —*Josh Billings*

*K*oyaanisqatsi is a Hopi Indian term that roughly translates
in English as "life out of balance." I learned this from
watching a 1982 documentary film directed by Godfrey
Reggio, which shows, without commentary, a series of powerful
images edited to the music of Philip Glass, reflecting the impact
of humans and their technology on the planet. The subtext, of

course, is that the rise of technology has knocked life on earth off-kilter.

Don't worry, this isn't an environmental book. It's a book about the connection between dogs and people. But the term *Koyannisqatsi* has a special resonance for me because, in a way, much of this book is about how we humans are living our lives out of balance. We are in the process of losing the instinctual sides of ourselves that make us animal first and human second. And instinct equals common sense.

I believe a healthy human being must be balanced in four areas of his or her life. First, there is the intellectual area. This is the side of our natures that most Westerners have down pat. We are masters of reason and logic. In America especially, the lifestyle most people lead here is very intellectual one. We communicate with one another almost exclusively through language. We send worded messages on the Internet and on cell phones; we read; we watch television. We have lots of education and more information at our fingertips than ever before, which allows some of us to live almost 100 percent in our minds. We agonize about the past and fantasize about the future. All too often, we become so dependent on our intellectual sides that we forget that there is much, much more to this amazing world we live in.

Next there is the emotional side. Growing up in Mexico, I was taught that only women can have emotions. Women carry the whole emotional load there, and in many other third world countries, as well. My father taught me that to cry was to be weak, to be a sissy. Men in my culture are conditioned from very young ages to suppress our feelings and hide them under bravado. Pretty soon, we are so distanced from our emotions that we don't even recognize them when they come up. When I came to America, I saw that compared to what I'd known in Mexico, everybody seemed free to show their emotions—even men. I saw Dr. Phil telling men that it was okay to cry, and asking them to talk about what they were feeling. "What?" I wondered. "How do they even know what they're feeling?" That's how messed up I was in terms of emotions. Once I married my wife, I had to get with the program and learn to communicate, learn to use my emotional side. Until I was able to access my emotions, I couldn't really become balanced. I believe that countries like Mexico can never be healthy societies until they learn the importance of emotions—and to value women and children, which is where most of the world's emotional power currently lies.

Another part of being human is our spiritual side. Of course, many of us fulfill our spiritual needs by going to a church, synagogue, mosque, or temple, or engaging in other forms of meditation or reverence. This is often a peaceful respite where we can get in tune with a deeper part of ourselves than the mundane part that gets up, reads the newspaper, and goes to work every morning. But spiritual fulfillment doesn't have to mean belief in a religion or disbelief in science. In the words of the late Carl Sagan, "Science is not only compatible with spirituality; it is a profound source of spirituality." Spirituality takes many forms, but one thing is known—it is a deeply ingrained part of being human that has existed since early civilization. Whether one believes in an unseen, all-knowing force, or the wonder of science and the universe, or simply the beauty of the human spirit, nearly every one of us feels an inner longing to feel part of something bigger than ourselves.

Finally, there is the instinctual side of our human nature. To be instinctual means to be clearheaded, open, and aware of the signals we are getting from other people, animals, and our environment all the time. It means understanding our connection to our natural selves and the natural world, and acknowledging our interdependence with that world. I spent much of my childhood in a third-world, rural environment where we had to be in tune with Mother Nature for our very survival. When my family moved to the city, I began to feel a barrier come up between my instinctual self and the civilized life I was now supposed to live. And once I moved to urban Southern California, I observed yet another layer of intellectual, "rational" living that separated people even farther from their instinctual side.

Humans will follow intellectual leaders. They will also follow spiritual leaders, and they will follow emotional leaders. Humans are the only species on earth that will follow a totally unbalanced, unstable leader. Animals, however—though I believe they possess an emotional and spiritual side—will *only* follow instinctual leaders. *I believe it is our loss of connection with our instinctual side that prevents us from being effective pack leaders for our dogs.* Perhaps it is also why we also seem to be failing at being positive guardians of our planet.

Without being in touch with our instinctual side, we are dangerously unbalanced. Most of us probably aren't aware of it. But believe me, our dogs know it; we absolutely cannot fool them. And in all the unstable behaviors that my clients call me in to "fix," they are unknowingly sounding the alarm for us to get back to our instinctual side and realize balance. Balance comes from having all four parts of ourselves—intellectual, emotional, spiritual, and instinctual—in alignment. It is only through balance that we can become fully realized creatures of Mother Nature.

The good news is that our instinctual selves are lying deep within us, just waiting to be rediscovered. And our best friends and companions—our dogs—can be our guides to reawakening our instinctual natures. In this book, I invite you to learn about true life balance from those who have already learned these lessons from their dogs. Our dogs are our mirrors—but do we dare look into their eyes and truly see our reflections?

The Tycoon

I was in New York City with my wife and kids to attend the fifth anniversary party for the National Geographic Channel, when I got a call from a former client. She had referred me to a friend of hers, a tycoon and a very powerful man.* He wanted to see me right away, because, in his words, "My dogs are about to kill each other." When I heard the amount of money he wanted to pay me, I honestly nearly fainted. Though of course the money was very tempting, that wasn't the only reason I went. I was by now insanely curious. What would make such a rich and powerful figure want to throw away that kind of money to a "dog behavior expert" he doesn't know, just to help two dogs? And how could a man who obviously was a supersuccessful "pack leader" in his own life have let his dogs get so far out of control?

When I arrived at the Tycoon's penthouse apartment, I was stunned by the high ceilings, marble floors, and dazzling, priceless artwork everywhere. I'd never seen a place like that before in my life. But instantly, my instinctual side began to pick up on an unbalanced energy. The maid who opened the door and took my

*Names and details of this case have been changed.

coat seemed quiet and nervous, as if she was afraid to do something wrong. And when the man himself came out and introduced himself to me, I could see her body language diminish even more. (Body language—no matter what species is displaying it—is the secret language of Mother Nature.) When the Tycoon addressed himself to me, I could clearly tell that he saw me, too, as a kind of servant.

I looked him over as I always do a prospective client—simply observing energy and body language, and comparing how they do or do not mesh with the words coming out of his mouth. The Tycoon wasn't a tall man but he carried himself proudly; his advancing age only evident by the thinning hair on the top of his head. Most interesting were his eyes. They were incredibly intense—showing an amazing intellect—but as my observant wife later described them, "They had a glaze over them, as if he were looking at you, but calculating his next deal at the same time. He wasn't *with* you, he was trying to figure out if he could make you into an asset."

Whenever I'm in a situation such as this one, I remind myself that I'm there for the dogs, *not* the powerful client. I also remember that the dogs do not recognize wealth and artwork and what we call power in the human world. They only seek out balance. And of course, by then, I knew for certain that I was not walking into a balanced household. All I could do was remark on how lovely his home was and ask him, "So how can I help you?"

The Tycoon told me his dogs were impossible and couldn't be in the same room together because they'd attack and try to kill each other. He immediately blamed the situation on his assistant, "Mary," saying that she had caused the behavior because she spoiled the dogs too much. That was another red flag for me.

Whenever a client immediately blames another person for a dog's problems, I remember the age-old adage "Point a finger at me and there's three more pointing back at you." It's a sign that a person isn't grounded and isn't looking to take responsibility for his or her own actions. But of course, I had to meet the dogs for myself.

Willy and Kid were both little gray miniature schnauzers, living in the lap of luxury, each in his separate room. They were absolutely cute and beautifully groomed. As soon as they appeared, this Tycoon who had appeared so intimidating a minute ago turned into a total softie. "Hey, Willy, hey, Kid." His voice got higher and his face relaxed. Even the glaze over his eyes disappeared. "You gotta fix these dogs, man. These dogs are my life." And by the desperation in his previously gruff and cocky tone of voice, I knew how much he meant it.

Privately, I was already wondering why this man seemed to have no emotion invested in any human being around him but had such a huge amount of emotion invested in these little dogs. But first, I had to deal with the immediate issue: Could these dogs be together without a fight? Of course they could! I first established dominance with Willy in one room, then with Kid in another room. Within a few minutes, I created a strategy for them to be together by addressing the behavior of the dog who was at the highest level of energy and aggression at that moment—in this case, it happened to be the Tycoon's favorite, Kid. The Tycoon had been blaming Willy all along, since Willy was the newer dog, but it turned out that Kid was starting most of the conflicts between the two dogs. Kid was not a dominant or aggressive dog by nature, and needed very little correction to get the picture. I was now the one in control, and I was telling him, "No fighting with your brother." Suddenly, right in front of the Tycoon's eyes, there were Willy and

Kid, getting along just fine. Was the Tycoon appreciative? Certainly not at first; that wasn't his style. It became apparent that he equated showing favor toward anyone to be a show of weakness. "Maybe *you* did that, but my staff can't. There's no way in the world we can put them together like that. They're going to kill each other." No matter what I tried to say to him or to explain to him how simply he and his staff could do exactly what I had just done, he kept returning to his negative, fearful memories. He kept being panicky, but with an angry, accusatory edge.

During that first session, I came to realize I had very little hope of getting through to him at that moment. After all, like most of my clients, he had hired me to help *his dogs,* not to help *himself.* But while most other clients eventually open up to at least looking at how their own behavior is reflected in their dogs, it was clear that Mr. Tycoon was certain *he* didn't need any help. He continued to blame his assistant, his staff, practically the rest of Manhattan for the problem. While I tried to get through to him, I noticed he would not make any eye contact. He was looking at his watch, eyes darting distractedly all around the room. In the animal world, we call that avoidance behavior. Nature deals with threats in four ways—fight, flight, avoidance, or submission. I was threatening his vision of the world, and he was fighting, fleeing, and avoiding—right on cue. Today wasn't the day for this powerful tycoon to face how his own problems were reflected in his dogs' behavior.

But that day was about to arrive.

Dogs Under Pressure

Like Willy and Kid, many of America's dogs are living under the pressure of too-high expectations from their human owners.

"Pressure?" you ask. "I treat my dogs better than my kids. My dogs get anything and everything they want. What kind of pressure is that?"

I've got news for you. Every time you humanize your dog and expect him to fulfill the position of an absent child, lover, friend, or parent in your life, you are putting unrealistic expectations on him. You are taking away his dignity, the dignity of being a dog. And a dog is part of Mother Nature, which means he is naturally wired to expect order in his life, to expect that he must work for food and water and must follow the rules and guidelines of an orderly social system, under the watch of a trusted pack leader. If you are not giving your dog these things, yet you are projecting on him all the emotions, affection, and intimacy that you lack with the humans in your life, then you are being very unfair to your dog—and you may well be the cause of his or her bad behavior.

What evidence do I have that we in Western society—particularly in America—are pressuring our dogs to fill inappropriate voids in our unbalanced human lives? First of all, I have my clients. In the following pages, you will read about some case studies from both my private work and my television series that dramatically illustrate how the owners' various psychological needs were being unfairly projected onto their dogs. But there's other evidence, too.

Take, for example, this survey of 1,019 pet owners, conducted by the American Animal Hospital Association in 2004.[1] The study asks this question: *You're stranded on a deserted island. Which would you rather have for companionship—a human or animal?* Think about it for a minute. These respondents could choose whomever they wanted to share the island with—Angelina Jolie,

Brad Pitt, Jennifer Lopez, Antonio Banderas. As devoted as I am to my Dog Psychology Center pack, I would choose my wife, Ilusion, hands down.

But who did the survey respondents pick? Fifty percent of them picked their *dog or cat*!

The survey also showed that 80 percent of the pet owners listed "companionship" as their primary reason for owning a pet, as opposed to a playmate for a child, protection, breeding for profit, or other reasons. Seventy-two percent of pet owners cited "affection" as their pet's most appealing trait; 79 percent routinely gave their pets holiday and/or birthday gifts; 33 percent spoke to their pets through the phone or answering machine; and 62 percent admitted signing letters or cards from themselves and their pets.

Here's another fascinating statistic: A 2006 study by geriatric studies researchers at St. Louis University School of Medicine found that senior citizens in nursing homes felt much less lonely after spending time alone with a dog than they did when they visited with a dog and other people.[2] The upside is that the animals relieved their loneliness. And animals do have that power; I'll talk about that later in the book. But the downside is they identified more with the animal than with other members of their own species.

People Who Live in Glass Houses . . .

There's a saying that "People who live in glass houses shouldn't throw stones." Well, I have to reveal my own glass house. It's a pretty fragile one, but through the school of hard knocks, I've finally learned that it's not a weakness to admit a weakness.

DOG PSYCHOLOGY BASICS

- Dogs come into the world using their nose first, then their eyes, then their ears. Smell is their strongest sense. "I'll believe it if I see it" for dogs translates to "I'll believe it if I smell it." So don't bother yelling at them; it's the energy and scent they pay attention to, not your words.

- Dogs are communicating with one another (and other animals) all the time using scent, body language, and energy. They are also communicating with *you* all the time, though you may not be aware of the signals you are sending. You absolutely *cannot lie* to a dog about how you are feeling.

- Dogs have an ingrained pack mentality. If you're not asserting leadership over your dog, your dog will try to compensate by showing dominant or unstable behavior.

- Dogs never "think they are humans," as many pet owners would like to imagine. They are exceptionally happy just being dogs. If you are telling people your dog thinks he's a person, chances are he's a dog who knows he's *your* leader.

- In a dog's world, you're either stable or unstable, a leader or a follower.

- A dog's natural "goal" is to be connected, to live harmoniously, grounded, and balanced, in tune with Mother Nature.

- Dogs live *in the moment*. They don't reminisce about the past or worry about the future; therefore, they can move on from unstable behavior very quickly—*if* we let them.

When I first came to America, I totally believed that my relationships with dogs would ultimately mean more to my life than my relationships with humans. I mean, women were for pleasure, and men were for interacting with in the working world. Nothing more. Why bother with people when you had dogs?

I grew up in Mexico, where my family went back and forth from my grandfather's farm in the countryside to the bustling city of Mazatlán, where we went to school and my father made his living. I never liked the city and always longed for the simpler, more natural life at the farm. In the city, among the throngs of people, I learned all the human ways of gaining power and status—work, money, jobs, grades, sex—but I never felt that the "real me" fit into that equation. My affinity with dogs was my center—it kept me going and moving toward my dream. It also gave me nonhuman companions who fulfilled my emotional needs for acceptance and love. Among the dogs, I didn't have to worry about being judged like I did when I was with people. The dogs accepted me as their pack leader without question or judgment.

I think many people can identify with my feelings back then. A dog is not critical of you, and he lives in the moment, so he naturally forgives any mistakes you might make. He is always loyal and trustworthy. Since I viewed peopled as critical, unforgiving, and untrustworthy, dogs were for me, by far the better choice for companions.

Years later, my wife, Ilusion, woke me up to the realization that you can't just "dump" your whole species simply because you've had a few bad encounters with some of its members. What other species on the planet does that? None! *Intimacy* is a greater goal to seek—with one's wife, children, parents, and friends. That true knowledge of intimacy within our own species will allow us to pass it along to interspecies relations. After years of working with but being puzzled by American dogs, I soon realized that there was a line that separated people who loved animals into those whose cups were almost equally full with human and animal love, and those whose cups were very much weighted in one direction. Without Ilusion, who knows which way I would have gone? After all, animals do offer us unconditional love. But they do not fulfill all the needs of our species. And more importantly, just because you and your dog share unconditional love does not mean you have a healthy or balanced dog.

The Tycoon Transformed

Clearly, my new friend the Tycoon is a prime example of a person whose emotional cup was tipping over when it came to his dogs, but running on empty when it came to his human relationships. He left the first session still blaming his assistant, Mary, for the dogs' behavior.

The next step in my relationship with the Tycoon was part two of the dogs' rehabilitation process: socializing them with other dogs at my Dog Psychology Center in Los Angeles. Believe it or not, he put each dog separately in his private jet and flew each one across the country to Los Angeles, accompanied by his assistant. Think about it. Four cross-country trips made by a jet carrying only one dog and one assistant each time! This was a man who guarded every one of his billions of pennies dearly, so you can imagine how much those dogs were worth to him psychologically and emotionally. Unfortunately, there were few people in his life whom he could feel this way about. While working with the dogs at my center, my most important job was to teach

his assistant Mary how to handle the two of them together with
calm and assertive leadership. But there was a huge roadblock—
she was clearly terrified of failing. If she failed and the dogs got
hurt, she would be the one blamed, and her boss would not only
be enraged over the situation with the dogs, he would also un-
leash all his frustration from everything else in his life on her and
the rest of his staff. Between the time I saw the Tycoon again and
while I was working on the dogs, I had a chance to interview several members of his staff, who all shared the same extreme fear of
this man. Of course, they were all grown-ups, and they did have
free will. Any one of them could have quit at any time. They
didn't have to be victims. But I know from my work with dogs
and with people that even the slightest bit of negative energy can
have a ripple effect in any community, whether it be a classroom,
a company, a country, or a dog pack. Extreme negative energy,
like psychological depression, can truly make people *or* animals
believe they are helpless or "stuck." And clearly, this man's negative energy was powerful. His staff members even claimed the
lights in his penthouse would blink on and off when he was on
his way home. Whether they were imagining it or not, he definitely was controlling them through their fear.

Once at the center, my regular pack of dogs helped both Willy
and Kid finally learn how to be *dogs* again. Willy and Kid each
learned how to approach other dogs politely, nose first, smelling
in order to get to know each other—not immediately going into
defensive or attack mode. They learned how to walk with a pack
and feel part of a "family." They learned how to play with others
of their kind and to respect all humans as pack leaders. But of
course, the dogs weren't the only ones who needed rehabilitation. As is almost always the case with my clients, the humans

were the root of the problem. Since I didn't have access to the Tycoon quite yet, I did an energy makeover on Mary. Mary was a smart, efficient, extremely capable woman. She could do a million things at once. But with Willy and Kid, she lost all her confidence. She was terrified that if anything went wrong with them while they were in her care, her boss would fire her. Mary and I worked on her calm and assertive energy. We worked on breathing and posture, and on taking the mind to a place of pure positivity and superconfidence. Mary was already a pack leader at heart—she just didn't know it! Later, Mary's new calm-assertive energy would pay off in ways that she never imagined. But by the end of our time together, she felt totally confident in handling Willy and Kid.

Now it was time for me to meet the Tycoon again, face-to-face, at his mansion in Beverly Hills. All the warnings from his staff had made me even more determined to confront him about how his unbalanced life was hurting his dogs—not to mention everyone around him. "No one talks to Mr. Tycoon like that!" Mary warned me. But hey, that man had entrusted me with a task, and I was going to complete it to the best of my ability. He was definitely going to get every penny of his money's worth—whether he wanted to or not. I had nothing to lose—and the dogs had everything to gain.

Facing the Mirror

The Tycoon and I sat together in his posh living room and I calmly but firmly addressed him, suggesting that perhaps he was the problem, not his dogs and not his assistants. Once again the avoidance behavior began: eyes roving, foot tapping, constantly looking at his watch. He didn't want to hear what I had to say. In his mind, he had sent the dogs out like appliances to be fixed. I was to give his assistants precise instructions that there would be hell to pay if they didn't follow, and that would be that. But this time, every few seconds in the midst of his avoidance strategy, I would stop and address him firmly. "You're not listening, are you?" I'd ask. "No, I'm listening," he'd reply, clearly annoyed that anyone would dare challenge him like that. I would continue talking, then stop again. "If you're not paying attention to me, how can I talk to you?" Now he was getting really mad. "But I *am* listening!" he'd respond. "No, you're looking up there, over there. You're looking everywhere else. I really need you to pay attention to what I'm saying." Eventually, Mr. Tycoon blew up. "You dominant motherfucker!" he said to me. From him, that evidently was a compliment, because he didn't usually surrender to other people. Somehow, by standing up to him, I had won his respect—at least for that moment. "All right," he said, gruffly. "I've got five minutes." "Fine," I said, "you give me five good minutes and we can get some quality work done. We can create a lot. We can accomplish a lot in five minutes, but we need five one-hundred-percent minutes."

When I talk with a client, I have an advantage because I can get to his or her own personal issues in a roundabout way. We start talking about the dogs, then we get to the real heart of the problem, the human. That's how it worked with the Tycoon. I was fascinated by the way he had transferred all his emotional needs to those dogs, yet he didn't have many family members or confidantes whom he trusted. Little by little, the story came out. As a boy, he had overcome major insecurities and fear by constantly achieving. That was where all his focus went, all his life:

I've got to be the best! And it worked. It made him powerful; it made him rich. But it also pushed a lot of people away. He could compete with them or control them, but he could never be close to them. And so his life played out that same old story, over and over again. It didn't suprise me at all that underneath the intimidating exterior lay a good heart. It was his good heart that he desperately wanted to share with his dogs. But you can't fool animals. The negative energy was stronger, and that's what was making them—and everyone else around him—unstable.

I am certainly not a human psychologist, but I don't need to be because so many times, even the most unobservant person can see an owner's own issues totally mirrored in his or her dogs' problems. The tycoon was unconsciously favoring one of them— Kid. He couldn't believe that Kid was the one attacking Willy, and not the other way around. Just like the Tycoon, the dogs' lives had become all about competition, not cooperation.

The Tycoon had a hard time hearing what I had to say at first. After all, how could I be telling a man brilliant enough to make hundreds of millions of dollars and run dozens of successful companies that he is unbalanced? How could I be telling him that he wasn't being a good leader, when all he did all day was run the show? Doesn't wheeling and dealing in the world of international finance take leadership? Doesn't it also require instinct? I tried to explain to him that, yes, in the human world he was perceived as a leader and of course he had exceptional business instincts. But the strategies and instincts that work in the business and political world are not always those of Mother Nature. Mother Nature is ruthless to the weak, but is not arbitrarily cruel or negative. Mother Nature saves aggression for extreme situations, and instead uses dominance—consistent leadership—to help keep things running smoothly. Mother Nature does not rule by fear and anger, but by calm strength and assertiveness.

The amazing thing about the Tycoon is he loved his dogs so much that he was willing to change. I finally *did* succeed in getting him to listen to me. He was used to telling, ordering, and lecturing—but never listening. And in listening, he showed another side of himself. I learned that he is an incredibly charitable man; that his passion is sending poor kids to camp—yet he doesn't like to share that part of himself with most of the people he interacts with in his life. Perhaps he views this "soft side" as a weakness, when I see it as a strength.

I started this book with the example of the Tycoon because he is the most extreme example I have ever encountered of how an unbalanced human can create a ripple effect of dysfunction within both his dogs and all the humans around him. He is also a powerful example of how looking honestly at ourselves can restore us to balance and create a positive ripple effect in our worlds. I'm happy to report that since I worked with him and his dogs, he's showing the wonderful softer side of himself much more often. According to his assistant, Mary, with regard to the people closest to him, the Tycoon truly has changed. She told me that for the first time, he actually listened to her—not only to her gratitude for the money he pays her, but to her candidly expressing her need to be appreciated and treated better by him. She had always known that there was a human being underneath that suit of armor. And that human being was the one who needed to listen to all these people so he could feel how much he influenced them—feel not only their fear and their gratitude but also the pain that he caused them. According to his assistant, he's made a lot of progress in that area. The whole tale sort of reminds me of Charles Dickens's *A Christmas Carol.* The Tycoon is now like Ebenezer Scrooge after he's been visited by the three ghosts on Christmas Eve. But the Tycoon didn't need ghosts to see the hard truths about himself—he had his two dogs!

And there's another happy ending to the story. Not only are the dogs doing great, but Mary got up the courage for the first time since he hired her to tell him she was taking a vacation! And she did it from a place of strength. She approached him and told him what the options were for her vacation dates, case closed. That's what calm-assertive energy will do for your life—it works on much more than your dogs. You'll read more such inspiring stories in future chapters.

The moral of the story is no matter how much money or power you have, how many academic degrees, or how many priceless works of art you own, *your dogs don't care.* They *do* care how unstable you are, because, being pack-oriented, it directly affects them. Dogs do know how comfortable you are with yourself, how happy you are, how fearful you are, and what is missing inside of you. They can't tell you, but they absolutely know exactly who you are. You can ask a human, "Are you happy?" Some, like my friend the Tycoon, will say "Of course"—either hiding or unaware of the fact that he's not. Then you'll see the dog. The dog can't hide his emotions, and he's *clearly* not happy. It becomes very obvious, by reading a dog, how stable or unstable his human companion is.

Our dogs are our mirrors. Have you looked in yours lately? If my friend the Tycoon could face himself in a mirror, confront a lifetime of demons, and make a better life for not only his dogs but also for the people around him, then any one of us can. That's why I say that harnessing the power of calm-assertive energy can not only improve your dog, but change your own life as well. Our dogs can lead us back to the balance that nature intended for us, if only we are willing to follow.

PART ONE

BALANCING YOUR DOG

In order to really enjoy a dog, one doesn't merely try to train him to be semihuman. The point of it is to open oneself to the possibility of becoming partly a dog.
—*Edward Hoagland*

A dog is not "almost human" and I know of no greater insult to the canine race than to describe it as such.
—*John Holmes*

As the story of the Tycoon has taught us, our dogs are our mirrors, and in order for them to have a balanced life, we need to address our own issues as well as theirs.

This book is about your dog and you—his bad behavior and your own helplessness. Or permissiveness. Or anger. Or frustration. Let's start with the easiest part of the equation to face—your dog, and *his* problems. Because probably, at this point, you might be thinking that his problems have nothing to do with you.

I believe that 99 percent of all dogs are capable of living full, happy, balanced lives. These chapters are designed to give you a better understanding of your dog's mind, needs, and what you can do to fulfill them.

1

Identifying Instability

There was something I had never told him, that
no one ever had. I wanted him to hear it before
he went. "Marley," I said, "you are a *great* dog."

—*John Grogan*, Marley & Me

How do you know that your dog is unstable? If you are like
the majority of my clients, you just *know*. Your dog gets
aggressive with other dogs on walks and at the dog parks.
Or howls for hours when you leave the house. Or compulsively
runs away. All this is puzzling to you, because the family dog
from your childhood was perfect—or that is the way you remember him. In the amber glow of your memory, your beloved

Blackie was mellow, obedient, and content to stay in the background. He was naturally social, and always got along with strange people and dogs. He fetched and returned the tennis ball, walked beside you to school, and never peed in the house. So why does your current dog dig up your garden? Why does he hide under the table when the garbage truck drives by? What in the world is up with him when he manically spins in circles when he gets excited? Of course, like most of my clients with unstable dogs, you simply accept that your dog was born with something missing—or has some sort of mental disorder. Or, if your dog was adopted from a rescue organization, you create a story— that he had such a traumatic experience in his past placements that he will never be able to forget the terrible abuse he suffered during those dark, lonely years before he met you. So of course, he will never be stable, and you should not complain, but instead, remain tolerant and feel really sorry for him when he pees all over your sofa whenever you turn the television on. How could you criticize him when he bites anyone who comes near his food dish, knowing what he's been through in his short but traumatic life? You decide you have to pay the price to live with an unstable dog, because of everything that happened to him before. You owe it to him.

They're *All* Great Dogs

The truth about dogs is, they don't feel bad about the past. They don't dwell on their bad memories. We are the only species that does that. Dogs live in the moment. If they feel safe and secure in the moment, then any past conditioned behavior can be reconditioned, provided we give our time, our patience—and our consistency. Dogs move on—often, very quickly. They—like everything else of Mother Nature—naturally want to return to balance. Too often, it is we, the humans, who are unknowingly preventing that balance from occurring.

We are human beings, and one of the most beautiful things about our species is that we have empathy. When someone—including an animal—who we care about is in distress, we feel bad for them. We hurt when they hurt. But in the animal world, hurt is a weak energy. Feeling sorry is a weak energy. The kindest thing we can do for our animals who have suffered in the past is to help them move forward into the present. In short, that uncontrollable, neurotic monster you are living with is just waiting for you to help guide him on the way to becoming one of the world's greatest dogs!

Marley & Me

John Grogan's book *Marley & Me: Life and Love with the World's Worst Dog* hit the best-seller list in November 2005 and, as of this writing, is still in the top ten. It's easy to see why—this fun-to-read, touching tale of a lovable but out-of-control family Labrador, Marley, could easily be the life story of many of my clients' dogs. Marley is usually destructive, rarely obedient, sometimes obsessive, and always unpredictable. He's even described on the book jacket as *wondrously neurotic.* To me, joining the words *wondrous* and *neurotic* is part of the reason that there are so many unstable dogs in America. Many people who love their dogs think that their pets' unhealthy issues are just "personality quirks." When author Grogan first published his tribute to the recently deceased Marley in the *Philadelphia Inquirer,* he initially thought that his former companion was one-of-a-kind—"the world's worst dog." He was soon flooded with letters and e-mails informing him that he was actually just one member of a giant "Bad Dog Club."

"My in-box resembled a television talk show," Grogan writes, "'Bad Dogs and the People Who Love Them,' with the willing victims lining up to proudly brag not about how wonderful their dogs were but about just how awful." Like many of my clients, however, all these well-meaning dog lovers may not understand that their dog isn't happy being "awful."

I was thrilled last year when the wonderful Grogan family actually became my clients. Through my National Geographic Channel series, *Dog Whisperer,* they contacted me and invited me to their home in Pennsylvania to help them with Gracie, their current dog. Also a gorgeous yellow lab, Gracie had a very different issue than Marley (which I'll get to in chapter 4). But as different as the two dogs were, Gracie and Marley's problems were both caused by the same *human* issues—lack of leadership. When I finally met John Grogan and his wife, Jenny Vogt, Marley's story made more sense to me. They are highly intelligent, compassionate people who see the world through the eyes of talented journalists. They observe, analyze, and describe—but they don't interfere or try to change. They assumed they were stuck with Marley the way he was—that, in the words of John's father, Marley just "had a screw loose." Indeed, as the couple laughingly said to me, if it hadn't been for Marley's quirks, there wouldn't have been a wonderful book for so many people to identify with, and to bring tears to so many people's eyes. That's the catch, isn't it? We don't want to change our dogs because they make us laugh, or feel unconditionally loved, or needed. But very often we don't put ourselves into the position of how the dog feels. When a dog has a fear, or an obsession, or any of the many other problems I am called in to solve, most of the time we're not talking about a "personality quirk." We're talking about an unfulfilled and sometimes unhappy dog.

After I finished wiping the tears in my eyes and put down Grogan's book, the first thing that came to my mind was that Marley was perfectly capable of being that "great dog," all the time! In the book, John's wife, Jenny, goes through postpartum depression after the birth of their second son and, overwhelmed with the frustration of caring for two babies and a dog that destroys furniture on a daily basis, she finally breaks down and orders the uncontrollable lab out of the house for good. Previously, Marley had been kicked out of obedience class, but John knows that if he can't get the dog to follow some basic commands and learn not to jump up on people who come to the house *this* time around, he's going to lose his best friend. So John actually did it. With grim determination, John buckled down, worked really hard to become a serious "pack leader," and finally helped Marley to graduate from obedience class at last—even though he was seventh in an obedience class with eight dogs in it. With the help of a friend, John breaks Marley of his habit of tackling people who come to their front door. The point is, John *was* a pack leader when he absolutely needed to be—and Marley was perfectly capable of being an obedient dog. Together the two of them rallied to the challenge and did what needed to be done in order to keep the pack together. In my reading of the book, however, once Jenny recovered from her depression and things mellowed out at home, John stopped following through in his leadership. So Marley only went so far in learning how to obey household rules, boundaries, and limitations.

John and Jenny also had an advantage that many people who adopt older dogs or shelter dogs don't have—the opportunity to condition Marley to be a well-behaved dog from puppyhood. Again, seeing their dog through journalists' eyes—in a detached way—they failed to interfere with what they assumed was Marley's natural development. They observed all his antics with wonder and good humor. Plus, he was so darn cute! The endearing photograph on the cover of the book says it all—the curiously cocked head, the pleading brown eyes ... how could anyone with a heart ever want to correct or give discipline to that adorable, floppy-eared pup? John and Jenny made the well-meaning but common mistake of believing that Marley's destructive antics as a puppy were evidence of his developing personality, his "spirit." When you study dogs in nature—from wolves to wild dogs to domestic dogs that raise each other, like some farm dogs do—you will witness discipline and order instilled in their lives from their very first days on earth. You'll also see the elder canids putting up with an awful lot from the pups—they won't deny their innate playfulness, but instead will allow the little ones to crawl on them, tug on them, even nip. However, they set definite limits on it. When playtime is over, the elder dog lets the pups know it right away by nosing them to the ground with a gentle bite or lifting them up by their scruffs, if necessary. Sometimes, only a growl will get their point across. The older dog always follows through and the pups always back off. If danger is imminent, the elders manage to get the pups immediately herded together and inside the safety of the den in the blink of an eye—to the envy of any kindergarten teacher out there who daily tries to get a pack of five-year-old kids to come back into class from the playground! The point is, the pups get the message very, very quickly that they *must* follow the rules of the pack. At no point in time is their playful "spirit" ever diminished, but they do come to understand early on in life that there is a time and a place for everything. Mother Nature has no trouble setting limits in a firm but loving way. But when it comes to cute puppies (and often, our own cute kids), most people just can't bear to set them on the road to good behavior—especially when their antics provide such memorably humorous moments. But when those pups reach one hundred pounds, the fun and games that used to seem cute suddenly become destructive and sometimes dangerous.

John and Jenny had a wonderful companion in Marley. They accomplished trust, love, and loyalty with him. What they didn't accomplish was *respect*, however, and respect is an essential ingredient in the structure of any healthy pack. When students don't respect the teacher, a school class doesn't learn. A military unit cannot function at its best when the soldiers do not respect their commander. Parents cannot properly guide their children if the kids do not respect them. In the same way, your dog will not feel safe and calm and stable if he does not respect you as pack leader.

Part of the reason John and Jenny did not gain Marley's full respect was that they always addressed themselves to *Marley*—the name and personality, first. Marley to them was just plain old, goofy, not-exactly-a-rocket-scientist, loyal Marley. They were not addressing themselves to the animal in Marley, the dog in Marley, or even the breed of Marley, a Labrador retriever.

Remember this key concept:

When you interact with your dog—especially when you're trying to correct out-of-control behavior—you *must* train your mind to relate to him in this order:

1. Animal
2. Species: dog (*Canis familiaris*)
3. Breed (Labrador retriever)
4. Name (Marley)

First, it's important to address yourself to the "animal" in your dog because that is what you have in common with him—you are both animals. We'll talk later about how to project the kind of energy that any animal will recognize. Second, your dog is a *dog*—not a baby or a small furry person with a tail. All dogs have certain traits in common and certain ingrained ways of behaving. Learning to recognize what is "dog" and what is "Marley" is the key in distinguishing unstable behavior from normal behavior. Then there's breed. Recognizing breed is especially important if, like the Grogans, you have a purebred animal. The genes that make him "pure" also give him special needs that you must know how to fulfill in order to ensure his happiness and balance. We'll talk more about fulfilling the breed in your dog in chapter 4.

After animal, dog, and breed, finally, there's Marley—the name, the irrepressible "personality." Most of the time, what we think of as a dog's personality is in our own heads, the story we made up about the dog. Often it's based on how the dog looks or acts, and I'm sorry to say that, far too often, what we think of as personality is actually based on the dog's own issues of instability.

ISSUES

- *Aggression:* Directed toward other dogs and/or people. Includes fear-biting, growling over food, lunging at strangers or strange dogs, aggressive possessiveness.
- *Hyperactive Energy:* Includes jumping on people upon meeting them or when they enter the house; compulsively spinning or twitching, destructive activity such as chewing and digging; overexcited panting, etc. *Don't confuse overexcitement with happiness!*
- *Anxiety/Separation Anxiety:* Includes barking, whining, scratching, etc.—whether you are there or after you leave the house; pacing; destroying things when you're away.
- *Obsessions/Fixations:* Includes an "addiction" or unusual preoccupation with anything from a cat to a tennis ball, expressed by tense body language, obliviousness to owner's commands, food rewards, even physical pain.
- *Phobias:* A fear or traumatic incident that the dog has not been able to move beyond—anything from shiny floors to thunder to the UPS truck.
- *Low Self-esteem/Timidity:* Weak energy, irrational fear of anything, total freezing up. An extreme degree of fear.

So how do you tell your dogs' "personality" from your dogs' "issues"? What are "issues," anyway?

Any kind of behavior that falls into these categories is *not* "just your dog's personality." It is a *problem.*

It's important to remember that each of the issues described

above *can* have a medical component. A disease or parasite can
cause your dog to act in an unstable manner, as can an inborn
neurological disorder. In my experiences with hundreds of dogs,
neurological disorders account for a very small percentage of behavior problems. However, it's always important to have your
dog checked out on a regular basis by a vet, especially if there is a
sudden behavior change. Chances are, using the leadership
methods I describe in my teachings will help rehabilitate your
dog—but make sure you get a medical opinion first, just in case
there is a health issue. I have several wonderful vets who I work
with and I like to think medicine and behavioral therapy can go
hand in hand in creating a world full of healthy, happy dogs.

Personality Versus Issues

What characteristics actually comprise your dog's natural
"spirit," or "personality"? First of all, you must understand that
"personality" has a different meaning to a dog than it does to
you. If you are a human who would like to date a person who
complements your personality, you might place a personal ad
and say things like, "I like to work out in the gym, go hiking,
enjoy romantic sunset jogs on the beach; I like action movies"—
indicating that you are an active, high-energy-type person who is
looking for someone to match your energy. If you place an ad
that says, "I like drinking hot chocolate by a fire, staying in and
renting videos, and doing crossword puzzles," you are indicating
that you are a lower-energy person who wants to meet someone
with a similar energy. You might describe yourself or another
person as laid back, or high-strung, or shy or outgoing. As a
human, you regard all these things as *personality*.

Personality is similar in a dog's world, but it is not expressed in words or in likes and dislikes, but rather by scent and energy. When two dogs in my pack make friends with each other, they will first use their noses to sniff each other's genitals, which will give them all kinds of information about the sex, energy level, rank, food the other dog ate, places the dog has been, and so on. The energy level is important because the dog will get along best with another dog whose energy is compatible. Have you ever seen two dogs playing where the energy level is not a good fit? This happens often with an older dog who is with puppies. Naturally, the older dog has less energy, even if he was a higher-energy dog in his youth. The puppy almost always has a higher energy and will be driving the older dog crazy wanting to play, when the older dog just wants to chill out. This happens to a different degree with the dogs in my pack: The dogs naturally seek out as "friends" the dogs who can match their level of play. Even though all the dogs in the pack get along, certain dogs will gravitate to certain other dogs based on their energy levels and how they like to play. A great example of this kind of attraction happened when I was working with Punkin, a Rhodesian Ridgeback who had developed a dangerous obsession over rocks. My goal was to bring him to the Center to learn from the pack's role models—balanced dogs who couldn't care less about rocks, but who have learned to play with tennis balls in a disciplined way (meaning play always has a beginning and an end, as determined by me, the pack leader). Punkin was an anxious, high-energy-type dog, and when we got to the dog park, he immediately was drawn to LaFitte, a very large, very high-energy standard poodle. It was like the stereotype of the "two eyes meeting across a crowded room." They instantly recognized in each other's scent and energy that they would match each other's level of play and have a great time romping together. Recently, I had a high-energy Jack Russell named Jack staying at my center, whose favorite play friend was a huge but medium energy pit bull named Spike. Even though Jack was half Spike's size, the two just meshed together perfectly. Scent and energy combined to make up a dog's individual "personality."

As humans, we naturally strive to create symbols and put names on things, and we tend to associate personality with names. As far as current science knows, we are the only species that started describing our world with symbols, artwork, and most of all, with labels and names. Today, we *Homo sapiens* have millions of different languages and symbols that we use to communicate with each other. Just look around you—we have the little man and woman on restroom signs; the NO SMOKING logo; even the American flag, to tell us where we are and how we should be relating to our environment at that moment. We have millions of different words and phrase combinations to describe things. As people, we tend to organize and personalize pretty much everything that happens around us. It's how we understand things, how we see the world through our human eyes. For example, we give hurricanes names. We classify flowers and trees.

In the dog world, however, trees don't have names. They have a scent, and they have a specific use for the dog in its environment. *Is this tree poison, or will eating the bark of this tree make my stomach feel better? Is this tree at a crossroads so I can mark it with my scent?* This is how a dog views the tree: from the point of view of his survival. Dogs don't need names to understand and identify each other, either. They look at the big picture—their own survival and the survival of the group. Your personality—your "name" to your dog—is how you fit into his life; your energy, your scent, your role in the pack is what is important to him.

Dogs don't have a name within the pack; they have a *position* within the pack. Some people who study dogs would name the ranks "alpha, beta, omega," and so forth. Other labels that we create would define them as number one, number two, number three, and number four. Many people misunderstand me and say that I'm looking at dogs simplistically, as if it's all about dominance. What they fail to realize is I believe that all the dogs are important within the pack. Dominance doesn't mean the alpha dog is "better" than the others. In charge, yes; better, no. Every dog serves a purpose within the pack. The guy in the back is the most sensitive of all; he's often the one that keeps everybody aware of possible intruders. The dog in the front—the pack leader—makes sure everybody gets fed, finds food and water, and is defended from rivals or other predators. It's not a democracy, but it's definitely all about the whole being better than the sum of all the parts. It's all about the "we."

From "I" to "We"

Humans—at least in Western culture—tend to see the world in a very "me versus you" context. Especially in America, where rugged individualism is what everybody strives for, the almighty "I" is the center of the universe. To my mind, that's what makes our interpersonal difficulties so common: Divorce rates are higher than 50 percent, kids rebel against their parents, people fight with their bosses and quit their jobs in anger—because at the heart of our relationships, it's almost always me against you. Quite differently, if a dog could have an inner voice expressed in words, he would be thinking of his world in terms of "we" all the time. Pack first, individuals later. Even the pack leader operates this way. Perhaps that's partly why so many of us insecure humans gravitate to dogs when we have difficulties with people. When a dog comes into your home, you instantly get a "we"—and that never changes. It's just in the nature of the dog, and it is really comforting when our relationships with people seem to be always fraught with tension.

This is not to say that every dog isn't an individual—of course he is! But how do you distinguish what is your dog's true uniqueness from what may or may not be his "issues"? There are certain characteristics that vary from one dog to another, which become how we humans usually gauge our dogs' "personalities." Every dog is curious to a degree—that's a part of a dog's spirit. Every dog is joyful to a degree—dogs live in the moment and every day for them is a kind of Christmas morning, even if they are a lower-energy or older dog. Every dog is playful to a degree. How he likes to play is partly determined by the breed and partly by the energy. Every dog is loyal to a degree—because in nature, the pack needs loyalty in order to stay together and survive. Every dog knows how to learn—that's part of survival, too—and he always likes to be challenged. Every dog knows how to follow a leader's directions and rules and understands the importance of such rules. Every dog is affectionate to some degree. Every dog likes and needs to walk with a pack leader in migration mode—how much, again, depends partly on breed and partly on energy. Every dog needs to be useful, to work for food and water—to be a helpful, productive member of your pack. Dogs are not solitary like many species of cats; they are *social* carnivores and their deep social needs are hardwired into their brains. Being social means they *need* the pack to be happy and fulfilled. Because we have domesticated dogs, we have become their default pack members throughout our long history together. If we were not around, they would still form packs. During the Hurricane Katrina crisis some of the dogs left behind did exactly that temporarily in order to survive. But we've been "pack leaders" to them and/or their ancestors for at least tens of thousands—and perhaps as long as hundreds of thousands—of years, so although they absolutely realize that we are not dogs but humans, they will naturally follow us if we provide them with the correct direction.

Exercise

On the next page you'll find two columns with single adjectives. One describes a normal dog's characteristics or traits that you might define as a dog's true "personality"; the other describes traits that are more likely to be issues of instability. It is a very general list, of course, as many of these traits vary depending on the breed, but I think it's a good overview for assessment. Read the list and note the adjectives that you would apply to your dog at least 75 percent of the time. Then make an *honest* assessment of what you and your dog need to work on.

Once again, the news is good—in 99 percent of the cases I've dealt with, all of the issues listed on the following page can be resolved with my three-part fulfillment formula for any dog:

1. Exercise (the walk)
2. Discipline (rules, boundaries, and limitations)
3. Affection

. . . in that order!

Normal Dog Traits, or Personality	Dog Issues or Instability
Active	Hyperactive
Playful	Jumps on people
Responsive to general commands and signals	Disobedient—doesn't come when called
Eager to join in "pack" (family) activities	Runs away
Sometimes cautious	Overly fearful—fear-biting, barking, or peeing; shies away from people, animals, or objects
Barks to announce newcomers	Obsessive barking
Sociable with dogs and people	
Curious	Antisocial—"doesn't like" dogs or humans
Happy-go-lucky	Aggressive or predatory
Alert	Overly territorial
Exploratory	Possessive of toys, food, furniture
Patient—practices waiting	Obsessive over object or activity (compulsive retrieving; chewing; tail chasing)
Responsive to food	
Affectionate	Shrinks from touch

When you provide the fulfillment formula for your dog, you are taking a positive step toward becoming an effective pack leader. Strong pack leadership depends on understanding the importance of remaining calm and assertive and remembering not to "punch out" on your responsibilities for your dog any more than you would punch out on your parenting duties with your children. I've heard children described as "little cameras that never turn off"—and dogs are exactly the same way. Living in the universe of the "we," they are always observing you and processing your signals for clues to how to behave. When we send dogs inconsistent signals, we create instability in them.

Once again, we're back to the part of the fulfillment formula that many of us have a problem with—discipline. Discipline isn't about showing a dog "who's boss"; it's about taking responsibility for a living creature you have brought into your world. Many of my clients think that if they set any boundaries for their dogs, they automatically become the bad guy. That's certainly the problem John Grogan and Jenny Vogt had. Without discipline, they could not accomplish respect. They could not give Marley the rules, boundaries, and limitations he needed in order to live a more peaceful life. He ended up full of what they saw as "personality quirks" but what I would call instability. By giving a dog rules, boundaries, and limitations, you don't "kill his spirit." You just give him the structure he needs in his life in order to find peace and allow his true dog self to emerge. Your dog can be that "great dog" you imagine—but you've got to be the one to lead him there!

BE THE PACK LEADER SUCCESS STORY

Tina Madden and NuNu

IF YOU'VE WATCHED the first season of my show, you probably remember NuNu the Demon Chihuahua, whose pint-sized aggression was making the lives of his owner, Tina, and her roommate, Barclay, unmanageable. Three years later, Tina Madden's life has changed dramatically since she became the pack leader. Now she not only works at my Dog Psychology Center, but she rehabilitates dogs herself. But what's more important is how she feels about herself—empowered as a woman and a person. Here's her story in her own words:

Before NuNu, I was extremely insecure. I didn't leave the house very much. I had issues with myself, my body image, what people thought of me, how they viewed me. I was always insecure and anxious. I cried all the time. Anyway, I decided I'd rather be around dogs than people, so I quit my bartending job and went to work as a vet tech assistant.

I was okay at work because the animals needed me. But outside of the work environment, I was afraid of the world. Even going to the grocery store scared me. I was isolating myself, and it was just getting worse. This kept going in a downward spiral. I wasn't rock bottom. But I was heading there.

I got NuNu in February. He comes in. I'm insecure. I'm nurturing bad behavior in myself and in him, and I think, there's got to be something I can do. Everybody kept saying, "Put him down. He's terrible. He's too damaged to ever be a good dog. Just put him to sleep." And then in April, in walks Cesar, and when he walked out of my house, my life changed that day. It was because he had such "can-do" energy. He wanted me to become more confident and show more leadership—something I would have found impossible to imagine before. But his words to me were, "No matter what, you can do this. You just have to do it." And if I wasn't going to do it for me, at least I could do it for my dog, whom I loved.

First of all, I *immediately* had to get over my fear of going out. Cesar absolutely ordered me to walk NuNu every day, and so that's what I started doing. Cesar said forty-five minutes. I said an hour. So at least two to two-and-a-half hours a day, before and after work, seven days a week, we'd be walking. And in my walking, because NuNu's so cute, people wanted to approach him, so I began to meet people that way. I started making friends in my neighborhood. Suddenly I had a social life—people were inviting me to their houses. And I had a ritual. Before I would go out on my walk every day, I would visualize. "This is going to be a great walk. This is going to be a perfect walk! Any

obstacle we come across, we can handle. I have the knowledge and the presence to handle it." I used to walk by dogs
behind fences and even face-to-face with dogs, and I would
be terrified they were going to bite NuNu. I thought I
didn't know how to handle it. But little by little, I noticed I
did know how to handle it. And the more I did it, the better
it became and the more confident I became.

NuNu didn't completely change the next day. He wasn't
all "fixed" the next week, or even the next month, but the
more I changed my behavior around him, which meant
being more confident, he started to really change. I'm
proud of NuNu for changing—but the big energy change
came from me. From empowering myself.

My self-confidence has increased so much. And not just
around dogs. The way I connect with other people has
changed completely. I think one of the hardest things for
some people is to be able to read another person. Are they
good? Are they bad? Can you trust them? But really, understanding other people begins with understanding yourself.
Learning to be aware of my own energy has really made
that easier for me . . . and that's something I learned from
Cesar and NuNu. And I don't feel like a victim anymore. I
feel in control of myself, in just about every situation.

I did "transform my dog," and then "transform my life."
I am very happy now. And all because of one little dog. One
little three-and-a-half pound dog.

2

Discipline, Rewards, and Punishment

Man is an animal that makes bargains; no other animal does this.
No dog exchanges bones with another. —*Adam Smith*

Nature's laws are the invisible government of the earth.
—*Alfred Montapert*

When it comes to becoming our dogs' pack leaders, the equation is not complete without understanding the concept of discipline. As we learned in the last chapter, your dog cannot be balanced and reach true peace in life without rules, boundaries, and limitations as part of her daily routine. For rules and boundaries to exist, someone has to set them—and that is the job description for a pack leader.

Many animal professionals who say they disagree with (what they perceive to be) my techniques follow the "rewards-only" trend of dog training—*training* being the key word. Remember, *I don't "train" dogs.* True, that was my original ambition when I came to America, but I quickly came to see that my own special skills could be put to much better use. It appeared to me that this nation's dogs needed much more to make their lives complete beyond the ability to sit, stay, heel, roll over, and fetch the newspaper. What I do is *rehabilitation,* although I absolutely 100 percent believe in positive reinforcement techniques for *training* purposes and rehabilitation, too, whenever possible. My philosophy about discipline and correction with any animal, for any purpose, is that they should always be applied with the *least force necessary* to accomplish the behavior you are asking for. And I do use positive reinforcement and food rewards all the time, in the appropriate situations. But I also believe there is a time and a place for every technique. The issue that many in the "positive-only" school of behavior seem to have with me is that they believe I should be using treats and clickers to redirect some of the behaviors that I choose to correct with energy, body language, eye contact, and physical touch. I believe my techniques work on very difficult aggressive, obsessive, or anxious cases because they are a simple, common-sense approach based entirely on Mother Nature.

I believe there is an enormous difference between the idea of *discipline* and the concept of *punishment.* To me, *discipline* is part of the order of the universe: It is the very core of how Mother

Nature works to make the planet operate. Discipline is order. Discipline is the rotation of the earth, the cycle of the moon, the rising and setting of the sun. Discipline is one season turning into another—a time for planting and growing, and a time for harvesting. Within this bigger context, discipline is how all members of the animal kingdom survive. Every morning in your backyard, the squirrels set out early and begin to forage. Some birds come to the bird feeder hanging on your porch; others peck along the ground, looking for worms and other goodies. If you take the time to observe them every day, you'll see that their routines rarely vary much, except when dictated by other factors such as raising their young, migrating or getting ready for winter, keeping out of the rain, finding a new tree after one has been blown over in a storm. None of these animals takes Sundays or holidays off. They live every moment to the fullest, and all those moments are guided by *discipline*. Their natural wiring tells them what to do to keep order in their lives. When there's a squabble over food or territory or a mate, they keep discipline among each other, and the environment maintains discipline among them all.

In the natural world of the social carnivore, discipline and order are incredibly important. In their world, the rules are set in two ways: by their "programming" (their survival instincts), and by the others in their group. Dogs, being pack animals, are finely tuned to the rules of the group. Cooperation means survival. Social animals rely on knowing their place and their role within the group in order to ensure the group's survival. If a dog doesn't have a solid sense of where she fits in the pack order, she almost always exhibits some sign of instability. This instability comes from a deep, primal place—a need to guarantee the group's continuation, no matter what the cost to the individual dog.

As opposed to the discipline that the natural world provides, *punishment,* to me, is mostly a human concept. Punishment is when I send one of my sons, Calvin or Andre, to his room, and tell him to think about what he's done. There is reason involved in this kind of punishment—based on Calvin and Andre's abilities to make thoughtful, conscious decisions and connections. When we send a man to prison because he has committed a crime, we assume he knows right from wrong, and that prison is a consequence for making the wrong choice. The concept behind prison is to keep the criminal away from society and—at least in an ideal world—to give him time to reflect on what he's done, so he won't make that bad choice again. But punishment is often a terrible choice for conflict resolution—any marriage counselor will tell you that. If my wife and I have a fight and I decide to "punish" her for a week by being sarcastic or rude to her, am I helping to solve the original problem? Of course not. More likely, she'll end up being even angrier with me than she was in the beginning. This is the danger of thinking "punishment" when we talk about disciplining dogs.

Animals do not have the ability to make conscious choices between right and wrong, good and bad. Giving a dog a time-out after she's chewed up your best pair of shoes is the kind of punishment that might work with your kids, but it doesn't work with dogs because they can't make that kind of intellectual connection. Yelling at or hitting a dog in anger only confuses the dog or frightens her. When someone adopts a dog from a shelter, then returns her because she is too aggressive, the dog has no idea why she's being brought back to a cage. She has no ability to reflect on how she blew yet another chance at a nice home and she can't feel bad and resolve to do better the next time. In the simple cause and effect universe that guides much of dog behavior, these "punishments" do not make it clear to the dog what behavior is unwanted and what behavior needs to be substituted to take its place. They are left to their own devices to figure that out, and often, neither they nor we are very happy with the solutions they come up with. That is why I personally prefer the words *discipline* and *correction* instead of *punish* when I talk about rehabilitating dogs.

Simple Math—Negatives and Positives

After the second season of my show aired, I was flattered to learn that clinical psychologist Alice Clearman, Ph.D., often uses episodes from *Dog Whisperer* to help illustrate principles of *human* behavior to her first-year college psychology students. A dog owner and rescuer herself, she has worked therapeutically with all kinds of people—from severely mentally ill patients to children with learning disabilities to law enforcement officers who deal with unstable members of the public. As someone who has focused her life work on studying the mechanics of learning and behavior, Dr. Clearman was very helpful to me, a layman, in breaking down the principles of reward and punishment as they apply both to humans and animals.

According to Dr. Clearman, there are two basic ways of changing all behavior—reinforcement and punishment. In human psychology, there is positive punishment and positive reinforcement, and there is negative punishment and negative reinforcement. Positive and negative work the same way that they do in simple math. If you add something, it's a positive. If you subtract something, it's a negative. Positive reinforcement means adding something I like to encourage me to repeat a behavior. If I do a seminar and get a standing ovation, it reinforces my experience of giving the seminar, and I'll want to do it again. Negative reinforcement is often thought of as equivalent to punishment, but it is absolutely not punishment. Negative reinforcement is when you reinforce a behavior by *removing* something someone *doesn't* like. Dr. Clearman uses the example of taking aspirin for a headache. If she has a headache, takes an aspirin, and her headache goes away, she has successfully reinforced herself for taking aspirin. The aspirin removed the headache—the thing she didn't like.

Positive punishment, on the other hand, is *adding* something I don't like to discourage me from repeating the behavior. If I give a seminar and everyone in the audience hisses and boos and throws things at me, that's positive punishment. I am now going to rethink my approach for the next seminar, to avoid an experience like that again. Negative punishment is subtracting something I like. When I tell Andre he is not allowed to play video games for three weeks, that's a negative punishment. Don't forget, the words *positive* and *negative* don't have anything to do with whether the consequence could be considered nice or not nice. It's not a judgment call—although we often react to those words with judgment. It's strictly math.

Based on Dr. Clearman's explanations, some of my techniques in working with problem dogs would be correctly termed *positive punishment*, but because the word *punishment* connotes something human to me, I prefer to think of these techniques as simple *corrections*. For example, I will curl my hand in a clawlike position to simulate the mouth and teeth of a mother dog or a more dominant dog, and firmly touch the dog on the neck.

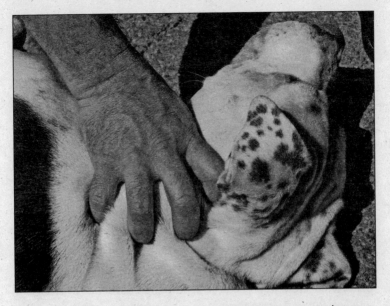

"THE CLAW" HAND POSITION, USED TO SIMULATE ANOTHER DOG'S BITE.
THE GRIP IS FIRM, BUT *NOT* A PINCH.

It's important to be clear on this: *I am not hitting or pinching the dog!* I am simply replicating what among canines is a natural correction, which has a primal significance to them. It is a form of touch with a very clear meaning behind it—"I don't agree with that behavior." If a dog is out of control on a leash, I might give a slight tug to the side on the leash or choke chain (see chapter 3), or I might use my opposing foot to tap a dog on her hindquarter. This has the effect of snapping her out of whatever she is fixating on, and also communicates, "That is not an acceptable behavior in my pack." Again, this is *not* a kick. It is a *touch*. It is the same kind of touch you use when you tap a friend firmly on the shoulder to get his attention. Above all, the energy *behind* this touch is absolutely key—it cannot be angry or frustrated, tentative or fearful—it must always be "calm-assertive." I am not correcting the dog because I'm mad at her or at my wit's end, or because I'm embarrassed about what she's doing or terrified at what she might do next. As a pack leader, I am always focused. I have a vision in my mind of proper behavior in my pack, and I am reminding her to pay attention to me while I communicate to her what that behavior should be. The reward for the correct behavior could be treats, affection, praise, or simply my silent, internal pride and happiness in her accomplishment. That, in itself, *is* affection to a dog! Many dog handlers in professional situations—on hunts, in search-and-rescue or law enforcement missions, or on stage or movie sets—aren't within reach of the dog to give praise through treats or even words. But they communicate their great appreciation of the dog's hard work through a nod of the head, a hand signal, and most of all just their focused, pure, positive emotion. Remember, your dog will always be reading your energy and emotions—and mirroring them right back to you.

When visitors come to my Dog Psychology Center and are about to walk through my pack of thirty to forty dogs for the first time, in addition to telling them "No talk, no touch, no eye contact," I always remind them to keep moving forward, even if dogs approach them or bump into them. Dogs don't take it personally when you touch them in a firm manner or if you bump by them as you're walking, as long as you don't do it with an energy that's abusive, angry, or overly aggressive. If your energy is truly calm-assertive, a touch to them is simply communication. Dogs communicate all the time with each other using touch as well as energy. They push and shove and nose each other constantly. It's a way of claiming personal space; of showing interest or affection; of agreeing or not agreeing with a certain behavior of another dog. In fact, the very first communication between a mother dog and her pups is based on touch, as they wriggle toward her to nurse, or as she pushes them away when she's had enough.[1] I regularly use my body simply to block or redirect a dog that is engaging in a behavior with which I don't agree. In the animal world, it's a very simple, no-nonsense way of getting a message across.

Positive reinforcement holds great power for changing the behavior of both humans and animals, and is usually the form of "discipline" people feel most comfortable about using. Positive reinforcement makes both object and subject feel good—but it is important that it's applied within limits. Take this example from the human world that Dr. Clearman shared with me. If her son comes home from school with a painting and she says, "That's a beautiful painting; you did a good job trying to draw those palm trees. Those are hard to do," that's a good, limited use of positive reinforcement. It's positive *feedback*—and it's powerful. However, if every day he brings home a painting and she fawns over every one, saying, "That's brilliant! You're the best little boy in the world! You're a genius! That's fabulous! Everything you do is perfect!", how much impact is her praise going to have when she really needs to use it? How does she get him to believe her when she tries to encourage him after he's actually failed at something? Since she is always rewarding him no matter what he does, she has lost total credibility. Too much positive reinforcement can create the appearance of weakness in the one giving the praise—or the treats, or the applause, or whatever that reward might be.

I have seen this kind of response in dogs that have never achieved total respect for their owners but are constantly being reinforced with treats for practically every behavior they do. The owner uses food treats for conditioning the dog to sit and stay, but also in situations where the cause and effect for the dog is often unclear. If a dog is growling at another dog, the owner will redirect the behavior with treats. If the dog is chewing on something, the owner will offer treats to give him something else to chew on. If the dog is on a sofa, the owner will throw treats on the ground so the dog gets off the sofa. The problem is, the owner may have temporarily redirected the behavior, but he hasn't addressed the state of mind that was causing the behavior in the first place. He hasn't earned the dog's respect by letting her know through energy and body language that no, it's not okay with me that you sit on this couch. He's also "numbing" the dog to the reinforcement method, making it ultimately less effective—and he may also actually be nurturing the dog's bad behavior at the same time! I wouldn't be surprised if many of these dogs go right back to growling, chewing, or jumping right back up on the sofa as soon as all the treats are eaten. Like the mother whose words lose their power because she praises her child constantly no matter what he does, the treats lose their meaning because they are not seen by the dog as directly connected to the unwanted behavior.

Positive reinforcement can actually backfire by nurturing a behavior that you don't want your dog to assert. In the human world, if a child hurts himself and begins to cry, his parents will naturally comfort him, stroke him, and say, "It's okay, it's only a boo-boo," and words to that effect. But most parents understand that if they go too far in their nurturing behavior—if they panic and get overly emotional themselves—it will only serve to heighten the child's distress. Though stroking a dog can have a calming effect on her, it also indicates affection—and affection is a powerful positive reinforcement tool. Remember it's positive—which means you are *adding* energy. In *Cesar's Way,* I gave the example of Kane, the Great Dane that was afraid of slippery floors. After he slipped on linoleum and collided with a glass door, he might have recovered on his own, at least if his life were ordered in the way it would be in the natural world. He may have been more cautious in the future, but would not have become completely phobic. Because his owner made a huge event out of the collision, however, his shock and trauma were intensified ten times over. Every time he and his owner returned to the "scene of the crime," she would reinforce Kane's insecurity by babying him and giving him extra amounts of stroking, comfort, and affection. Dr. Clearman gave me another example from the human world: a student who is nervous about failing an upcoming final exam because she doesn't feel prepared for it. If her roommate says, "Oh my God, you are so right to be worried. I had that teacher, too, and he is a nightmare—you'll never be prepared and you'll probably fail," the roommate is *agreeing* with the behavior and acknowledging the feelings, but reinforcing the fear. Likewise, petting or giving treats to a dog in a fearful state may be distracting her in the short run, but it can also be communicating to the dog that you actually agree with that state of mind.

Treat-based positive reinforcement training has been around for as long as there have been dogs and humans who wanted to control them. Across all species, tasty nourishment is a no-brainer when it comes to an incentive for an animal—any animal, from gerbils to bears to children—to do something. Clicker training is a more sophisticated step than simple treat-based training. It was originally developed over thirty years ago for trainers of marine mammals, to get them to perform certain tricks and behaviors. The clicker—or whistle, in the case of the performing cetaceans and pinnipeds—serves as a bridge between the food reward and the behavior. The clicker allows instant, split-second feedback between the animal and the trainer, so that the very moment the animal "hits her mark," so to speak, the clicker makes a sound that signals that food is coming. In the early phases of clicker training, a food reward instantly follows the clicker when the animal has performed the behavior. Once the animal has been thoroughly conditioned and is totally comfortable performing the behavior, often only the clicker is needed for positive reinforcement, since it is associated with the reward, and promises a reward is eventually on its way. In controlled situations, clicker training is incredibly effective and has even been shown to *accelerate* the process of learning in many species of animals. The clicker works most efficiently at adding behaviors, not removing them, although it can be used to remove unwanted behaviors by shaping and rewarding new responses.

Treat-based or clicker-based positive reinforcement techniques are ideal for teaching a dog to do tricks, to track, to hunt, to fetch—basically anything she is already capable of doing naturally in some shape or form. It also works to manage behavior and basic obedience in low-to-medium-energy, happy-go-lucky, already balanced dogs. But many of the dogs I work with are highly unstable and won't be tempted to change their behavior by a treat, no matter how tasty. You could throw a juicy steak in front of a red-zone dog—a dog that wants to kill another dog— and she wouldn't even notice. Can you imagine trying to click and throw treats while you are struggling with all your might to keep your dog from attacking someone or another dog? A client of mine from a New York City *Dog Whisperer* case actually faced that exact situation, minus the clicker. Pete had been at his wits' end with his red-zone Lab-greyhound mix, Curly, and had consulted several trainers. One trainer told him to throw treats on the ground whenever Curly's aggression toward other dogs flared up on walks. Pete told me, "It only took him a couple of times before he realized if he ate the treats really fast, he could get a snack and *then* attack the other dog. A two-fer."

I believe there are many ways to help dogs become balanced—and they include both positive reinforcement techniques *and* humane corrections. Ultimately, the goal is the same—to help the dog.

Four-alarm Wilshire

The story of Wilshire the fire dog is a great example of what I consider to be the perfect combination of positive reinforcement training *plus* my three-part formula of exercise, discipline, and affection. Wilshire, a Dalmatian puppy, was about two months old when he showed up on the doorstep of Fire Station 29 in Los Angeles. His owners had bought him from a breeder—no doubt on a whim after the kids had watched *101 Dalmatians*—but had quickly found him way too high-energy for their family life. When the family brought him to a shelter, however, they were informed that if he wasn't adopted in twenty-four hours, he would have to be put to sleep. Wracked with guilt, the family was driving by Station 29 when it occured to one of them, "Dalmatian = fire dog!" They brought the feisty pup to Captain Gilbert Reyna at the station and pleaded for him and the rest of the firehouse crew to take the dog in. At first, Captain Reyna said, "Absolutely not." How was this extremely busy fire station going to deal with raising a hyperactive, excitable, orphaned Dalmatian puppy? But then, a few more of his crew wandered out to take a look at the little guy. They held him, played with him, passed him around, fed him a few snacks. You know the formula. Forty-five big, beefy, macho firefighters plus one adorable little puppy equals love at first sight. How could they possibly turn him away?

Wilshire instantly won the hearts of the forty-five firemen at this landmark station, but the humans definitely didn't win *his* respect at first. In fact, by his second day there, he was running the entire firehouse. He would climb all over the tables in the lunchroom, eating food off everyone's plates. He would teethe on coats, hats, and valuable, life-saving hoses, cables, and wires. He ran wherever he wanted and he peed wherever he wanted—a violation of city health codes. All the firemen were constantly on edge, because whenever a call came in and they had to get the engines out of the garage, Wilshire would dash out the door and make a run for it, straight toward busy six-lane Wilshire Boulevard and its deadly traffic. Sometimes he'd run right in front of the enormous fire truck's wheels—in the middle of the driver's blind spot. One day, a group of schoolkids came by for a tour of the firehouse, and Wilshire got so excited, he ran all the way down a long hallway and launched himself through the air like a rocket—hitting a little boy full in the chest and actually knocking him to the floor! The Los Angeles city attorney's office made a warning call to Captain Reyna—get this dog under control, or he's out of there. Of course, all the guys had bonded with Wilshire by this time, and there was no way they were going to let that happen. Wilshire had to be rehabilitated!

When the firemen called me in to help, Wilshire was only three months old and was already king of the firehouse. He had all the guys running around, flailing their arms, yelling, "Oh my God, Wilshire! No, Wilshire! Oh no, stop, Wilshire!" I had to laugh—these are the same guys who risk their lives every day rescuing people from the worst imaginable disasters, all the while staying calm, cool, and collected. And now here's this little dog sending them into a panic. When I pointed this out to them, they were all very embarrassed, but they had to laugh, too. I said to them, "When you pull someone out of a burning building, do you say to them, 'Oh my God, you look awful! Those are horrible burns, oh no, what are we going to do?!' " Of course they don't! They show leadership and share calm-assertive energy—exactly the kind of energy required to be a perfect pack leader. These were men who already had all the skills they needed to manage Wilshire. They just didn't have the right information to put it into practice.

In fact, the firehouse is an ideal example of how a smoothly functioning human "pack" can work. The captain sets the rules, but only enforces them when necessary. Every person knows his or her place and job. The whole operation has the steady but soothing hum of an efficient, productive beehive. The day begins and ends in a routine, but emergencies are the stock and trade. When a call comes in, there is a rush of activity, but the firefighters react in a totally organized, disciplined fashion—much the same way that wolves or other social carnivores perform together in a hunt. Wilshire, as a pack animal, could not have found himself in a more perfect place for a dog than this firehouse. But Wilshire needed to become a disciplined member of the pack—not its out-of-control, underage pack leader!

My job was to get Wilshire's behavior under control, then show the firemen how to follow up after I left. Of course, because

Wilshire was still a puppy, he was hungry for knowledge. He was practically crying out for some rules, boundaries, and limitations. I began conditioning him with a firm touch, with my hand curled in the teeth position, to keep him away from the firemen's food on the table in the firehouse kitchen. He learned right away to be submissive. After a couple of touches, all I needed to do was raise a finger, move my body toward him, and send him my calm-assertive energy. Because he was a puppy, he had no lifelong habits to break. What I was telling him to do—to submit to the laws of the pack—was already prewired into him. With only one or two touches, and later with body language alone, I was able to create for him an invisible boundary in the garage through which he was not allowed to pass. He learned very quickly, and so did the firemen.

This is the wonderful advantage of having a puppy—you have the perfect opportunity to mold his behavior. The ability and desire to cooperate and get along—to fit into a social setting—is already there, programmed into every dog's brain. When adult dogs nudge or growl at young pups to let them know they are playing too roughly or otherwise breaking the pack rules, there's never any negotiating—but the pups don't take it personally. Again, this is not punishment—it's discipline. Humans can learn much from natural dog-on-dog puppy training. If you watch puppies of any canid species—whether African wild dogs, wolves, or dingoes—you'll notice how little rebellion they give the adults in the pack that set the rules for them. The more naturally dominant or higher-energy puppies may put up a little more challenge—testing their limits, so to speak—but they instinctually know that their survival is dependent on following the rules and rituals of the pack.

Another aspect of rehabilitating Wilshire was finding a way to get his very high energy level under control. Puppies need a lot of exercise, and Wilshire was no exception. When the guys came to work at the firehouse, there wasn't always time for one of them to take him on a brisk walk through the neighborhood. Fortunately, the firemen's own rules and discipline provided them with the perfect solution. It's a mandatory condition of employment that every Los Angeles firefighter does a run on the treadmill every day when he or she comes to the station. Fire Station 29 has two treadmills, side by side. First, I taught Wilshire to run safely on the treadmill—using a food reward to keep him interested for the first few minutes until he got into the flow of it. After that, it was up to the firemen. During the three weeks before I returned, the guys decided to designate one of the tread-

mills as "Wilshire's treadmill," and almost any time one of the crewmembers came in to run, Wilshire would follow along, jump up on "his" treadmill, and plead to be able to join in. Wilshire had a lot of energy to burn, and his daily runs went a long way toward making him more controllable. It wasn't long before Wilshire was running on the treadmill without a leash, and the act of him running side by side with every member of the fire crew created an amazing bond among all of them.

When Wilshire first came to the firehouse, Captain Reyna and his counterpart, Captain Richard McLaren, decided to make him a teaching aid so that he would have his own special job in the unit. One of the jobs of Los Angeles firefighters is to give educational presentations to schools and other groups in the community about fire safety and survival. Captain Reyna wanted to train Wilshire how to stop, drop, and roll on cue. Since adorable Wilshire would be a surefire attention-getter for kids, they'd be more likely to remember the lesson. But with Wilshire's behavior so erratic, there was no way he would be able to focus long enough, even to learn to "sit." That's why it was smart of them to bring me in first to train *them* how to give Wilshire rules, boundaries, and limitations and to make him part of the team. During the three weeks after I left, these guys proved to be the best students ever. The men on each shift left notes for the others, so everyone would be consistent in how they treated Wilshire. They settled on a routine for him, and began to put up signs around the station, reminding their brother firemen of the one-word commands that would now be in place. *Down* was to get Wilshire to stop jumping up on people. *Bed* was to send Wilshire to his bed. No one was allowed to sneak food to Wilshire in the cafeteria anymore. Consistency is of great importance when a dog has more than one pack leader. Everybody had to be on board—nobody could be a softie and let Wilshire break a rule once in a while, because then the whole program would fail. Fortunately, the life of a fireman is based on discipline and teamwork, and they stayed consistent 99 percent of the time. When I returned three weeks later, Wilshire was as energetic as ever, but now a well-behaved, respectful puppy—and a true member of the Fire Station 29 "pack." He was what I'd call *excited-submissive*. Now, he was finally ready to be trained.

When I returned, I brought along Clint Rowe, an A-list trainer who has been working with animals in Hollywood movies for over thirty years. His resume includes films like *White Fang, Turner & Hooch, The X Files, The Journey of Natty Gan,* and *Man's Best Friend.* Clint even trained the luckless bear in *Borat.* Clint has wrangled and trained animals from deer to cougars to wolves, and of course dogs, which are his specialty. Clint brought one of his tools—his clicker—along with some treats, and started Wilshire with just the "stop-and-drop" part of the routine. Training a dog to perform tricks on cue can be a time-consuming exercise, and it takes patience, timing, and a lot of repetition. It's also best not to overload an animal with long "cramming" sessions, but to do a little bit, maybe ten minutes or so, two or three times a day. I really enjoyed watching Clint work, and he was clear and concise as he explained and demonstrated his methods to the firemen.

One difference between Cesar and me is that he works in "real time," which is pretty impressive. In training animals to perform in films, the only real time that exists is on the set, on the actual day of the filming. People don't realize that most of our work is done in preparation, behind the scenes, day after day.

In what I do—especially in films—you really want the animal to enjoy what he does; you want him to actually pull you to the set, he's so excited to get to work. With Wilshire, the first thing I had to find out is what drives him; what motivates him. Luckily, I saw right away that he had a great food drive.

We started with just stop and drop. We gave Wilshire a little blanket for his comfort, and we set a little mark on it to be the spot he'd go to that would start the behavior sequence. I used the clicker, then rewarded him with food at each stage. Stop on the mark, click, and reward. Down ("drop"), click, reward. Eventually we phased out the food. What the clicker provides is a neutral environment. It works to separate out any tension that occurs naturally or unnaturally between you and the animal. It allows the animal to work on its own, responding to its environment on its own. The learning process becomes relaxed. When learning happens in a relaxed way, the lessons are retained both quickly and smoothly.

The key to working the clicker is keeping your emotions "neutral." Cesar might call it calm and assertive; to me, it's just a nonemotional place. I've seen people yelling at animals, getting upset with animals, and they still don't get why they fail. I agree with Cesar—it's really about the energy you're sending the dog, not the tool you're using—that determines the outcome. If I get frustrated or angry or tired—say, it's been a long day—it doesn't matter how great my timing is, or his food drive, or anything. If I get too excited and overpraise or overreward, it's the same problem. You have to keep your emotions—your "energy"—steady, or it's just not going to *work. The animal's trust and security—both in you and in himself—is always built around and grounded in your calm emotions.*

Cut to four weeks after Clint first came to work with Wilshire. Our *Dog Whisperer* crew, ever mindful of television deadlines, were there to film Wilshire's first on-camera performance, at a local elementary school. Clint was there, too. I couldn't have been more proud to watch a lanky, maturing Wilshire do his perfect stop, drop, and roll routine in front of a classroom of delighted preschool and kindergarten children. But remember, it all began with the simple rules, boundaries, and limitations the firemen and I had set into place during my first visit. Before that, Wilshire had no attention span, no focus and, most importantly, no respect for humans. Though it is possible to *force* new behaviors or tricks on a dog that isn't balanced—I witnessed this once at a facility where I worked when I first came to America—that dog will be much less likely to retain the behaviors, and may also become inconsistent in responding to commands. As I've mentioned before, a dog that is "trained" is not necessarily balanced; just as a Harvard graduate isn't necessarily mentally healthy. Balance can be achieved, however, with exercise, discipline, and affection, and in training with *the right blend of both positive reinforcement and well-timed corrections.*

Clint tells me that Wilshire has proven such a great student; he's still adding even more difficult tricks to his routine. When we filmed an episode for *Dog Whisperer,* either Clint, or the fireman who was Wilshire's trainer for that day, would have to be right next to him in order to get him to stop, drop, and roll on cue. But recently, Wilshire made a special guest appearance at a huge pet adoption fair with hundreds of people in the audience. Wilshire's trainer was a full ten feet offstage while Wilshire did a perfect stop, drop, and roll! Clint and the firemen have now taught Wilshire to "suit up"—meaning put his head into his own collar—and are working on teaching him to do an army crawl, another lesson in fire safety. Wilshire is the perfect example of how the formula of exercise, discipline, and affection, consistent calm-assertive leadership, and reward-based behavioral conditioning can all come together to create a happy, balanced, and psychologically challenged dog. From a pup whose very life was on the line, Wilshire promises to become a role model for all firehouse dogs—as well as a real Los Angeles institution. Captain Reyna says that when the fire truck drives up with Wilshire in the front seat, people spontaneously jump to their feet and cheer.

Once a dog is stable and balanced using my exercise-discipline-affection formula; once the human pack leader has earned his or her dog's trust and respect—*then* the benefits of reward-based training and conditioning are endless. Dogs need psychological as well as physical challenges, and learning new behaviors—especially those that make a dog feel useful or proud of herself—are all a part of that. Just like humans, dogs are social animals that flourish when they know what their job is in keeping the pack running smoothly. Recently, most ethologists and other experts who study wild animals in captivity are becoming champions of the common-sense notion that *all* animals need some sort of "job," or purpose, to be psychologically healthy, especially when they're living in our artificial, human environments; that is, behind walls. Behavioral enrichment for animals is a new field where experts study what tools, games, and challenges work best to keep captive animals en-

gaged in and excited about their environments. Those of us who work with animals have known for a long time that a happy animal is one that feels she has a purpose. For years, trainer Clint Rowe worked on training a tightly knit pack of wolf hybrids to play the parts of real wolf packs in movies. Wolf hybrids are some of the most difficult dogs to train, since they are genetically as close to their wolf ancestry as a dog can come, and always retain many of the raw survival instincts and sensitivities that undomesticated animals tend to have. Yet Clint describes performing with this pack as one of the most profound experiences of connecting with animals that he has ever had in his life. "Working with the wolf hybrid pack preparing for a film, and on the set itself, was like a ballet. They anticipated what the next steps were and so were totally tuned in to their environment and of course me, since I was a key in their focus—their leader. The pack knew everything I was thinking and wanted them to do—and I knew that they were going to follow through beautifully. We were just so completely connected—there was an energy field between us that nobody could see, but even the film crew could sense there was something powerful happening there."

A warning about wolf hybrids to readers who might be interested in these magnificent animals: Clint says he always treated his wolf hybrid pack as if they were *pure wolf*, not part dog, and stresses that wolf hybrids should never be obtained by people unfamiliar with handling dangerous wild animals. Many nonprofessionals have adopted these beautiful animals for the "thrill" or the status of owning them, and have ended up having terrible experiences and sometimes even fatal accidents. Wolf hybrids' unique genetic mix keeps them squarely in the wild domain. Some experts theorize that wolf hybrids are so potentially hazardous because they combine the predatory instincts of wolves (which aren't predominantly aggressive) and the aggressive instincts of dogs (which aren't predominantly predatory). Don't be fooled by some of their doglike features: They should be treated with the same caution and respect given any wild animal.

Like Clint and his pack of wolf hybrids, therapy dogs, agility dogs, hunting dogs, farming dogs, police dogs, search-and-rescue dogs, and even dogs of war often develop these incredibly deep, fulfilling bonds with their human handlers. Giving your dog a "job" means having to become an even stronger pack leader than a mere "pet owner" usually does. You, the owner, are actually creating a kind of purpose and structure for dogs that most closely reflects the kind of lives and functions that they were originally built for.

Turning a Negative into a Positive

The point of *all* behavioral work with animals is to end up with a positive experience and a win-win situation, for both the animal and the handler. In nature, discipline, rules, and boundaries are positive things, because they ensure survival. When a more dominant dog corrects a more submissive dog, the payoff is that the second animal learns how to get along better within the pack. The dominant dog helps create an environment with less conflict. Through a momentary correction, a positive result is reached. That's why I always say, when working with dogs, you must always envision the positive outcome that you desire, which will allow you to turn any negative into a positive.

If an experience is made positive, it can even override an animal's natural instincts, to help her assimilate better into our human world. For example, the three female sea lions in the Central Park Zoo in New York perform dozens of variations on their natural play behaviors at feeding time, three times a day. But the animal professionals at the zoo also need to give the sea lions a daily medical checkup, and that's something that sea lions wouldn't submit to in nature. Remember, in the wild, an injured or diseased animal can attract predators, threaten the security of the group, and even be targeted by the group itself—so animals instinctually don't "advertise" when they're not feeling well. Except for human beings, you won't find any whining hypochondriacs in the animal kingdom. Therefore, the trainers at the Central Park Zoo must encourage the animals to display behaviors such as opening their mouths wide for checkups and teeth cleaning in exchange for positive encouragement and food rewards. There is a huge amount of trust and respect between the sea lions and their handlers—because they are turning what, in nature, is seen as a negative behavior, into a positive one.

When I feed my pack at the Dog Psychology Center, I make everyone wait, then I feed the calmest, most submissive dog first.

In nature, of course, the most submissive dog would eat last. By doing this, I encourage the rest of the pack to mirror the behavior that was rewarded with food. Though I continue to believe that you should always work with Mother Nature, never against her, when it comes to dogs, I also think that making the decision to work around instincts that are no longer advantageous for an animal that must survive in the midst of our often alien human world is *not* an exception to that rule. In this case, we are manipulating instincts to make life better for the animal so she can live more peacefully and stably in *our* environment—even if our modern world comes in a sloppy second to the place nature might have chosen for her to live.

Canine Democracy

It seems to me that in our current "politically correct" climate, many of us, especially in America, have somehow concluded that it is wrong to assert leadership over our pets. We've gone from the old-fashioned authoritarian extreme—where animals existed only to do our bidding—to another unhealthy extreme—where animals are considered our equal partners in every area of our lives. This is not to say that we are better than animals in any way, shape, or form. Absolutely not! We are simply different. But one very clear reason we need to be in control of our pets is that we have brought them into *our* world, not the other way around. We have brought them into a world fraught with strange dangers—concrete floors, moving vehicles, electric wires, and high-rise apartments. Everything about our world is unnatural to them. Sure, with our guidance they can learn how to navigate around that world safely; they can become accustomed to it and even come to live happily in it. But it is still not the way Mother Nature intended them to live, and it never will be. The more we understand the way our dogs think, the more we can learn to fulfill their needs, despite the fact that they are living with us in a world that is foreign to them—and on a deeper level, to the animal within us as well.

Saying that we must take the leadership role with our dogs is not saying we must become ruthless dictators over them, and saying our dogs should be calm-submissive does not mean we make them "lesser" than us, either. Like all social animals, both humans and dogs need structure and leadership or their lives dissolve into chaos. Though democracy may be the highest ideal that most human societies strive for, even democracies have leadership figures. And trust me—your dog has no desire to live in a democracy! Every cell in your dog's body would rather have a clearly defined social framework, with a fair, consistent pack leader whom she trusts and respects at the helm—more than she would ever want an "equal vote" in how your *human* household is run. Human beings would be wise to worry about perfecting the concept of democracy among one another first, before they start imposing it onto other animal species.

Punishment, Abuse, and Out-of-Control Emotions

Showing an animal strong leadership and giving it rules is not the same thing as instilling fear and punishing it in an abusive fashion. A quick, assertive touch is not the same thing as a strike. Creating respect is not the same thing as creating intimidation.

The first time I witnessed animal abuse was when I lived in Mazatlán, Mexico, as a child. It tore me up inside to see people throwing rocks at dogs and swearing at them. Later, as an adult, I witnessed firsthand the effects of abuse on dogs. I have seen animals that have been hit and kicked, neglected puppies tied to trees in backyards for days, and dogs denied food and water. One memorable case is Popeye, a pit bull. Popeye lost an eye in an illegal dog fight. After this, his owners abandoned him. With his new vision impairment, Popeye felt vulnerable, grew suspicious, and became very aggressive toward other dogs in an attempt to intimidate them. Rosemary was also used in illegal pit bull fights. When she lost a particularly important fight, her owners poured gasoline over her and set her on fire. A rescue organization stepped in and saved her life, but the horrific experience turned her into a dangerously aggressive dog.

Thankfully, I was able to rehabilitate both Popeye and Rosemary and provide them with the proper leadership they needed to be fulfilled and feel safe. However, not all dogs are this fortunate. Out of fear, abused dogs may attack and kill other dogs, and sometimes even humans. Society often sentences these dogs to death, despite the fact that it was because of humans that they became dangerously unstable in the first place.

The way I see it, most animal abuse comes from unbalanced human emotions and our own repressed, negative energies. Just as it is ineffective to punish a child when a parent is out of control, it is useless to vent your rage or unhappiness on an animal that can't possibly understand what you are upset about. And, as hard as it is for most of us to face it, love is not enough, either— for animals, or for humans! I always say, if love were all it took to change unwanted behavior into good behavior, then there would be no unbalanced people in the world! Likewise, if love were enough to make your dog into the perfect pet, she would be

SOME BASIC DOS AND DON'TS OF DISCIPLINE

- DO establish your house rules, boundaries, and limitations between the *human* members of your pack *before* you bring a dog into your home.
- DO make sure all the humans are on the same page as to what is or isn't allowed.
- DO remain clear and consistent with your dog about the rules.
- DO begin enforcing rules from your dog's first day at home—your dog doesn't understand the concept of a "special day" or "holiday" from rules!
- DO always call up your calm-assertive energy when you notice a behavior you need to correct.
- DO offer your dog an alternative to the disallowed behavior.
- DON'T enforce rules if you are frustrated, angry, emotional, or tired. Wait until you can respond unemotionally to your dog's behavior.
- DON'T yell at or hit your dog out of anger, ever!
- DON'T expect your dog to read your mind.
- DON'T expect your dog to follow rules that aren't consistently enforced.
- DON'T reinforce or encourage a fearful or aggressive state of mind.
- DO reward your dog with treats or affection, but only when she's in a calm-submissive or active-submissive state.

thinking, *My owner loves me so much, I'm not going to chase the cat today.* Of course, your dog doesn't think like that. She can't rationalize or ponder her own behavior. That is reason enough never to let any animal "push your buttons." Never, ever correct an animal out of anger or frustration. When you try to correct your dog out of anger, you are usually more out of control than your dog is. You are fulfilling your own needs, not the animal's— and in a profoundly unhealthy way. Trust me, your dog will sense your unstable energy and often escalate her unwanted behavior instead.

Remember, your dog is your mirror. The behavior you get back is usually, in some way, a reflection of your own.

SUCCESS STORY

Bill, Maryan, and Lulu

We rescued our dog Lulu from the local shelter. When we first brought her home, she would roll over and pee if you tried to pet her. . . . She was especially afraid of me and would normally roll over on her back, tail tucked between her legs, when I entered the room she was in.

Outside the house she was very difficult to control on the leash; off the leash she'd tear off across our yard, then the neighbor's yard(s), and I'd end up down the block before I'd be able to get her back.

Both Maryan and I were very concerned about our inability to control her, and that she seemed interested in the cats more as a meal (or a snack) than in having them as friends.

As we'd both seen the *Dog Whisperer* show, and had been impressed with what we'd seen, we decided we'd try out a few of Cesar's methods. Cesar's philosophy of exercise, discipline, and then affection is so simple, it's hard to believe the difference it makes.

Two [methods] in particular stood out to us. The first was the *tshhhst* sound he makes on the show; it always gets the dog's attention, and nearly instantly. The second was using the leash, but up high, right behind the ears, instead of lower, near the base of the neck.

A third method, using a treadmill to provide exercise when you're otherwise unable to take the dog for a walk, seemed like something we'd like to be able to use (as Maryan has had great difficulty walking for any extended period of time), *if* we could figure out how to get her [Lulu] to do it. Initially she'd try and get off, but with her on the leash, and keeping her up there, she eventually started walking. Today, she'll actually get our attention and then go to the treadmill as if she's asking for a session. It has been a truly amazing transformation.

I'm happy to report that in just a few short weeks these three seemingly small techniques have transformed our life with Lulu. She's far more confident, calm, and far less of a "handful." Maryan is now able to take Lulu with her when she walks to the mailbox; Lulu is attentive, calm, and incredibly gentle on the leash now. No longer tugging or refusing to move . . . instead she's become a great walking companion.

She and the cats have made friends. Our cat Precious and Lulu have become such good friends, they actually will sleep next to one another at times! Now we've all become "a pack"—my only real wish is that these same methods would work on the cats!

Cesar's overall philosophy, one of balance, ties closely to my own. I'm of the belief that in order to achieve balance we need to live "in the now." It's a belief most often touted by Eastern religions . . . that once it's examined, causes you (or at the very least it caused me) to realize that the "now" is all we ever have. The past is gone, and nothing about the future is guaranteed; all we ever have is the moment we're living in, right now.

3

The Best Tool in the World

Training is a term we have been conditioned to
accept as something we do through tasks and by using
tools. This is true, but sometimes the tools we use, we
cannot see, taste, hear, smell, or physically touch.

—*Brandon Carpenter, horse trainer*

Often when I'm doing a public appearance or leading
one of my seminars, I'm approached by people who
want to know what I think is absolutely the number
one, best, most consistently reliable tool for training or rehabilitating a dog. They are often surprised when I tell them that the
best tool they could ever have for controlling their dogs is some-

thing they already own. They carry that tool with them every day, everywhere they go. That tool is their *energy*. In fact, that is the one and *only* tool that I will always come out and advocate every time.

You—meaning your energy, your beingness—happen to be the most powerful tool that has ever been created. You, as a human being, have ability that is unique in all of the animal kingdom. Only a human—no other animal—is able to put several different species together in one place—species that might be killing each other in nature—and influence them to get along. Have you ever seen a movie—for example, *Ace Ventura: Pet Detective* or *Doctor Dolittle*—where there is a chicken, pig, horse, cat, dog, snake, and cow all together in one room? Of course, it was a human who came up with the intention to film that scene, who developed the strategy to make it happen, and whose energy created the possibility to make it all happen. All those animals on that movie set had human handlers—trainers like my friend Clint Rowe—who are able to control the animal that they are in charge of without leashes or collars or cages—at the very least, for the period of time in which the scene is being filmed. If any of those human handlers in charge of the animals became nervous or frightened, or somehow woke up one morning thinking, "I'll never be able to control that pig today!", the scene wouldn't happen.

Excluding your energy, I define a *tool* as any item we use to establish a physical link to our dogs. Like our energy, tools are intended to *communicate* our intentions and expectations to our dogs. Techniques are how we apply our chosen tools and other methods to become more effective pack leaders.

My Grandfather's Rope

I always say that companies like Petco or PetSmart would never make as much money in rural Mexico as they do here in America. That's because, instead of a fancy leash, we just use the same old rope, over and over again, for generations and generations: "Hey, go and get me Grandpa's rope out of the barn." That's why I so often use a simple, thirty-five-cent leash—to show that it's not the leash that's controlling the dog; it's the energy behind the leash. In *Cesar's Way*, I talk about the fact that the homeless in Los Angeles are among the best pack leaders for dogs that I've seen since coming to this country. They lead these dogs with their energy—and the dogs follow, off leash. These homeless pack leaders have a simple mission: to move forward and do whatever they need to do to survive. Their energy is reflected in their mission, which in turn is reflected in the dog's mission. In many primitive cultures, dogs still roam free in villages, scavenging for scraps. They follow along with humans without a leash when it comes time to go hunting or tracking. These human pack leaders are instinctively aware that the best tool they have to communicate with another species is their energy.

Before human civilization began encroaching on animals' territories, forcing them to become unnaturally aggressive in order to survive, most animals—even some of the most fearsome beasts on earth—were naturally afraid of humans. Wolves, leopards, lions, and elephants all instinctively understood that humans had something they didn't—a combination of powerful instinctive, psychological, and intellectual energy—that overrode the fact that we *Homo sapiens* are slower, weaker, and have no teeth or claws with which we can truly fight back. Today, we modern humans just go down to the store and buy special leashes and collars that we *think* give us more power over animals. In truth, most of us have lost the instinctual energy that gave us our natural advantage in the first place. We have forgotten what our ancestors already knew about animals—that the only surefire way to outwit them was by using our minds.

Throughout years of civilization, humans have invented thousands of tools for controlling or influencing various members of the animal kingdom. Some of those tools are now thought of as inhumane; others are still in use today. I'm sure there will be more and more tools developed in the future. But there will never be a better tool than what you already have within you. There is no work of art that exists in the universe that is better than you in that regard. Remember, you are part of Mother Nature and you have the ability to connect with Mother Nature at any time. Who you are in the animal world is your energy—and that energy has no limits. They key is learning how to break the code and tap into the animal in you. Your instinctual energy is the number-one most important tool you can have when it comes to controlling or influencing the behavior of your dog.

Tools Are for Empowerment

A tool doesn't become energy until you touch it. A tree branch is just a tree branch until a chimpanzee breaks it off and uses it to dig for bugs. It has no special function until the chimpanzee uses the branch with *intention*. A cheese knife can be lying on the cutting board next to a row of cheddar and crackers, but if a man takes it and stabs another man with it out of anger, it becomes a weapon—again, simply because of intention. Is using a cheese knife to cut cheese inhumane? Of course not! Is using a cheese knife to stab someone inhumane? Yes! What I am getting at here is that whatever tool you choose to use with your dog was not invented to hurt the dog. The tool was made to empower the handler, given the possibility that the handler cannot control the animal with energy alone. If a handler comes to certain tools with anxious energy, frustrated energy, anger, or a feeling of helplessness, then I would argue that the handler's negative energy is far more inhumane toward the dog than most tools out there. If a tool isn't used correctly and with calm-assertive energy, not only will it not work, but it can indeed become something that harms the dog.

There are many cases in which a dog owner legitimately cannot control the animal with energy or just a simple rope—and no one should be ashamed of that. After all, there are leash laws throughout America. Even the lawmakers pretty much assume that a good percentage of people out there may not be able to control a dog in an emergency. Leashes, collars, and other tools act as our backup. In some cases, a dog is just way too physically strong for a human. My friend and client Kathleen is a good example of such a case. Kathleen adopted Nicky, a ninety-two-pound Rottweiler that had been abused by his previous owner, and there is no doubt that without Kathleen stepping up to rescue him, Nicky surely would have been put to sleep. Kathleen is a delicate, tiny woman who also has osteoporosis. And since Nicky is a powerful, high-energy dog, he needs to walk regularly. Kathleen is not strong enough on her own to stop Nicky if he gets excited and rushes toward another dog while on walks. Kathleen is exactly the kind of person who needs the correct tool to empower herself, and to keep Nicky and other dogs safe.

I applied a three-part strategy to help empower Kathleen to be a wonderful, responsible owner for Nicky. First, I took Nicky to the Dog Psychology Center for two weeks, to better socialize him with members of his own kind. Because his previous abusive owner had kept him chained to a post for literally years, he had a staggering amount of pent-up energy and frustration, which he was releasing on other dogs. Nicky turned out to be a friendly, playful guy once he experienced "the power of the pack," vigorous daily exercise, and a balanced, predictable routine. Next, I worked with Kathleen on channeling her own calm-assertive energy. Kathleen is a strong, determined woman, but her medical condition had left her feeling a little unsure of herself. She was also very much ruled by her sorrow for what had happened to Nicky in the past. I helped her to draw on the resilient, survivor part of herself when dealing with Nicky, and helped her start living in the moment with him. Finally, I taught her the correct use of the tool she had chosen for Nicky—the prong collar. The collar helped Kathleen give Nicky stronger, quicker corrections than she would ever be able to do on her own, especially given her osteoporosis. In turn, knowing she had the collar to fall back on further empowered Kathleen to feel stronger and more confident when walking Nicky. Ultimately, it was Kathleen's increased confidence that turned Nicky into a more obedient dog—not the collar at all! Once again, it's not the tool, but the energy behind the tool, that matters. Would it have been more "humane" for Kathleen to give up on Nicky, possibly condemning him to death? I believe she made the right choice, finding a tool that she could use without harming her dog, learning to use it correctly, empowering herself and making her a far more effective pack leader to her dog. But it wasn't the collar *itself* that turned Nicky around—the collar was simply one step on her journey to Kathleen's acceptance of her own strength and potential.

Dillinger's Gun and Grandmother's Newspaper

People often forget how much the power of intention, psychology, and energy contribute to the effectiveness of a tool. It became legendary when infamous Depression-era outlaw John Dillinger broke out of the "escape-proof" jail in Crown Point, Indiana, using a wooden gun painted with shoe polish. If this colorful story is true, you can bet that it was Dillinger's determination, charisma, and fearsome reputation that *really* got him out of jail—and probably prevented his jailers from examining the "weapon" in his hand too closely. If your eighty-year-old grandmother had a dog, it's likely she kept a rolled-up newspaper nearby. That's the old-fashioned way of disciplining a dog (many of my elderly clients still use it) and I certainly don't advocate it, for very practical reasons I'll share later in the chapter. But is it wrong? If it's used abusively, of course it's wrong. Still, clients who've had a parent or grandparent use this method tell me that Grandma usually didn't even touch her dog with the newspaper. She'd just move toward the newspaper. From that point on, the dog realizes that Grandma is serious—even when she never even touched the paper itself. Because the simple act of moving toward the newspaper empowers Grandma in her *own* mind, the dog changes. The dog feels the switch of Grandma's energy, and understands that she now seems more powerful. Once again, it's the energy, not the newspaper, that caused the shift. If you think any tool alone is going to do the job for you, forget about it. It's not going to happen. The calm-assertive energy you put into the tool is much more important than the tool itself.

I can make any tool work for me, but that doesn't mean it will be the right tool for the person I'm trying to help. When I go to the homes of my clients, I always ask them, "What is the tool that makes *you* the most comfortable?" I prefer to work with the tool they are already familiar with, but of course, to train them in the correct method of using that tool—since incorrect use of any tool *can* be harmful for a dog. Sometimes I might feel that the clients would do better with a different tool because, perhaps, they may not be at the correct level to master the tool they are currently using. In that case, I will suggest what I believe is a better method for them to obtain control and, more importantly, the self-confidence they need in order to be effective. Again, it's the confidence—the calm-assertive energy—that is the key. The ideal goal—and this is a goal that truly is possible for many people—is to recover the primal connection between human and dog in order to master the off-leash experience. The dream is to be able to use your energy to connect and communicate with your dog in such a way that your need for any tool is minimal.

Take, for instance, my relationship with my pit bull Daddy. Although I use a simple thirty-five-cent leash with Daddy in situations where it's either necessary by law or is for his own protection, basically the only tool I need to influence Daddy is my mind, my energy, and my relationship with him—which is based 100 percent on trust and respect. When Daddy and I are walking together, I feel there is no boundary between him and me. He reads my energy and I read his energy and we move forward together as one. If I have an intention, I can almost always communicate it to him with a gesture or a thought. To me, this is the ideal relationship between human and dog—and a goal we all can strive for.

While I've focused on one's energy to control a dog's behavior thus far in this chapter, I do want to clarify that I am in favor of leash laws. Having grown up in a country without leash laws, I believe America does exactly the right thing in requiring owners to keep their dogs on leashes while out in public. Dogs are animals, and animals are controlled by instinct, not by reason. Even the most diligent owner could experience her dog being attracted to a child who's eating a piece of chicken or a baby in a stroller with a bottle of milk or another dog across the street. The dog could bolt away and hurt a child or another dog, or could dart into the street and get hit by a car. Sadly, experience has proven that most owners have little control over their dogs in such a situation. Another advantage to a leash law is to help control the dog population. One of dogs' strongest natural urges is to mate, and without leashes, an unspayed female in heat can be impregnated in the blink of an eye. To sum it up, a leash law is about facing reality and preventing accidents, and I am 100 percent supportive of this important safety measure.

Now that you understand my overall philosophy about tools—it's not the tool itself, it's the energy behind it—let's review some of the most common tools people use for correcting their dogs, examine their pros and cons, and discuss situations when they may or may not be appropriate.

The Rope or Simple Leash

From my grandfather's rope in Mexico to the thirty-five-cent nylon leashes you can pick up at any pet store, this tool can be

anything you can simply loop over an animal's neck to make sure
that he follows you. The purpose of this kind of leash is just very
basic communication between you and your pet—so you can
tell him in the simplest way to trust you and to follow you, or to
go in the same direction you are going.

A simple leash is the basic way to ensure that an animal
doesn't run away from you. Usually, this is for the good of the animal. I remember experiences on my grandfather's farm where a
cow or a horse would fall into a ditch. The animal would panic
and thrash around and do things that were obviously going to
hurt him. My grandfather would go get the rope, loop it around
the animal's neck, and use his calm-assertive energy to get the
animal to relax. Then he would use the rope to lead the animal to
safety. The rope accomplished trust, respect, and leadership—
and it allowed my grandfather to communicate directly with the
animal about what direction it needed to go in order to get out of
any given dangerous situation.

The simple leash is my tool of choice when I take my pack on the road. When I am going to walk Coco the Chihuahua, Louis the Chinese crested, and Sid the French bulldog in a strange city, I will loop my little nylon leashes over their necks and we'll "migrate" for a few blocks. I like to keep the loop part of the leash high up on the neck, to give me more control over the animal's head and to keep him from wandering or tracking or sniffing the ground. Just as Daddy, Coco, Louis, and I are totally in tune using leashes, so I could just as easily have them follow me off-leash in places where that is legal. Sid, however, is another story. We only adopted him a few months ago, and unfortunately, he's got a long way to go in learning to understand limits and boundaries—those are the areas where I need to work with him. Sid is a retired show dog—a prizewinner, in fact. His experience of life up until recently was mostly inside the show ring. He never wandered in open areas or spent time in the outdoors, so if a squirrel passes by, it is a major event and distraction for him. Sid doesn't yet understand that when he is outside, he can't just tear off in any direction. Until he and I spend more time together, repeating over and over the exercises that will help him understand the concept of invisible boundaries, the only thing that is going to communicate boundaries to him is the leash, and the leash is going to save his life.

The Simple Collar

The next most basic tool for influencing a dog is the simple collar or buckle collar—the one that looks like a belt. This collar enables the dog to carry his tags. Most collars you can purchase have a feature where you can clip a leash on to it, creating a collar-leash combination. If an animal isn't tame, he will fight a collar that is too restricting, but your average dog will have no problem with it. It is a step up from the little nylon leashes I use, and for most owners, it provides more security. Plus, collars come in thousands of styles and can cost anywhere from less than a dollar to thousands of dollars. Some stud collars can prevent another animal from hurting your dog's neck if he happens to be attacked, but most of these collars are purely for aesthetic purposes. When Daddy and I were presenters at the Creative Arts Emmys in Los Angeles, I put him in his swankiest studded collar for the occasion. Did Daddy know the difference? Of course not. But the paparazzi did find him to be extra photogenic when he was walking down the red carpet!

A very important thing to remember when using any leash or collar on a dog is that you *never* bring the tool to the dog; you invite the dog to come to the tool. You can make it a positive experience by using treats or just your own energy. Chasing after a dog and trying to force something foreign around his neck will not accomplish trust or respect. The dog will either believe you are playing a game with him, or come to fear the tool itself. Never let a tool be associated with a negative in your dog's mind.

The Flexi Leash

Flexi leashes were first created for tracking purposes. Before the flexi leash, handlers of tracking dogs would have to carry twenty-, thirty-, or forty-foot leashes to allow the dog to follow a scent; then they'd have to go through the long and tedious process of winding the leash back. The flexi leash became the perfect solution because the handler was able to command the dog to search and let the dog go, and once the dog had located its goal, the handler could just follow the lead to where the dog was waiting, reeling the leash in as she walked. Since its invention, the flexi leash has become very popular among pet owners because of what I believe is a myth: that a dog needs "freedom" on its walk.

Yes, dogs need freedom; all animals do. But the term *freedom* can have different definitions. The purpose of a walk with a pack leader is not to let the dog wander; it is to give the dog a powerful, primal, structured, bonding experience between human and dog. Most people don't understand that the structured walk in itself can be a truly "freeing" experience for a dog. Often, the owner who is so concerned with her dog's "freedom" is really secretly guilty for having left the dog alone in the house all day while she was at work. Somehow, letting her dog pull her all over the neighborhood in the name of "freedom" manages to soothe her guilty feelings.

When a dog is being walked on a flexi leash and pulls way out in front of the owner, then the dog is in charge. The dog is not tracking, which is a controlled, structured activity; it is simply sniffing. Many owners approve of this behavior because they believe they are allowing the dog to "read the newspaper," or what some people now call reading her "pee-mail." Yes, your dog *does* get her "daily news" from sniffing the ground, bushes, trees, hydrants, and other landmarks. She *does* find out who's been around recently, whether someone has a health problem, and the rest of the juicy canine "Page Six" gossip tidbits that dogs pick up from scents and their environment. However, there is a right way and a wrong way for you to allow your dog this opportunity to catch up on the local news. First of all, your dog can get the same information when he's walking behind or beside you. He doesn't have to be pulling you along, acting as your pack leader. Second,

I always recommend that a human "pack leader" allow her dog a short break or two in the middle of a walk to wander around and explore, to smell and to urinate. The difference is that the owner controls the behavior—gives her dog permission when and where to explore, then decides when it's time to return to the structured walk. This way, you can maintain your solid pack leader status at the beginning and end of the walk, while rewarding your dog at the same time.

There are other negatives involving both control and safety using flexi leashes. A flexi leash gives you the minimum amount of control over your dog. People often get tangled in the leads, and sometimes, so do dogs. A very high-energy, active, dominant dog has the greatest likelihood of getting into trouble with so much space between the leash and the handler. The stronger the dog, the more likely he is to pull away from the handler, dragging her or even yanking the leash out of her hands, defeating the purpose. Flexi leashes work best with medium-energy, happy-go-lucky dogs or very lightweight dogs that don't have dominance issues and are basically obedient in most situations.

The Choke Chain

The choke chain, probably the training tool with the most negative name in the world, originated from the same basic idea of the loop around the neck to control an animal's movement. We're back to the concept of my grandfather's rope again. When used correctly, this tool is not supposed to cause an animal to "choke," cut off an animal's breath, or even cause momentary discomfort. The premise is that tightening the chain around the neck sends a message of correction, and releasing it implies that the correction

has been heeded. Of course, if the chain is used incorrectly—pulling the dog's neck upward with too much force—it can indeed cause a choking reaction. It's intended to be used with a firm but gentle, split-second pull to the side; a "snap-out-of-it" kind of movement that has the sole purpose of simply getting the dog's attention. I just wish they had given this tool a different name—loop chain, a neck chain, a control chain—anything other than a name that implies giving pain to a dog. But it seems we are stuck with the term *choke chain,* so that's how I'll refer to it here.

A choke chain doesn't even have to be a chain to serve its purpose. While the traditional choke chain is made out of metal, some people believe chains made out of heavy cotton or interlocking loops of thick nylon are more humane for the dog. The choke chains handlers use in dog shows are made of little snaking pieces of metal, woven so closely together that they look like a continuous line. These serve the same purpose as a heavier chain.

The heavier the chain, the less likely the dog will be to chew through it or to pop it off accidentally by pulling away. Logically, it follows that the more powerful the dog, the heavier the chain you will want to choose. The heavy metal choke chain concept was originally developed for really powerful dogs—dogs that can hurt a person, another dog, or themselves if they get away.

As always, it's important to remember that when choosing a slightly more advanced tool like a choke chain, the owner should have a professional, or at the very least a salesperson at the pet store, instruct her hands-on in the correct way to use it. Most vital of all, the energy behind the chain *must* be calm and assertive, not upset, tense, anxious, or angry. If someone flails around, yanking a dog's chain with anger and frustration, then this very useful, innocent tool can indeed choke—and become the instrument of cruelty that its unfortunate name implies.

A Note About Chains in General

My Dog Psychology Center in South Los Angeles is in the heart of some pretty hardcore gang territory. It seems that throughout history, aggressive men have gravitated toward big, tough dogs to make them seem more powerful. In this day and age, pit bulls seem to be the tough dog of choice—for gang members, drug dealers, and other antisocial types. In the past fifteen years, the brutal, underground culture of dogfighting has become a big source of income for gang members and other criminals. Many of my dogs at the center are survivors of such brutality—and if you go into any major animal shelter or pound in much of Los Angeles, you will see a majority of pit bulls who will probably lose their lives to euthanasia because they happened to have owners in that culture. I am strongly against this way of life. It is not only inhumane to animals, but many who attend dogfights bring their children to watch, creating a new generation of people who are desensitized to animal cruelty. It also creates a climate of prejudice against pit bulls, or the dogs sometimes known as "bully breeds," that is not the fault of the breed but of the owner.

Chains seem to be a big part of this destructive culture. Gang members will put huge, heavy chains around the necks of their dogs to make them seem fiercer, or because they believe it makes them stronger for dogfights. It's a misconception that putting weight on a dog's neck makes it a better fighter. If the neck is strong but the body is lean, the dog will not be a good fighter. Heavy chains can give dogs head and neck problems. Chains are also used on dogs to chain them up in a yard, either for guard purposes or just to get the dog out of the way for a period of time— usually by criminals and people who are either uninformed or immune to animal cruelty. This is a very dangerous and cruel practice—the more tightly a dog is chained, the more pent-up energy he will have; the more pent-up energy, the more the aggression. A frustrated dog on a chain becomes a weapon, and is nearly three times more likely to attack or bite a person than a dog that is simply loose in a yard.[1] Many activists in Los Angeles are working to set laws against this practice, and I support their efforts.

Back before I began rehabilitating dogs, I trained attack and guard dogs. As any police dog handler will tell you, a dog conditioned in human aggression does not have an easy on-off switch. The people who work with these dogs are experienced handlers and have specialized training to work with controlling such dogs. As I've written in *Cesar's Way*, anyone should think long and hard before deciding to use a dog as a weapon.

The Martingale Collar

The martingale collar was designed to help a dog stay comfortable while remaining securely on the leash. It has a longer, wider section, usually made of leather, chain, or nylon, joined through two loops—the larger one placed loosely around the dog's neck; the smaller one clipped onto the leash. If the dog pulls away from the leash, the tension pulls the small loop taut, tightening the larger loop around the neck. The wide section both prevents the chain from tangling in the dog's coat and prevents the collar from becoming so tight it cuts off the dog's airways. In my experience, martingales are a good alternative for happy-go-lucky dogs that don't need a lot of correction, and for dogs that are basically well-behaved and just need an occasional reminder.

The Illusion Collar

A few years ago, my wife, Ilusion, suggested to me that I invent a leash that would help owners to hold a dog's neck in the highest position during a walk—the way I do it on our television show. I suggested that she take a stab at it herself. With the assistance of designer Jaci Rohr, Ilusion perfected her original design of the Illusion collar, which helps you, the owner, put the natural architecture of a dog's neck to use in your favor.

In terms of handling and leash work, a dog's neck has three parts—the high, the middle, and the lower part.

The lower part is the strongest part of the neck, where the dog has the most control. Trying to control an unstable dog with a leash in this position can cause the dog to choke, pull, and

wrestle—and you are likely to be the loser of this wrestling match. But when the leash is attached to the very top of the neck, you're dealing with the most sensitive part. It takes very little effort for you to communicate, guide, and correct your dog when holding the leash in that position. It is more natural for the dog to give

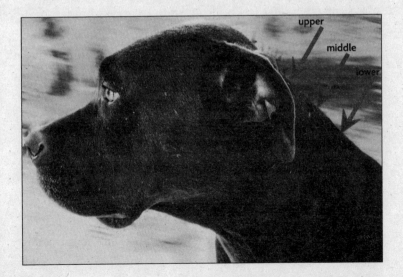

in and have a positive learning experience. It also removes the dog's nose from the ground, redirecting him from the distractions of the environment around him. The Illusion collar is designed to use the lower part of the neck for support, while at the same time relying on the upper part of the neck for communication and control.

The Illusion collar also helps a dog to achieve a body language where she looks proud. I believe that's why dog show handlers put their leashes at the top of the neck—to keep the dog's head held high and to signal to the judges and the audience that the dog is a proud and confident contender. Any leash or collar placed high up on the neck will do this; we've just designed the Illusion to be more foolproof about it. When a dog holds her head up and looks forward, her entire body language changes. You can visually see it change. Her tail and chest often follow the head in being lifted higher. Once the body language changes, the energy follows suit. When a dog holds her head up, she is communicating a sense of pride about herself.

Is saying that dogs feel pride an effort to project human emotions onto them? In my opinion, it is not. We see displays of body language that communicate pride all throughout the animal kingdom. You know the phrase "proud as a peacock"? When a male peacock expands his multicolored wings, throws out his chest, and struts, he is out to attract a mate. That, to me, is an animal's version of pride. Pride in the animal world is self-confidence, self-esteem, energy level, and assertiveness or even dominance. The "dominance" part of it can even come from a more submissive-type dog—because with the kind of pride or self-esteem I'm describing, there's also playfulness involved. It's not 100 percent dominance, requiring submission from others—it's simply a dog feeling his best about being a dog.

Come to think of it, what I just described is not too different from what we call *pride* in the human world. I believe that feeling proud of one's self is a natural state that encompasses the whole animal kingdom. So is low self-esteem. And the body language that signals both of these states doesn't vary all that much from animal to animal, or even from animal to human.

Harnesses

Recently, I was in Central Park in New York, observing all the thousands of dogs and their owners. New Yorkers are great! Much more than Angelenos with big backyards, New Yorkers intuitively understand that dogs have to walk. Obviously, if a dog lives in a small apartment all day, he has to walk. New Yorkers are big walkers, too. However, only a small percentage of the dogs I saw in the park were being walked correctly. There were lots of owners being pulled all over the paths by their dogs. I also noticed that dogs with harnesses seemed to be very popular.

When it comes to the harness, we need to remember that harnesses were invented for the purpose of tracking and/or for pulling. They were not created for the purpose of controlling a dog. Huskies used the harness before any other breed, for pulling sleds over snow in cold climates. Cart dogs like the Swiss mountain dog and German shepherd dog in Germany were harnessed in order to carry loads for people. Saint Bernards wear harnesses so they can rescue people from the snow. The harness allows the dog to use the entire weight of his body as leverage to perform that task. Obviously, whatever is being pulled is behind the dog, even if it's the owner.

In tracking, the harness allows the dog's nose to have full contact with the ground. A collar or leash around a dog's neck doesn't allow him free use of his nose, which is essential in order to track.

In my experience, people who don't know how to use a leash or collar properly may hear their dog coughing and fear the dog is choking. Some dogs do have softer and more sensitive throats than others, or medical conditions—or simply have not been correctly conditioned to accept the leash. Many owners of such dogs choose harnesses as their primary tool. This can be a wise choice if the proper walk etiquette is established, with the dog walking at the side of the owner. An easygoing, happy-go-lucky dog without obedience problems does fine with a harness. The problem is in many dogs the harness can trigger a pulling reflex. From my observations, it seems as if some people actually like being pulled by their dogs! This may be fun—like waterskiing—but it will never earn your dog's respect.

I see a lot of people, especially men at the beach, with fighting-type dogs in harnesses, pulling them along. It looks to me as if they want to announce to everyone else, "Look at me—I must be tough because I have a tough dog." The dog becomes a macho status symbol, like a motorcycle or a Ferrari. I'd like to remind anyone who fits that description that your dog is a living, breathing being with needs of his own—not a shiny new piece of stereo equipment. Also, if your dog doesn't respect you, that's not very "macho," now is it?

The No-pull Harness

There are several different brands and styles of no-pull or anti-pull harnesses on the market. They are designed to be more humane and feel more natural on the animal's body (you can even buy them for pigs, cats, rabbits, etc.!) than regular harnesses, leashes, or other types of leads. This type of harness is supposed to gently squeeze the dog's chest when he starts to pull. It creates an uncomfortable sensation that is supposed to discourage him from pulling. Many owners swear by this tool, but like every tool I've listed here, it can have its downside. I saw a lot of dogs in Central Park wearing no-pull harnesses that were having no problem pulling their owners! The dogs were just contorted into strange positions and pulling hard to one side. I would not recommend this tool for very-high- or high-energy-level dogs. Though they do offer more control than a regular harness—especially for an average walk—they aren't ideal for an animal that you already have a hard time handling.

The Halti

Leading an animal by the head instead of the neck is not a new concept. People have been doing this for thousands of years. It is our primary way of managing horses, animals that are much larger and stronger than we are. The halti, or head collar, comes in several forms and has many names, including the "gentle leader." Like any other tool, the halti works when it's used properly, with the right energy, and it works best on dogs of a certain type—particularly long-nosed dogs. There are dog owners who swear by the halti and claim it is by far the best tool for controlling a dog. But in the wrong hands, it can be as ineffective as any other tool, and sometimes uncomfortable for a dog.

One positive aspect of a halti is if you are not strong enough to use a regular training collar on a hard-to-control dog, a halti can allow you more direct access to keep him from pulling you around. The halti is designed to fit around the face of a dog, positioned far down on the nose. It works on the same principle as any device that allows you to give a dog a correction when he behaves in a way that you do not agree with. When the dog pulls, the halti tightens around his the mouth; when he relaxes, the halti automatically loosens. The cause-and-effect correction is intended to keep the dog in the position where the owner wants him to stay.

One downside of a halti is that some dogs automatically feel uncomfortable wearing it—it's not natural to have something foreign around their mouths—and it's an easy device for them to revolt against. They can use their front paws to try and rub it off, or they can twist their heads around trying to shake it off. The best remedy for this is to make sure to associate early experiences of the halti with very positive rewards, such as food and a massage. As always, I recommend a professional trainer or behaviorist, vet technician, or at the very least, reputable pet store representative make sure you have the halti that correctly fits your dog so there is no possibility of physical strain or damage. And anyone who chooses this tool must be sure to work on their leadership skills in the home, to make sure that the dog doesn't become dependent on the halti as its only excuse for good behavior.

The Muzzle

Wearing a muzzle is not a natural sensation for a dog. Unlike a halti, it totally blocks a dog from using his mouth and can be very uncomfortable at first. The muzzle was created specifically for prevention—to prevent a dog from biting another person or animal. I only advocate a muzzle as a temporary Band-Aid while working on a dog to achieve overall rehabilitation. If the only way you can go outside with your dog is to have him in a muzzle, then you probably have a bigger problem than just not having the right tool.

Since a dog is naturally going to fight a muzzle, it is imperative to introduce it to him slowly, and make it as pleasant an experience possible. I recommend exercising a dog with a vigorous walk or run before introducing any new item such as a training tool to him. The dog should not be overheated or thirsty, just fully exercised and relaxed. Then, armed with some exotic treats like hot dogs, hamburgers, or real cooked chicken, introduce him to the muzzle by letting him smell and explore it on his own. Then reward him with food.

Next, put the muzzle over his head but not around his face. He might be uncomfortable with it at first, but leave it there until he relaxes, then reward him with food. You can only give him food when he's relaxed. The goal is for him to associate the muzzle with pleasure (food) and with relaxation. The next step is to put the food into the muzzle, and work up to putting it over his face while you keep feeding. Leave it there a little while until he's totally relaxed, then take it off and come back again later. Don't expect to have your dog accept the muzzle and be out on a walk right away. Come back to your dog an hour or two later, then start the reward process with the muzzle on the face. Once you have the muzzle tied and your dog is walking with it, reward him with food every time you take it off as well. Many dogs will fight any item you put on their bodies—even if it's for their own good. Nothing like boots for snow or extreme heat or a bandage ever feels natural to a dog the first time out. It's up to you to take

BASIC GUIDELINES FOR MUZZLING

- Try to do it after exercise.
- Begin when your dog's body is relaxed.
- Finish when your dog's mind is relaxed.
- Reward the experience.
- Never rush the process.

the time and the patience to build up an association for the dog that any tool you use has a positive reward attached to it.

The Prong Collar

The prong collar—often known as its more negative name, the pinch collar—is another tool that can be invaluable when used correctly, or potentially hurtful when used incorrectly. Kathleen and Nicky, in the example I gave earlier in this chapter, were ideal candidates for a prong collar. A prong collar isn't necessary for a happy-go-lucky dog; a small, lightweight dog under thirty pounds; or most important, an uninformed handler. In other cases, however, such as Kathleen's, it can make the difference between responsible dog ownership and an accident waiting to happen, between saving an unstable animal and being forced to return him to a shelter where the only choice he has left is death.

The prong collar was designed to mimic the bite of a mother dog or a more dominant dog, much like the "claw-hand" correction I use as a natural rehabilitation method. Most carnivores—even those with powerful claws—use their teeth as their primary disciplinary tool. They bare their teeth as a warning, and they

bite—either firmly or gently—to signal displeasure with another animal. Mother bears, mother tigers, and mother dogs all
bite the necks or scruffs of their young to tell them to "stop that!"
It's not a bite that breaks the skin or even causes pain, but it gets
the point across. Used correctly, I believe a prong collar can create an instant reaction much more quickly than many other
tools, simply because it's based on nature.

The basic prong collar operates on the same principle. It is
made up of chain links that are pointed toward the loose skin
around a dog's neck. When the owner tightens the collar, it gives
a quick, startling correction like a bite—if done properly, it
should never be painful. In fact, an ideal prong-collar correction
should feel like pressure rather than pinching—digging into the
muscle in such a way that it actually creates relaxation. Imagine

an experienced masseuse digging her thumbs into the tight mus-cles in your neck. You first feel pressure, then an immediate re-lease. An informed prong-collar user can create such relaxation in a tense dog, but an incorrect use of the collar can actually cre-ate more tension and lead a dog into a fight.

Once again, a correction given with the wrong energy (frus-tration, anger) or timed wrong (given intermittently, not at the instant that the behavior occurs) is going to hurt the dog. If the handler is flailing about, making a correction over and over be-cause the dog isn't responding, it's possible to make a dog be-come numb to the correction. A prong collar that's too loose can fall out of position. Repeated, violent tugs on a prong collar *can* puncture a dog's skin, especially if the collar hasn't been fitted correctly. The objective is pressure, never pain. Fortunately, prong collars with plastic prongs and rubber bumpers over the points now exist, so the dog doesn't even have to feel metal; he can just feel rubber or soft plastic.

In general, owners who have dogs that react in violently terri-torial or dominant ways around other dogs should be trained by a professional in the proper use of a prong collar before using it, since in my opinion, it can put the idea of a "bite" into the head of a dog that's already wound up.

Like all tools, the ideal use of a prong collar is to further the relationship between human and dog to the extent that a dog learns to understand what behavior is and isn't accepted by the owner. The goal is for the dog to come to respect the human as pack leader, so the human will be relying more on her own lead-ership skills and energy—not on any tool—to communicate her wishes to her dog.

The Electronic Collar

Perhaps no behavioral tool invented by man has been vilified more than the e-collar—or, as its opponents call it, the *shock collar*. I absolutely, positively agree with critics of this tool that, used incorrectly or put in the wrong hands, it can not only traumatize your dog, but permanently damage the trust you desire to build with him. However, when used by a proper handler, under proper circumstances, I believe that this tool can truly mean the difference between life and death for your pet.

The e-collar was originally invented for hunting. The first patents for the e-collar concept can be traced back as far as 1935.[2] The whole point of the tool was to be able to correct a dog that may be following the wrong scent, which is now, say, half a mile away. How can you reach the dog and give him some signal that he's on the wrong track when you can't even see him? In addition, hunting breeds have highly developed noses and once they are on to a scent, redirecting them is next to impossible even when close up, let alone far from the handler's physical reach. In these cases, not only the hunt, but the dog itself can be at risk. He can get lost, he can get killed—the risks for a dog obsessively following the wrong trail are many. The e-collar solved that problem by being a remote-control way to communicate with a dog and get him back on the right track.

Many people unfamiliar with the correct use of this tool are also under the misconception that an electronic collar administers a pain to a dog. The myth is that a dog suffers what we imagine electroshock therapy may have been like in the early days of primitive mental hospitals. Since these collars have been in use for several decades, the earliest models had no options for variation in length or intensity of stimulus an owner could send to a dog, and were certainly far less considerate of the dog than the ones on the market today. But as technology has changed, so have our tools. The truth is, the grade of electrical current produced by reputable e-collars is more comparable to the kind of stimulation from a TENS unit that humans voluntarily use on themselves during physical therapy. My cowriter gets TENS intramuscle stimulation for twenty minutes twice a week when she goes to her chiropractor. She describes it as a "pins-and-needles" type of feeling.

Another thing to remember about the corrections administered by a reputable e-collar (and an educated, responsible handler) is the duration of the pulse. An effective correction should take only one-fortieth of a second—or less time than it takes the average person to snap her fingers. As I have mentioned earlier in this chapter, effective corrections of *any* kind should always be this quick. Because dogs live in the moment, a correction has to come in the split second when unwanted behavior begins. This is how the dog puts two and two together and becomes conditioned to the change in behavior.

So why, if an electronic collar is used correctly, do we witness a dog jump, startle, or even yip when a pulse is administered? It seems impossible to most onlookers that we are not, somehow, "hurting" the dog—something that, of course, we all want to avoid at all costs. The answer comes from the very basic difference between human and animal—the ability to reason. Most humans learn about electricity at an early age. We hear the story of Ben Franklin flying his kite in a thunderstorm and about Thomas Edison and his lightbulb. We learn that we shouldn't put our fingers in light sockets and shouldn't use electronic appliances when we're in the bathtub, and know never to carry a metal umbrella in a lightning storm. In other words, we have knowledge about electricity's causes and effects that our dogs don't. The sensation of a mild electric shock—like that of scuffing our feet on a carpet or of a TENS unit relaxing our muscles in the chiropractor's office— is not a totally foreign sensation to us. In the latter case, we understand that it might feel a little weird at first, but that ultimately it's doing us good. To a primitive human living outside of our civilization, however, it would most likely produce the same startled, uncomfortable feeling that an e-collar produces in a dog. Fortunately, today's modern e-collars have graduated steps of stimulation which we can totally control, starting at such a low level that a dog barely feels any sensation at all. That's the correct place to safely introduce any dog to an e-collar.

Another important warning for those who choose the e-collar for appropriate situations is never let the control of the collar get into the wrong hands. The family member or members responsible for the e-collar conditioning should keep the remote control with them at all times, or keep it in a safe place, in case children or others who might not understand the process find it and misuse it.

As I discussed in chapter 3, positive punishment can be an effective training method. It can also be the most destructive method if used incorrectly or haphazardly. When a dog is startled by the e-collar's pulse, he instantly relates it to an object or a behavior he is engaging in at the time. Improper use of an e-collar can damage the trust between you and your dog. Therefore I recommend that anyone wishing to use this tool in behavior modification consult with an experienced e-collar trainer who knows how to minimize punishment. I also believe that the e-collar is *not* a tool to be used on a dog for any *long-term* period of conditioning. When used correctly by an educated handler, it can save a dog's life, but as always our aim should ultimately be to remove the need for its use by calm-assertive leadership.

Molly and the Combine

I'll give you an example from a recent case from the third season of *Dog Whisperer*. Molly, a one-and-a-half-year-old blue heeler from the Eggers farm in Omaha, Nebraska, was the perfect farm dog—except for one problem. She was obsessed with chasing tires—from the small tires on her owner Mark Eggers's pickup truck to the giant, seven-foot-tall tires on the farm combine. By the time I came into her short life, Molly had progressed to sinking her teeth into moving tires and had thus far lost an eye and had her lower jaw pushed up into her upper. And still, Molly's obsession continued—overruling what should have been her natural common sense. Her owners, Mark and Lesha, were incredibly distressed. Molly had earned a deep place in their hearts and lives, yet they knew that it was only a matter of time before one day she would get her teeth caught on a tire and not make it through alive.

When I visited the Eggers family farm, I learned that Mark and Lesha had tried an electronic collar on Molly the previous year. It had worked temporarily, but they had not followed through. The collar had been too large for Molly's neck, so the corrections she was receiving weren't consistent. The owners also weren't consistent about having her wear it every day, and they didn't make sure she wore it ten hours a day, which was what was needed. Then, the planting and harvesting seasons had come, one after the other. Being working farmers, the Eggers had to put their livelihood above Molly's reconditioning. So the collar idea was dropped—and it wasn't long before Molly got into another serious accident.

I brought Molly a Dogtra electronic collar that was the perfect size for her small neck. We made sure she was comfortable with the collar before starting the corrections exercise. Then we tempted her with the pickup truck tires. As soon as Molly made a move toward the tires, I pressed the "nick" button at level 40. Without missing a beat, Molly made a wide U-turn and tore away from the tires. Next, she approached the most dangerous item on the farm—the combine. I taught Mark and Lesha how to spot the split second when Molly began focusing on the tire— and instructed them to press. Again, Molly darted away. No expression of pain or discomfort, just a fast movement away from the object she was already beginning to identify with the stimulus. This is the power of an e-collar used appropriately and correctly. By the end of the day, Mark and Lesha were only having to press the very lowest "vibrate" level to have Molly get the message. Before I left, I was able to drive past Molly in the combine while she lay peacefully off to the side. This was a first for her.

I instructed the Eggerses to leave the collar on for ten hours each day for three months, and to continue to use the lowest level of correction necessary (in this case, vibrate) when Molly began to obsess about tires. Three months later, Molly's tire obsession was completely gone, and so was her need for the e-collar. With minimal discomfort, Molly can now look forward to the long, productive life of a cattle dog—and her family can look forward to many happy years of loving her.

Rocco and the Rattlesnake

An e-collar can also be used for very short periods of life-or-death negative conditioning. Recently, my friend Jada Pinkett Smith lost her beloved dog Rocco after he was attacked by a rattlesnake on her high-desert property. UC Davis School of Veterinary Medicine estimates that 150,000 domestic animals are bitten by poisonous snakes every year. That statistic shocked me, because the dogs I knew in Mexico all seemed to know instinctively to stay away from snakes and scorpions. Because I often take my pack up to walk on Jada's trails and in other parts of Southern California snake country, I wanted to know if they, too, might be vulnerable to snake attacks. In an experiment at the center, I brought in a rattlesnake in a cage and exposed my pack to it. I was stunned to learn that, if that snake had been uncaged, I would have lost at least five dogs in just a few minutes' time. That's because, being city dogs, most of the pack had lost their natural instincts to be cautious of snakes—instead, they were curious. In that split second between their initial curiosity and their instincts kicking in to tell them that the snake could hurt them, the snake could have taken any number of them out, the same way that rattler ultimately killed Rocco. Jada and I decided to hire a professional whose specialty is conditioning dogs to avoid snakes, and have him work with each member of both of our packs.

Bob Kettle was a rugged, salt-of-the-earth guy, and his tool was the e-collar. He would use more than one snake to make sure the dogs' associations with the snakes weren't too specific, since different snakes have different scents. He instructed me to take my dogs out on the field and approach the snake cages. Daddy

DOGS AT MY DOG PSYCHOLOGY CENTER WERE FAR TOO CURIOUS ABOUT THIS RATTLESNAKE.

was the first guy I took out there. The moment Daddy keyed in on the snake, Bob would yell "break" to me, and at the instant he would administer the pulse, I would turn and pull Daddy away from the snake. We did this for less than ten minutes, and by the end of it, the last thing Daddy ever wanted to do in his life was go near a snake. He passed the test with flying colors, and then played with me happily for an hour afterward. One week later, I brought a caged snake to the center to give Daddy a final exam. Daddy didn't even need to see the snake to get behind me and stay back. The conditioning took just ten minutes—but I gained a lifetime of peace of mind for myself when walking with Daddy and the rest of my pack in the snake-infested Santa Monica mountains. These are two examples where I believe the e-collar was a wise and humane choice for dogs. In life-or-death cases like this, and like Molly's situation, when people ask me whether or not I support e-collars, I would have to say yes.

Dangers of E-collars

As I have mentioned previously, in the wrong hands and used incorrectly, e-collars can have negative consequences. However, thanks to advances in the e-collar, correctly using techniques that apply only low-level stimulations have made it a useful aid in training and behavior modification for appropriate situations. The e-collar should always be introduced to the dog so he understands what the stimulations mean, by finding the level that the dog just barely feels. It should not frighten or concern him but instead be just a new and different sensation he responds to, like the feel of a new leash. Without a gentle introduction to gain understanding, you can ruin your relationship and possibly damage the all-important trust between you and your dog. I have to stress again that to use any tool effectively, we still need to be calm and assertive leaders. Trust and respect are the keystones of the human-dog relationship. If you don't have both, then you really don't have a balanced relationship between you and your pet.

The most ineffective use of the e-collar is to use it for compulsion. Yet there are people out there who practice methods like this. Why? Because often, they produce faster, though usually superficial and temporary, results.

When I worked in a dog-training facility that also trained guard and attack dogs, many of these methods that I now view as mostly dangerous and negative for dogs were used on a daily basis. The establishment was being paid a lot of money to get dogs to respond to commands in two weeks' time, and so we staff members were told to do whatever it took to get those results in two weeks.

That's one of the reasons I began to change my outlook on dogs and dog training, and develop my concept for dog rehabilitation instead. There is absolutely no point in giving an insecure dog a two-week deadline to learn obedience. Every dog needs its own period of time to learn and to become balanced—it's not something you can rush, and it's not something you can "send your dog out" to have done. As I've said before, dogs are not appliances. True obedience from a dog is something that requires patience and leadership and respect from the owner or handler. And though the electronic collar can often create fast results, again, unless the situation is a life-and-death one, it is a tool that is ripe for misuse and exploitation. Once again, if the energy behind an e-collar is angry, frustrated, or any other negative emotion, your chances of getting a good long-term result are close to zero.

As always, I believe your choice of tool—your choice for anything that you do for the animals you have taken into your care—is a matter between you and your conscience, you and your spirituality, you and your relationship with whatever higher power you believe in. If an e-collar still seems like the wrong tool for you, then thankfully there are many other options available. Whether or not you choose an e-collar, I recommend you find a professional whose methods and philosophies feel right for you, then get the correct, hands-on instruction before you attempt to influence your dogs' behavior.

The Electronic Bark Collar

Another use for electronic collars is to prevent a dog from obsessive barking, and yes, it *can* work for this purpose. It's my general observation, however, that an obsessive barker is almost always a dog that has pent-up frustration, is behind walls a lot, and doesn't get enough exercise—specifically, primal pack-type walking from its owner. Sometimes the owner wants to take the easy route, so when she leaves for work, she waits until she's outside the house and activates the remote control to stop the dog when he barks from inside the house. The collar is wired to give a sensation every time the dog barks during the day, whether the owner is nearby or not.

At one time, some bark collars could be activated by other sounds that weren't the dog's barking at all. It could be another dog barking outside, an echo inside the house, or even a reaction if the dog got too close to metal. Suddenly, the dog is not only being given the stimulation when it barks, but for a number of other inconsistent, unpredictable reasons. The dog can't make the cause-and-effect connection—which is what's crucial to any kind of conditioning. Dogs live in a very neat, clean cause-and-effect universe, and they naturally know that action equals reaction. Being given random, unpredictable punishments is just about the worst thing that can happen to a dog. This can result in a universally fearful dog; an anxious dog; a nervous dog; even, on rare occasions, an aggressive dog that may not have been aggressive before the irregular corrections began. Never use a bark collar that is based on a microphone alone. Fortunately, today's bark collars mostly use vibration sensors only activated by the dog's bark. This type of collar cannot be set off by other noises. I still believe there are other, more natural options to help a dog with a barking issue, but they will take a whole lot more time and intensive work from you, the owner. The first is—you guessed it—regular, vigorous walks next to you, for an hour a day, in your neighborhood.

The Citronella Collar

One option for people who don't feel comfortable with an e-collar for barking problems is a citronella collar, which has only been marketed in the United States since 1995. A study at Cornell's College of Veterinary Medicine found that this method—which uses a puff of natural citronella released under the dog's chin (the same plant-based substance used to make the anti-mosquito candles you buy for your patio in the summer)—is actually more effective than electronic collars for what they refer to as "nuisance barking."[3] A microphone in the collar activates the substance, which startles the dog because it is a strange, unfamiliar smell that irritates the dog's very sensitive nose. Because the dog's nose is uncomfortable, his brain gets a signal to stop barking and to just breathe, to remove the unpleasant sensation. Like the e-collar, it's a physical correction, just one based on an irritating scent instead of an irritating shock.

Based on the same philosophy of wearing an e-collar for ten hours a day whether it's activated or not, a citronella collar can be replaced by a "dummy" collar once the dog begins to respond to it regularly. But like older electronic collars, the microphone in citronella collars can be activated by other sounds—including the barking of other dogs—but only if the noise is within four inches of the unit. If you choose this device, make sure the microphone is adjusted by a professional so that you are being fair to your dog and not correcting him for something he has not done.

The whole point of both e-collars and citronella collars for barking is for the collar to be a temporary measure. But in both cases, a dog can easily outsmart his human and realize that when the collar's not on, he can do as he pleases. That's why consistency is vital in both cases.

The Electronic Fence

Here in the United States, there remain some places where, by law, you can't build a fence around your property. Likewise, building a fence can cost thousands of dollars, and some dog owners can't afford to do so. An electronic fence creates an artificial boundary, so that the dog learns the limits of its territory. The dog receives a mild shock every time it approaches the "border."

Electronic fences work very well for many people, and it can be argued that they mimic Mother Nature, which teaches animals boundaries all the time. When a dog in the wild sees a cliff, he knows if he goes too far, he's going to get hurt. If there is a thicket with thorns in it, he may venture too close to the thorns and learn through the discomfort that it's not a safe area for him. Dogs learn very quickly from their environments, which is the principle behind the electronic fence, and in my opinion this is a tool that can save a lot of lives. But again, owners need to learn to condition their dogs the right way when they install the fence for the first time. You don't want to "test" your dog by throwing a ball over the fence so he'll get shocked when he tries to retrieve it, because you don't want him to associate the shock of the fence with you. When you first introduce the dog to the fence, make sure he is either tired out or at a low energy level, because a very-high-energy dog might ignore the shock just because he is so excited. Dogs in excited and fixated modes can be impossible to condition. Let your dog get tired out and then let him explore the new boundaries on his own. You may only get one chance to do it right—and it may be a matter of life and death for your dog.

Scat Mats

Scat mats are based on the same philosophy as the electronic fence—the use of technology to try to reproduce the natural warnings Mother Nature gives to animals to stay away from certain things. The scat mat was originally intended for cats, which have a habit of climbing up on furniture, counters, bookcases— you name it—and it's made up of a plastic mat with a net of wire inside, usually powered by a 9-volt battery. It emits a three-second pulse—again, the level of the shock is about the same sensation as we humans would receive from a carpet shock based on natural static. The shock causes the cat to jump off the counter, and generally, after two or three experiences, to avoid that piece of furniture in the future. Of course, it serves the same purpose for dogs.

Like the electronic fence (but at a lower intensity), scat mats succeed because the animal associates the consequence with the environment. As in all electricity-based devices, it's important that you, the owner, make sure the product is in good working condition—that there are no loose or frayed wires—or anything else that could make this tool dangerous for your pet or your children.

Other Behavioral Tools

Granny's Newspaper

Your grandmother and grandfather used to swear by the rolled-up newspaper they used to swat the dog on its nose as the only "training tool" they ever needed. It's an old-fashioned, low-tech, low-cost form of discipline. It may have really worked for Granny. As I've already mentioned, the very act of picking up the newspaper was probably what empowered Granny—and that act became associated in the dog's mind with something he shouldn't do. *But any kind of discipline that involves hitting with the hands can cause very negative complications for dogs.* Being hit is not a natural thing in a dog's world—they don't discipline each other that way—so avoidance of hitting becomes not so much a consequence of breaking the rules in their minds, but an instinctual fear reaction that can cause shyness, mistrust, and other negative emotions. A hand flying toward them is a totally foreign experience to their instincts, so they might become shy of all hands, not just hands with newspapers in them. Fearing a hand can involve either avoiding a hand or biting a hand.

Startle and Sound-Related Tools

A more benign use of a newspaper for discipline is simply to roll it up and *thwack* it in your hand to startle a dog. Dogs have sensitive hearing—they're always on the alert—and they are easily affected by strange, loud noises. This is the philosophy behind a whole subgroup of training aids, like beanbags or throw chains. These devices were most often used for housebreaking a dog— when the dog went toward a certain area to relieve himself, the owner would throw an object to startle him. The problem with anything that's thrown is that the dog will usually not believe it came from outer space. Dogs have a very good sense of cause and effect, and a good sense of direction. Once the dog is associating this foreign object with you throwing it, you've begun the process of breaking your bond of trust with him, because having an object thrown at him makes no natural sense to a dog. It may startle him enough to stop him from repeating a behavior, but it's not going to make him respect you or accomplish calm submission.

Spend a day at the zoo observing any small society of primates. You'll see that throwing things to get another animal's attention is very much a "primate thing"[4]—go to a large kindergarten class at recess and you'll witness the same thing. It's a natural, inborn primate activity—but it's definitely *not* a canine activity! I'm a big believer in behavior techniques that mimic as closely as possible what dogs do with each other, or how they learn in nature. In order for this technique to be effective at all, first, you have to surprise the dog. Second, you have to be stealthy, like a hunter— throw the object so the animal doesn't know exactly where it came from. Third, you have to carry the objects around with you at all times; and fourth, you have to have absolutely precise timing for the correction. It's a technique that requires patience, precision, and a certain degree of inconvenience, and though it does work in theory and is, to most people, humane, in my experience, nine out of ten people will fail at it—they'll quit out of frustration.

Spray Bottle

The spray bottle is considered by many to be another humane way of addressing a dog's negative behavior, but it is by definition a more confrontational approach. Like any of the startle tools described above, its effectiveness depends totally on consistency and timing—which means the owner must carry the spray bottle around with her everywhere she goes. In my experience, this method is about 40 percent effective, and then for specific behaviors only. Also, it is not a 100 percent safe method. Dogs have developed eye, ear, and nose irritations and infections and other minor health problems from incorrect use of the spray bottle. In my opinion, like anything used to hit or throw at a dog, it is not a method of discipline that is natural in their world. And remember, the dog cannot help but associate you with the spray bottle, so remaining calm and assertive is a must.

Reducing the Need for Tools

This chapter was intended to introduce you to some of the basic behavior modification tools available to help you in your relationship with your dog. I don't advocate any tools more than any other tools overall, though as is clear from my descriptions above, I think some tools work better than others in certain situations and with certain types of dogs. Others may disagree with those opinions, and may have evidence or experience to back up their beliefs. I encourage you to do your research to become as informed about tools as possible.

My point is that the issue of which tools to use or to avoid is a very personal one. Every dog is different; every dog has different issues; every owner is different. For any advanced tool (such as an e-collar, a prong collar, a muzzle, etc.), I cannot stress enough that you should have some professional guidance in its use. If you need an advanced tool to handle your dog, there is no substitute for some professional guidance—even if it is just an extended session of one-on-one instruction with the salesman at your local reputable pet store. There are also thousands of qualified dog trainers and behaviorists out there just waiting for a phone call, and it's well worth the small investment for one of them to visit with you for an hour, show you the proper use of the device, and answer any questions you might have. With every trainer, as with every tool, you need to find the professional who fits your philosophy and your values, and you should first get a reference and have a conversation with him or her about views and methods before trying the trainer on your dog. It's been said that if there's one thing any two animal professionals can agree on, it's that a third animal professional is doing everything wrong. Trust me—there are enough viewpoints, methods, and philosophies out there for you to find one that you feel right about in your heart. With our pets, it is always a matter of balancing our hearts with our practical sides. A good professional should be able to help you combine both to form a stronger and healthier bond with your dog.

Ultimately, I think any tool you choose should ideally be just a step along the road to relying on your best, most reliable tool—your energy. The dream scenario is that you may start with a tool like the prong collar, gain your confidence, and establish a better bond of trust and respect with your dog, then downshift to a nylon choke chain. In a year or so, you can use a simple rope—and a year later, you'll be able to enjoy some off-leash experiences with your dog. Should you feel bad if, after three years, you still have to use a more advanced tool to control your dog? Of course not. Does that mean you should give up working on your leadership skills and trying to be a stronger pack leader? No! It is in our nature as human beings to always strive to make ourselves and our world better. I believe I am a good father to my sons, but I never for a moment stop thinking I could be a better one. I have found with my clients that, as their confidence increases, their bonds with their dogs improve, and they naturally find themselves relying less on tools and

DOS AND DON'TS OF TOOLS

1. DO thoroughly research the tool you are thinking of using. Don't take any one opinion as gospel—check out at least three sources.
2. DO contact a professional if you are unfamiliar with a tool.
3. DO remember that a tool is only an extension of you and your energy.
4. DO work toward reducing your need for tools, especially advanced tools.
5. DO continue to work on your calm-assertive energy and leadership skills, no matter what tool you are using.
6. DON'T use any tool if you are tense, anxious, angry, or frustrated.
7. DON'T think of any tool as punishment.
8. DON'T rely on advanced tools such as e-collars as permanent solutions.
9. DON'T use any tool that you are not 100 percent comfortable using—intellectually, morally, or spiritually, no matter what the experts say.

learning how to communicate rules, boundaries, and limitations through energy. There is no substitute for that energy and bond—no tool that money can buy—and almost no experience on earth can rival the kind of spiritual closeness that occurs when you and your dog are truly, naturally in sync.

4

Fulfilling Breed

A really companionable and indispensable dog is an
accident of nature. You can't get it by breeding and
you can't buy it with money. —*E. B. White*

W e have friends who are hunters," *Marley & Me* author John Grogan mused. "They come over here,
take a look at Gracie and say, 'Wow. What a waste.'
For a non-hunter to have such a magnificent hunting dog. Because they can see that she totally has that instinct."

It was the summer of 2006, and Marley, the beloved yellow
Labrador retriever who had won hearts all over the world, had

died. I had come to a peaceful corner of rural Pennsylvania to see John and Jenny Grogan, Marley's devoted owners, about their new Labrador retriever, Gracie. And while the beautiful Gracie was the same breed as Marley, her issues were very, very different. Or were they?

The Grogans, Gracie, and Me

After they had finished mourning the loss of their adored Marley, the Grogans realized like so many of us do that their house would not be a true home again without a dog in it. Nine months after Marley's passing, Jenny went to a breeder and picked out an adorable, purebred Labrador who resembled their lost friend. Because Marley had been so high-energy and rambunctious, Jenny was attracted to the apparent calmness of this puppy, and brought her home—figuring that, after thirteen years of Marley, the odds were in favor of them getting a "perfect" dog this time. The family named her Gracie.

True to Jenny's expectations, Gracie did grow up to be a much calmer and more sedate dog than Marley. Unlike her predecessor, she didn't devour furniture or clothes or injure herself trying to dig through walls to escape whenever there was thunder outside. Gracie didn't have Marley's fear of loud noises, his hyperactive energy, or his burning need to fling his entire body at every stranger who entered the house. Inside the house, Gracie was peaceful and obedient, although she sometimes acted a little aloof and chose to do her own thing, in stark contrast with Marley, who had always wanted to be right at the center of any family activity. But it was when she went outdoors that Gracie turned into a real problem for the Grogans.

John and Jenny own a sprawling two-acre property sur-
rounded by hills, trees, streams, and lakes, squirrels, rabbits, and
other wild animals—a peaceful, private oasis and perfect paradise for any dog. They installed an underground invisible fence
to create boundaries for Gracie, and allowed her to roam freely
on their land all day long. Like so many of my clients, they mis-
takenly assumed that she was getting plenty of exercise on her
own without daily walks with the family. Once Gracie left the
house, however, she transformed into a completely different dog.
She would refuse to come in when called, and the only way Jenny
could get her to go back in the house was to bribe her with slices
of bologna. "It works great—until you run out of bologna,"
Jenny told me wistfully. The other problem (which the Grogans
thought was completely unrelated to Gracie's lack of consistent
obedience) was Gracie's obsession with hunting. She would
spend all day stalking and devouring any small animal or bird
that passed through the yard. The family had several chickens
that provided them with eggs and that roamed free around the
property, helpfully eating bugs and other garden pests. Of
course, the family became attached to the chickens and treated
them as pets. Unfortunately, two of those pet chickens met their
maker after Gracie trained her predator's eyes on them. "She ate
Liberace," Jenny admitted with a grimace. "You look differently
at your dog once she's eaten another one of your pets." The Grogans moved the invisible fence so that the chicken's coop was
about four feet away from the boundary that Gracie wouldn't
cross, but she still stalked them obsessively, and therefore they
couldn't be let out to roam anymore. And, of course, when she
was deep into her predator mode, not even bologna could entice
her to obey her owners.

DESENSITIZING GRACIE TO ONE OF THE GROGANS' SURVIVING CHICKENS.

To me, the problem was clear. The obedience issue and the hunting behavior were totally connected. The Grogans had purchased a 100 percent, purebred, top-of-the line retriever, and when they brought Gracie home, they also brought home her genetic blueprint. Although Gracie was trusting, loyal, and friendly, the Grogans were not fulfilling her needs as what I call *animal-dog* first, with structured exercise and clear rules, boundaries, and limitations. Because of this, they were coming smack up against her *breed,* which took over as a way for her to drain all that excess energy and frustration. *The more purebred the dog, the more intense are the needs of the breed in her.* Gracie's genetics—her breed—were making her into a single-minded, focused, and exceptional hunter—but not a very respectful pet.

The Significance of Breed

In order to fulfill our dogs' needs so that they will happily and willingly fulfill ours, it is vital to begin by addressing the *animal* in your dog. All animals need to work for food and water, and they all communicate with other animals using energy. The next level of communication is to address the *dog* in your pet. A dog, being a social carnivore, innately wants to be part of a pack. Dogs strive to see the world in a very orderly fashion, with clearly defined rules to live by and a defined hierarchy of jobs and status. Dogs see the world through nose first, eyes second, and ears third. Believe it or not, by simply addressing and fulfilling the needs of your pet as an animal first and dog second, you can learn to avoid or conquer many of the problems you might encounter with your pet.

The next level in your dog's psychology, however, is her *breed*. Just as she receives "signals" from the animal and dog sides of her, the more purebred she is, the more attuned she'll be to the signals coming from her breed side, and the more she'll be driven to respond to those signals.

Breed Isn't Destiny

I don't agree with the common assumption that a dog's breed will dictate the rest of her life, especially if she is first viewed as *animal-dog*. When people say to me, "I'm terrified of pit bulls; pit bulls are killers," I introduce them to Daddy, the star pit bull of my pack, who is the sweetest, mellowest, most friendly and easygoing dog you'll ever meet in your life. Daddy is indeed a pit bull by breed, and with his giant head and neck, he looks like quite an intimidating pit bull at that! But those of us who know Daddy see him as just a wonderful, totally loveable animal-dog wearing the *outfit* of a pit bull. As long as I address and fulfill all his animal-dog needs first, the pit bull side of him will not surface in a negative fashion. But when those needs aren't fulfilled in a dog, *breed* can and often does become a factor in his physical and psychological responses to the stresses of life, and the pent-up energy that often follows.

The DNA of a dog's breed contains part of her "instruction manual," so to speak. Your dog's breed is made up of what she was built for, so the more purebred she is, the more likely she will draw on the characteristics of her breed in order to release excess energy and frustration.

I started working with Daddy when he was four months old. If I had not given him vigorous daily exercise when he was younger, if I had not been clear and consistent about his rules, boundaries, and limitations from the time he was a puppy; and if I did not stay on the job 100 percent of the time as his unquestionable pack leader, then, if he became frustrated, perhaps Daddy's pit bull genes could have driven him to become destructive. But the point is, with steady pack leadership, I freed him from the fate of living out the bad stereotypes of his genes. Even the half-dozen other pit bulls in my pack, all of whom were aggressive either to humans or dogs before their rehabilitations, are no longer doomed to forever play the role of the "killer pit bull." By fulfilling their most basic needs, I can peel away their pit bull overcoats and let them enjoy life simply being dogs among other dogs.

It's important to remember that we humans are the ones who actually created those breeds in the first place—we were the original designers of the very blueprints, or "instruction manuals," that make our dogs look a certain way or exhibit a certain skill. It's mind-boggling to think of all the processes and generations that it took to create the hundreds of breeds that exist today. Thousands of years before the nineteenth-century monk Gregor Mendel discovered the principles of modern genetics, humans somehow figured out that if you mated a fast mother dog and a fast father dog, you would probably end up with at least a few fast puppies in their litter. Or if you had male and female dogs that were both good at hunting, chances are their offspring would include some superior hunters. As humans and dogs evolved together, people began realizing that, hey, this dog can help me on the farm. This other dog can help me to guard my property. This third dog can fetch things in the water for me. Our ancestors started paying attention to and thinking hard about every particular skill that each individual dog seemed to be born with, and then they figured out how to adapt that skill for human benefit. Sometimes we just borrowed their natural talents—hunting, for instance—and conditioned them to perform those functions for us. In other instances, we took their inborn aptitudes and adapted them so the dogs would perform tasks that are man-made but feel primal. For instance, herding actually takes part of certain dogs' natural hunting behavior but blocks the act of killing. Retrieving is also a man-made act that feels primal to dogs. And finally, some jobs we've created are all man-made—like hauling. We chose dogs specifically for their sizes and shapes and bred them to do tasks like that for us.

In this process, humans created generations of dogs that were born with specific skills to do the jobs they were "built for"—and very powerful drives that went along with those skills. The problem is, in our modern world, many dogs don't get a chance to do those jobs or put those inborn skills to use. But all those drives are still lingering in their genes.

Remember, the breed part of your dog is much less primal than the dog or animal part of her. As in the case of Daddy, it is totally possible to block the brain from listening to the breed. How do you do this? By draining energy. Exercise, physical activity, and psychological challenge are the three ways to drain energy in any dog. Nothing trumps the vigorous walk—done correctly—as primal exercise for draining energy. If you walk for a longer period of time or at a faster pace, the dog has to use her energy for endurance, leaving less of it left over for breed-related activities. One of my favorite examples of good pack leadership are some of the members of L.A.'s homeless. You'll often see fearsome-looking pit bulls following homeless people around. These dogs are walking purposefully, focused and obedient. They don't pull, they don't jump, and they don't fight. They don't get distracted by cats or squirrels or cars or little kids. Because they walk for a long period of time—and walk with intention—all the energy that goes into the animal, the dog, and the breed is constructively channeled. What's important to remember is these dogs aren't just walking around the block to pee. They are walking with a powerful *intention*. They feel in a primal way that they are using their skills to survive. This is what I try to create for my pack when we hike for long periods of time in the hills, or when I let them run next to me while I Rollerblade for an hour. A focused, primal experience with the pack leader burns energy, challenges the mind, and calms the soul of even the most purebred dog.

But let's be realistic—most people can't walk their dogs all day. Their dogs may be huge parts of their lives, but they also have to make a living, take care of their families, and tend to all the various other details of being human in our complicated, modern world. Most of my clients fall into this category, so I try to help them create a combination of physical and psychological challenges for them to help their dogs fulfill their animal, dog, and breed sides, in that order.

The American Kennel Club has broken down groups of breeds into general categories, usually based on the original tasks the dogs were used for. Let's look at those categories and talk about things you can add to your routine beyond the walk— from organized "club" activities to simple things you can do in your backyard or living room—to help fulfill any breed-specific needs that your dog might have.

The Sporting Group

The dogs we call "sporting" are the descendants of dogs bred to work with human hunters to locate, flush out, or retrieve game— specifically, birds. Pointers and setters are the dogs that locate and "point to" game, spaniels are the groups that flush out game, and retrievers are the group that brings back the game once it's been shot. Remember, it's called *sporting* because they're not *killing*. Over time, humans have adapted these wolf-descended, finely tuned predatory instincts and behaviors and stopped them short of the actual kill. It becomes a sport to the animal; the only one who's a full-fledged predator in this process is the human.

I don't necessarily agree with the many guides to dog breeds out there that claim all dogs of a certain breed have a given preordained energy level. In the same way that there can be high- and low-energy kids born into the same family, there can be a whole range of different energy levels in every breed and even in every litter. Just because a dog has a blue ribbon lineage doesn't necessarily mean that dog is going to become the poster pup for all of that breed's ideal characteristics. If you breed together two prize-winning, sporting setters, you might get a litter of two energetic, potential prize-winning pups; one medium-energy pup that gets tired or bored after an hour on a hunt; and one mellow, laid-back dog who only wants to laze around the house and lie by the fire. I believe that, just as in humans, energy level is something you are born with.[2] As I discussed in chapter 1, energy is a part of identity and what we call *personality*. No energy level is better or worse than another, though certain energy levels are better "fits" for certain jobs. You need a lower-energy human to be happy sitting at a computer all day; and of course you need a higher-energy human to be an aerobics teacher. The same thing applies to dogs. However, people discovered thousands of years ago that higher-energy dogs are necessary to be successful sporting dogs, so they began selecting as best they could to ensure that energy level in as many offspring as possible. A good sporting animal needs stamina. Hunting is a sport that can take hours and hours at a time of intense activity combined with focused waiting, requiring lots of patience and concentration. You have to move forward and you have to make sure you're going on the right trail and following the right scent. That's why it's safe to say that sporting breeds are usually higher-energy dogs overall. The more purely they're bred, the more intense those breed-specific characteristics will tend to be.

Gracie and Marley—Two Faces of a Breed

Both Gracie and Marley are Labrador retrievers; they're from the sporting group, bred to find, track, and retrieve game. However similar they may look on the outside, though, they are great examples of the range of different temperaments that can be found in the same breed. Though Marley's breeders claimed he was a purebred, he was definitely the offspring of city dog stock, and he was raised in a city setting, without all the environmental cues to trigger his buried instincts. In fact, it seemed that Marley had only a few leftover instincts from his sporting past—but he had all the pent-up energy that went along with them. John Grogan writes of how happy Marley was to go on long, long walks along the Intracoastal Waterway in Florida—walks that could only begin to challenge his very high energy level. Playing with him in the backyard, the Grogans were both entertained and frustrated by Marley's inability to understand the concept of retrieving. That is, Marley didn't understand that retrieving doesn't just mean getting and *keeping* the ball; it means *bringing it back* as well! Marley's energy and instincts were bouncing all over the place—and they usually found their outlet in destruction. When the Grogans moved to their rural Pennsylvania retreat during Marley's later years, they saw him relax into his new environment that, on a very primal level, must have felt more familiar to him.

Gracie, on the other hand, was bred from hunting stock that had lived and thrived in the countryside for generations. She was a top-of-the-line dog who hit the jackpot when it came to hunting genes and energy level. And when you're talking about a dog of that caliber, you are going to see from an early age all the greatness of the generations of her breed. From a very early age, you'll see such a pup stalking a feather duster in the house; seeking out bird feathers in the yard; freezing and getting into stalking pose as they see birds and small animals wander by. It's very clear to them what the purpose of their life is going to be. If a dog like Gracie were living in the city with the same lax structure she was now experiencing, she would most likely become neurotic, developing obsessive, possessive, or destructive tendencies. But living in her country paradise, she had plenty of natural outlets for her frustrations. And as the Grogans told me, when she got that bloodlust look in her eyes, it was as if they didn't exist. She'd become a completely different dog, with one master only—her instinct. From an early age, the owners of such dogs have to learn to channel that energy and redirect such behavior if they don't want the dog to take over on her own.

The Grogans told me that Gracie was quiet and controlled inside the house, which makes total sense. Gracie's energy wasn't wasted in bouncing off the walls, as Marley's had been; she was carefully conserving it to use for the endurance that great hunting dogs need to track and stalk their prey. Her genes were telling her, "Don't squander your resources in here; save them up! There are chickens outside in the yard, just waiting for you to stalk them!" She wasn't going to sweat the small stuff by eating couches and knocking over tables like Marley did—because she had a clearer *purpose* for the skills born into her. That purpose lay in the great outdoors and all its temptations.

Both Gracie and Marley were frustrated dogs at heart. Though neither of them lacked for love from their family, both suffered from a lack of leadership, rules, boundaries, and limitations, and not enough physical and psychological challenges. But in Gracie's case, her purebred genes were determining a very specific outlet for her frustration. The *animal* in her wasn't being fulfilled because she wasn't getting enough physical activity to simulate the process of having to work for food and water. The *dog* in her wasn't being fulfilled because she lacked rules, boundaries, and limitations. But it was the *breed* in her that was telling her, "*This* is the activity that we practice in order to drain our excess energy." That's why I told the Grogans that we had to consider *breed* first in order to lower the intensity of her needs. And the way we'd lower the intensity and channel that excess energy is by giving her guidance in exactly what she was already doing, but from a sporting point of view, not a killing point of view. It was obvious to me that we needed to gain control over that side of her so we could decrease the frustration in the other areas as well.

Fulfilling Sporting Dogs

If you have a sporting-breed dog with a genetic drive as strong as Gracie's, you cannot be a true pack leader unless you have control over the activities that spring from that drive. When the lightbulb of that idea went on for John Grogan, he came up with a brilliant metaphor for it that I'm going to borrow here. What if two parents who are both very practical, math-science types have a child who is born with both the gift and the drive to be highly artistic? That child will flourish if the parents guide him in that talent—giving him crayons and paper, showing him art books, and encouraging him to take art classes in school. But what if the parents totally ignore the child's talent and his need to express it? That child is naturally going to be driven to find a way to express it on his own. If he doesn't get the support from school classes, he might create elaborate doodles on his notepad in class instead of listening to the teacher, causing his schoolwork to suffer. Or he might create graffiti art on walls to exercise his passion, causing him to get into trouble with the authorities. In the first scenario, the parents are a part of the experience, and are able to show the child how to incorporate his gift into a stable, well-balanced life. In the second situation, the child creates a life based on his talent

"HAWKEYE" RETRIEVING A BUMBER.

outside the world of his parents. Therefore, there are no rules, boundaries, or limitations. On top of that, the child becomes more distant from his parents and loses respect for them—because they are not respecting and seeing through to the person who he truly is. Now apply that metaphor to your relationship with your dog. If you fulfill all three of her drives—animal, dog, and breed—you are creating a bond based on trust and mutual respect. If you let your dog fend for herself in fulfilling her inborn needs, however, why should she ever learn to respect you?

The breed-specific drives of the sporting groups can be fulfilled in many different ways. Of course, draining energy through fulfilling animal-dog comes first, and for high-energy dogs, that means long, vigorous walks at least twice a day—for any of the breed categories. Tools and techniques that can help you reduce your walk time and distance, or simply create even more challenging experiences for your dog, include biking, Rollerblading, skateboarding, and putting a backpack on your dog during the walk. There are some dogs that simply need to run—or to turn up the volume on their exercise—and the bike, skateboard, and

USING THE BACKPACK TO DRAIN ENERGY

- Make sure your dog has a full physical at the vet to determine whether or not she has any back problems that might prohibit her from safely using the backpack, and to learn how much weight your dog can safely carry, and for how long.
- Select a backpack specially made for dogs. You can find one at major pet stores such as Petco, or online. Use a search engine to find *dog backpacks*.
- Make sure to find the right size backpack for your dog, based on size, weight, or breed.
- Add ballast, depending on how much of a workout your dog needs. I advise weights from 10 to 20 percent of your dog's total body weight. Some packs come with special weights included; others do not. You can add your own weights or anything you may need your dog to carry for you—water, packaged goods, books, etc.
- Firmly attach the backpack to your dog and enjoy your walk!

Rollerblades can help you accomplish that, but only if you have a good physical sense of balance yourself. The backpack creates added weight to make the walk more physically vigorous, but also creates a psychological challenge through the act of carrying. All of these activities can help tremendously in establishing your role as pack leader in the mind of your dog.

Once you have accomplished the primary task of draining energy on the walk, you can add specific activities to help your dog connect with the breed in her. For sporting dogs like pointers, I recommend structured games you can play in your yard or the park, where you introduce an object with a familiar scent to your dog, then hide it and guide her as she seeks it out and points to it. Reward the dog at the pointing phase only, to discourage the exercise from becoming a prey-oriented one. For the spaniel-type sporting breeds, the same exercise can be used, but with the dog actually physically finding the object or person that's been hidden. And for the retrieving dogs, the goal is to teach her to find the object, then retrieve it and bring it back to you unharmed. Frisbee playing and other backyard games are excellent—but remember, even if you are throwing the Frisbee back and forth five hundred times, if you're behind a fence and haven't accomplished the walk, you are only creating excitement, not removing it. Many of the retrieving dogs were bred to be water dogs—including Labrador retrievers, Irish water spaniels, American water spaniels, Nova Scotia duck tolling retrievers, flat-coated retrievers, curly-coated retrievers, and Chesapeake Bay retrievers. Swimming, dock-diving, and fetching items in the water are obvious breed-fulfilling games for them.

Sporting dogs often excel in search-and-rescue activities. Therefore, a variation on these games that I often recommend to clients is the "find my family" exercise, or what search-and-rescue trainers call a "runaway." Family members hide in various places, then the handler gives the dog a piece of clothing and the dog must find the family member whose scent is on the item. I believe the "find my family" activity—whether the dog is finding actual humans, or just objects that belong to them—encourages a deeper bonding between the dog and the rest of her human "pack." Since you are controlling the exercise, your value as pack leader is greatly increased in the dog's mind.

If your dog is a top-of-the-line hunter like Gracie, then fulfilling the breed in her is an exercise in which you might want to enlist the help of a professional. Not just any professional—every breed has specialists who concentrate on the intricate needs of one breed only. Specialists like these may come up with a whole new world of information and activities for you to explore in order to get to know your dog better with regard to the genes of his or her breed.

Grace for Gracie

By the time I came to the Grogans, I saw right away that Gracie needed someone who was an insider to her world. I worked with them for a day at their farm, showing them how to be pack leaders who "owned" their chickens, to give Gracie a sense that the chickens are off-limits. I gave them a beginner's course in cultivating calm-assertive energy, but I also left them with the somewhat difficult "homework assignment" of finding a professional hunting trainer who could teach Gracie and the Grogans how to channel Gracie's natural hunting energy into nonlethal outlets.

I'm always encouraging my clients not to give up on their dogs—and never to give up on themselves, even when others are telling them to quit. The Grogans didn't give up. Jenny later told me that she contacted nine different hunting and obedience professionals in her area, and all of them turned her down. "It can't be done," they told her, because the Grogans didn't actually want to teach Gracie to hunt with a gun; they just wanted to redirect her hunting instinct. Nine out of ten people told Jenny that it was impossible! But Jenny persevered until she found Missy Lemoi, an obedience and retriever field trial trainer from Hope Lock Kennels in Easton, Pennsylvania. Missy is experienced in training dogs to run competitions and field trials and hunt tests, and is one of my favorite types of people—she sees no limits and always sees a challenge as a possibility. She came to the aid of the Grogans by teaching them how to develop a dog's inborn skills in helping her become the best dog she can be.

One of the first things Missy warned the Grogans about was that it would take a lot of work and commitment to get Gracie from the dog she was to the dog they wanted her to be. Most people simply don't have the energy or the time to put such intense work into their dogs. But the Grogans—and especially Jenny—were willing to step up to the plate and face the daunting challenge.

Missy began with the same exercise as I did—trying to desensitize Gracie to feathered friends and reduce her obsession with fowl—except she chose a less excitable duck rather than a chicken. The goal was to desensitize Gracie slowly through obedience commands, until she ignored the duck. That went hand in hand with the basic obedience work Jenny was doing with her—basic commands that communicate to the dog, "You have to listen to me, and you have to take your cues from me."

The second phase of Missy's work with Gracie involved her hunting instinct. "We had to overcome the disadvantage that Gracie had," Missy told me, "since she was born with all the instincts, but hadn't been raised to hunt in a disciplined fashion since she was seven weeks old, like my own dogs. We had to find something to motivate Gracie, and I chose her family because her family motivates her. She loves her family. So using the search-and-rescue technique of the 'runaway,' we created a giant game of hide and seek where her family members run and hide, and Gracie simply goes and finds them. When she does, she gets lots of praise and a little treat."

WITH THE GROGANS AND MISSY LEMOI, WORKING WITH GRACIE.

According to Jenny, from the first day of working with Missy, Gracie became noticeably more obedient to everybody in the family. It was clear that Gracie had been a dog with special skills that were just aching to be channeled in the right direction.

After five weeks of working with Missy, the Grogans invited me back for a follow-up visit, to see what kind of progress they had made together. Gracie clearly still had a long way to go—Missy described her as between a 2 and a 3 on a scale of 1 to 10—but there was a noticeable change in her. Though her retriever instincts were still driving her behavior, she was beginning to understand and respect the concept of limits. But the day I came to call on the Grogans, Missy Lemoi had a special treat for all of us—and especially for Gracie! She brought along her champion Labrador retriever,

Hawkeye, who gave us an amazing demonstration of a blind search. Missy hid a retrieving bumper far away on the property, and then—using only hand signals and energy—directed Hawkeye to find and retrieve the object. We all were in awe of how well Missy and Hawkeye communicated, even though not a sound was uttered. Between them, there was the highest level of both respect and trust. The two were totally in tune with each other, the way that I am in tune with my pack. Missy was fulfilling all three dimensions of Hawkeye—as an animal, a dog, and a Labrador retriever breed—and Hawkeye was saying "thank you" with his enthusiasm and obedience.

Of course, I believe in the power of the pack—that is, that dogs learn from other dogs much better and faster than they do from humans. That's why, during the exercise, I held on to Gracie so that she could observe Hawkeye do his thing. Gracie was clearly fascinated. Something deep inside her really responded to the whole communication between Missy and Hawkeye. Gracie got an awesome lesson from both humans and dog that day. She experienced two handlers—Missy and me—who understood her and created a situation where she could remain calm and submissive. Missy was one and I was the other one. But Hawkeye the dog was the best teacher. Gracie witnessed what the end product of human-dog collaboration looked and felt like—and so did the Grogans.

Six months after they began field trial and obedience work, Jenny and Gracie have completed the intermediate class and Missy has invited them to continue on to more advanced levels. As for the small animal attacks, Gracie is an angel when the Grogans are around. Using the techniques I taught them, they turn her attention away from the object she is focused on. Jenny's next goal is to work with Missy in getting Gracie certified to do therapy work in human hospitals.

The Grogans are now recognizing a lot of the mistakes they made with Marley, and trying not to repeat them with Gracie. Of course, thanks to John's book, all of America and much of the world love and appreciate Marley for who he was—instabilities and all. But it's Gracie's turn now. And while Gracie was brought into the Grogans' home to fill emptiness, now they also see that she's here to give them the opportunity to break a cycle. By becoming her true pack leaders, the Grogans can have the dream dog they always wanted—and Gracie can finally be understood and fulfilled as the prize Labrador she was born to be.

The Hound Group

The hounds are believed to be one of the oldest groups of dogs bred for cooperating with humans. Dog skeletons resembling basenjis have been found in ancient burials alongside primitive humans, and drawings of canines that look like greyhounds or pharaoh hounds cover the walls of tombs from ancient Egypt. Hounds are hunters, pursuing their quarry—unlike sporting dogs, they're usually mammals, not birds—using sight, scent, or a combination of both. However, unlike the sporting group of dogs, these guys traditionally didn't wait for the slower humans to set off on the chase; they ran ahead of the hunters.

The Nose Knows

The family of scent hounds includes the basset hound, the beagle, the coonhound, the bloodhound, the dachshund, the American and English foxhounds, the Harrier, and the otterhound. As we've discussed, scent is the most important sense for all dogs, but the nose is everything for these guys—and the humans who began breeding them made the most of their biology. For dogs such as bloodhounds, it's said the wrinkles in the face function to steadily hold the scent they're following close to the nose, and the long, lazy ears keep them from being distracted by sound when they're on the trail. Some of them—like the dachshund and the beagle—were even bred with shorter legs, to keep them lower to the ground. Often, they prefer to hunt in groups—and if you ever get a chance to watch a pack of scent hounds go after something, you'll see the miraculous power of the pack at its finest. Every dog is single-minded in its pursuit of the prey, and cooperation within the pack is key. It's this kind of coordination and cooperation that has helped the canid family adapt and survive throughout the ages. If your dog is a purebred scent hound, then in some way or another, you will want to fulfill her need to use her powerful nose for a purpose.

Banjo's Homecoming

One of the most powerful, moving cases I had during the third season of *Dog Whisperer* was the case of Banjo from Omaha, Nebraska. Beverly and Bruce Lachney, two of the most selfless people in this country, foster abandoned dogs until they can find families to adopt them. While Beverly was working at the Nebraska Humane Society, she came across the cage of a black-and-tan coonhound whose chart told her he was scheduled for euthanasia because he was "too fearful of people" and so couldn't adapt to a human placement. Beverly was immediately taken in by Banjo's mournful brown eyes and soft, floppy ears, and so she began to look into his history. It turns out Banjo had spent his entire life as a laboratory dog in a research facility and was the subject of medical experiments. He was kept in a sterile, metal cage next to other animals in similar metal cages, with no contact or warmth from another being. The only interaction he had with humans was when a person in a white lab coat came with a syringe to draw blood. The lab workers were trained not to interact or develop any kind of emotional connection with the animals they used for experiments, so there was no warmth in Banjo's life—no respect or acknowledgment of his basic dignity as a living creature. No wonder he didn't trust people.

Beverly adopted Banjo and brought him home. She kept thinking that all it would take was time and comfort and unconditional love, and he would eventually come to trust her. But four years passed, and still Banjo shrank from all people—even her. He seemed to have a good time playing with the other foster dogs in the Lachneys' yard, but wanted nothing to do with people. At her wits' end, Beverly took him to a vet to make sure he didn't have any kind of neurological or physical problems that were causing his extreme fearfulness, and she was told that physically he was fine, but his experience in the lab had probably emotionally stunted his growth. This vet suggested that the best thing Beverly could do for Banjo was put him out of his misery and take him out of this world for good. But Beverly is not a person who includes the word *quit* in her vocabulary—especially when it comes to one of her animals. Instead, she called me.

Most of the cases I get involve dogs that love and trust their owners, but don't respect them—as in the case of Gracie and Marley. In Banjo's case, however, there wasn't even that basic foundation of trust. Part of the problem was that while Beverly

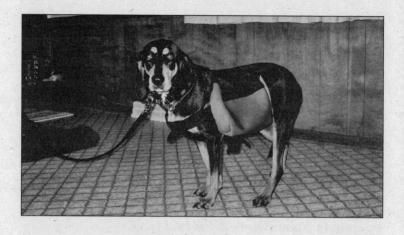

had been petting and comforting Banjo, she was nurturing his instability. Eventually, she could give him affection, but first, she needed to help him move forward on his own.

After I arrived in Omaha, I spent several hours working with Banjo, letting him gradually get to know me and developing the beginnings of what it would be like for him to actually trust a human being. I can't stress enough that we have to learn how to practice the highest levels of patience with any fearful animal. You have to let the animal use her own initiative to come to you and get to know you—you absolutely cannot force your presence on the animal.

The next step involved showing the Lachneys how to walk Banjo with a pack. Since Banjo already had a level of trust with the other dogs, if the owners established themselves as pack leaders of the entire group, then trust for them would eventually evolve naturally. Becoming a pack leader means earning both trust and respect—you can't have one without the other.

These exercises helped fulfill Banjo as an animal-dog and had an immediate effect on him. I was able to show the Lachneys how to help fulfill him as an animal through walking and through structure, and the other dogs in the household gave Banjo some identity as a canine. But what about Banjo's breed? One thing I immediately noticed about him was that, although he was clearly pure coonhound, I never once saw him use his nose to do anything. He didn't sniff me to get to know my scent. He didn't sniff the environment around him as a way to get to know it. How could Banjo have any sense of identity or self-esteem if he didn't even know what it meant to be a hound?

In the middle of a sweltering hot day in July, I asked Christina, one of our producers, to find me a bottle of raccoon urine. Yes, raccoon urine! It was probably the strangest request she ever got from me, but I knew that hunters used it, and there are a lot of hunters in the Omaha area. When the foul-smelling stuff finally arrived, I made a little trail of it on the grass leading to a tree. Then we brought Banjo to the area. By this time, he was noticeably more relaxed around all of us, though still tiptoeing around as if the sky would fall on him at any minute. But suddenly, he got a curious look in his eye. He put his nose to the ground, sniffed, and followed the trail I had made for a few steps, before looking up at us questioningly. The Lachneys rejoiced—in four years, they'd never seen him use his nose for anything—even food! And I couldn't have been prouder of Banjo. Although he was on the trail for only a few seconds, he had passed the test. He had taken the first step in awakening the coonhound inside him.

My work with Banjo only lasted a day, but I accomplished what I set out to do: open Banjo up to a new way of living and give him the foundation he needed to begin to trust humans and relearn how to be a dog. In the months since then, it's all been up to the Lachneys. Happily, they inform me that he has continued his miraculous comeback. He no longer keeps his tail between his legs, he walks confidently with the pack, and best of all, he trusts and gives affection to Beverly and Bruce. The point is, for Banjo to recover from the severe deprivation of the first two years of his life, he needed to have all three dimensions of his self fulfilled—animal, dog, *and* breed. By doing breed-related exercises, Banjo could begin to feel good about himself as a scent hound. The smell of the raccoon triggered his genetic memory, and suddenly he felt a sense of his own usefulness—the value of who he was born to be. In responding to the sensation of a life with purpose, Banjo is no different from any other animal—from rats to dogs to humans. We all need to feel that we have *purpose* in order to be truly happy and fulfilled on this earth.

Dachshund Therapy

When a dog has lost her identity as a member of a breed, another dog that strongly exhibits breed-related traits can be the best therapist to help her. Recently, I had a case of a dachshund named Lotus. Lotus's owners, Julie Tolentino and Chari Birnholtz, had been babying Lotus and treating him like a little human. There was no respect in the household, and Lotus was a very insecure little guy. Since the couple was going on an extended trip overseas, I took Lotus into the center for four weeks. There, I immediately noticed that he didn't feel comfortable about himself as a dog. He gradually adapted to the pack, but he still wasn't acting like a real dachshund.

There is a Buddhist proverb that promises "When the student is ready, the teacher will appear." Lotus's teacher appeared to me when I was working with an amazing rescue organization called

United Hope for Animals, which rescues stray dogs in Los Angeles, as well as from the inhumane death of euthanasia by electrocution in Mexico. The moment I saw Molly during the United Hope for Animals shoot, I thought of Lotus. Molly was yin to Lotus's yang—a purebred dachshund who had clearly lived a terrible life of deprivation—but somehow, she had really kept the dachshund side of her alive! She was doing all the typical little dachshund things like burrowing, digging, hiding, using her nose all the time when she walked. I decided to adopt Molly then and there—to become a member of my pack, and also, to become a "breed role model" for Lotus.

Once Molly arrived, Lotus seemed very curious about her, but reserved at first. He gradually began to hang around her and watched as she burrowed in my gardens—digging in so deep that it was almost impossible to find her! It only took a day or two before Lotus was burrowing, too—and suddenly, Lotus and Molly were a team! Normally I don't allow the dogs to destroy the landscaping, but in this case, it was for the sake of Lotus's therapy. Together, the two dachshunds would run through tunnels, hide under piles of cloth, and use their noses to lead them everywhere. Lotus had not been doing any of those things before Molly came into our lives. Molly was able to do what no human could do—to bring out the dachshund in spoiled, pampered Lotus.

Fulfilling Scent Hounds

Obviously, scent hounds need to use their noses—in fact, most of them will whether you want them to or not! After making sure you've fulfilled their exercise and discipline needs, the "runaway" game we used with Gracie is an ideal exercise to give the breed in them a challenge. Instead of letting them smell every single pole in the neighborhood on a walk, take items of clothing with members of your family's scent on them and present them to your dog. Then deposit each of them in various places along your regular route. Reward your hound every time she finds one of the objects. This now becomes her job—and a physical-psychological challenge. To find one scent and disregard all the others takes a lot of concentration. And the more your dog concentrates on something that you ask her to do, the more energy she drains. Higher-energy dogs can do the same exercise with a backpack on to make it even more difficult.

Fulfilling Sight Hounds

Sight hound breeds include Afghan hounds, basenjis, borzoi, greyhounds, Ibizans, Irish wolfhounds, salukis, Scottish deerhounds, and Whippets. Unlike scent hounds, which were bred to sniff out prey in brushy or wooded areas, the ancestors of sight hounds probably hunted in more open areas—deserts, plains, and savannahs—where they could see over long distances. Sight hounds are ancient dogs—for thousands of years, breeders have focused on refining their speed and abilities to chase and capture prey. They are amazing athletes and the fastest among them, the greyhound, can sprint at speeds of forty-five miles per hour. Since their prey drive is so strong, it can be hard to get a sight hound home if she happens to break away during a walk to chase after a squirrel or a cat, though it's the movement of the fleeing animal, not the scent of blood, that attracts her. Having been bred through the ages to hunt in packs, they tend toward sociability with other dogs.

Of course, all great hunters need a high energy level, and most sight hounds need some time every day to just cut loose and run.

Rollerblades and a bike will help you there—although many of the coursing breeds are sprinters, not distance runners. They tend to like a shorter vigorous sprint followed up by a normal-paced walk. Some dogs that have been rescued from the racing tracks have sustained serious repetitive-use injuries and should be checked thoroughly by a vet before they begin any exercise program.

While it's natural for sight hounds to have fun running after moving objects, historically, professional greyhound racing has been anything but fun for the dogs. While they're alive, many racing greyhounds spend their lives crammed into crates or pens with little human interaction, often without heat or cooling. A properly cared for greyhound can live thirteen years or more, but if she happens to be born into racing, she's likely to be disposed of—sometimes inhumanely—within three or four years to make room for "fresh dogs." Fortunately, animal activists have begun to convince some in the dog racing industry to create more humane conditions for their racers, "pension plans" for racers' retirements, and sanctuaries for retired dogs. It's only a beginning, but it's a step in the right direction.

However, loving sight hound owners can use their dogs' hunting instincts for breed-fulfilling pursuits that are fun for the dog, like *humane* lure coursing, which never uses a live animal as bait. Coursing for sport uses everything from fake fur to white kitchen trash bags as a lure, moved along a tracking line by pulleys and a motor. The mechanically inclined can hook up something themselves in their own backyard, or those who really want to get into the official sport can contact the American Sighthound Field Association (ASFA) or the American Kennel Club (AKC) to find clubs in their area.

With both families of the hound breeds, it's important to keep in mind that the hunting instinct can be powerful, and the bottom line is it should be regulated by the pack leader at all times. In nature, no dog in a pack simply takes off after a scent any time she feels like it. Hunts are coordinated efforts, with clear beginnings and endings. Any breed-related activity you do with your dog should follow the same patterns and rules that have worked so well for Mother Nature for many thousands of years. That means that you, the pack leader, are always in charge.

The Working Group

As humans evolved from primitive hunter-gatherers and began to raise domesticated animals and settle down into villages, they began to look for dogs to help them in other ways besides hunting and tracking. Hence, the working group of dogs were bred for guarding, pulling, and rescuing—some breeds for only one of those purposes; others, for two or three. The humans who created these breeds selected for body size and shape, strength, perseverance, and sometimes aggressiveness, in the case of guard dogs.

Here in America, it's been hundreds of years since most of us brought home dogs in order to hunt large game, fight other dogs, or attack men and animals. Yet some of our most popular breeds have such skills in their background. Akitas, Alaskan malamutes, Great Danes, and Kuvaszes were all bred for large game hunting, in addition to being watchdogs. Mastiffs and Neopolitan mastiffs both have ancient roots as war dogs and fighters who combated men, lions, tigers, and even elephants in the Roman gladiator rings. Guarding and security—including military use—is in the genes of black Russian terriers, Doberman pinschers, and Rottweilers. It's common knowledge that these dogs are popular

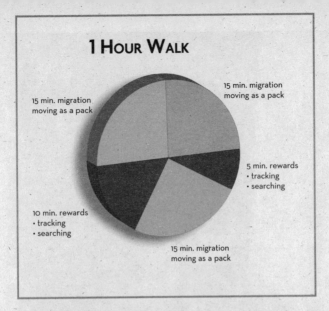

1 Hour Walk

15 min. migration
moving as a pack

15 min. migration
moving as a pack

5 min. rewards
• tracking
• searching

10 min. rewards
• tracking
• searching

15 min. migration
moving as a pack

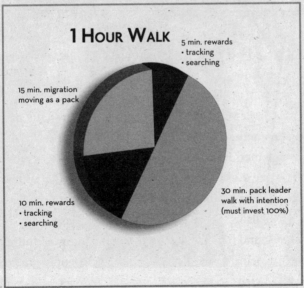

1 Hour Walk

5 min. rewards
• tracking
• searching

15 min. migration
moving as a pack

30 min. pack leader
walk with intention
(must invest 100%)

10 min. rewards
• tracking
• searching

MASTERING THE WALK

Allow a full hour and control the time your dog is allowed to wander or explore, as exemplified by the two pie charts. The top chart is for dogs who don't usually relieve themselves at the beginning of a walk. The bottom chart is for those that do.

PUTTING A LEASH ON YOUR DOG
Be strong, calm, and assertive from the moment you even *think* about taking a walk. Wait until your dog is in a calm-submissive state before putting the leash on.

WAITING AT THE DOOR

Once your dog is wearing her leash and is calm and submissive, then you may open the door. Is the dog *still* calm-submissive? If not, wait until she is. You move outside first, and then ask your dog to follow. Do not allow your dog to dart in front of you.

WALKING WITH YOUR DOG BEHIND YOU
Walk with your dog next to you or behind you, never in front of you.

RIDING A BIKE WITH YOUR DOG ON LEASH

Even if you are on a bike, your dog should remain next to you or beside you. Bike riding is a good way to give a high-energy dog a more intense workout.

LETTING THE DOG SNIFF
If your dog has maintained her wonderful state of mind during the migration part of the walk, you can reward her by letting her explore and relieve herself.

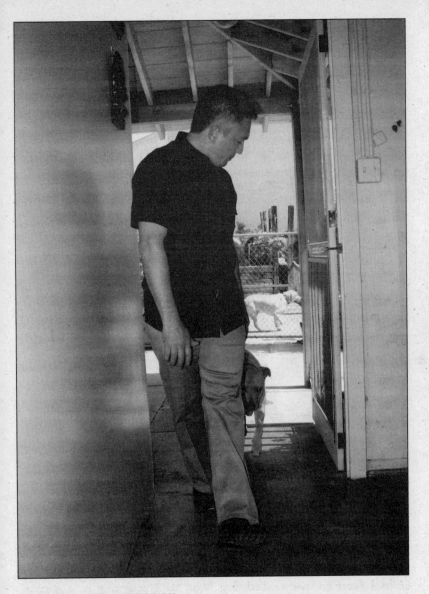

RETURNING FROM THE WALK
Coming home, follow the same routine as you did when going out. As the pack leader, you should open the doors and enter your territory first.

THE FEEDING RITUAL

Do not feed an overexcited dog. Wait until your dog is in a calm-submissive state before providing the meal. In the feeding ritual at the Center, I ask the dogs to look at *me*—not at the food dish—before I give the meal to them in order to prevent them from becoming obsessive about the food and to create an "appreciation" ritual between me and the pack.

for personal protection, but Rottweilers were also known as "butcher's dogs" for their excellence in herding and guarding cattle. The Rottweiler became so indispensable to the butchers that it's said they hung their profits in a bag around the dogs' necks when they went into the pub, knowing their money would be perfectly safe. The more purebred the breed, the more likely their breed-specific qualities will surface if you as pack leader do not fulfill animal and dog completely. And because of their size, these dogs obviously can do a lot more damage when their pent-up energy erupts than a beagle or a greyhound can.

Fulfilling Working Breeds

As with all dogs, draining physical energy is vital to living happily with a working breed—perhaps even more important for these breeds than other groups. Because they were bred for brawn—that is, strength, power, and/or ferocity—that's where breed-oriented activities should begin. Since so many of these dogs were draft dogs at one time or another, carting or pulling activities are something at which they usually excel.

In Dallas, Texas, the *Dog Whisperer* crew and I visited Rob Robertson and Diane Starke, who had brought Kane, a Greater Swiss mountain dog, into their home as a small puppy. Possibly a close relation to the mastiff and even the Rottweiler, Greater Swiss mountain dogs were once champion draft dogs, herders, and guardians. Unfortunately, though just over a year old, Kane had developed a dangerous possessive aggressiveness over his food bowl. After working with Rob and Diane on the principles of calm-assertive leadership when it came to feeding time, I helped them create a breed-specific activity for Kane to help work out his excess energy by calling up the ancient draft dog in him. Using a flatbed cart, our production team devised a makeshift cart for Kane to pull. Kane was a little jittery at first, but once he got used to the sound of the cart following behind him, he threw himself into the pure joy of his ancestral livelihood. He would have pulled that cart long into the night if we'd let him. Though we city dwellers usually balk at the idea of making our dogs into "beasts of burden," the truth is, working breeds such as Greater Swiss mountain dogs, Rottweilers, Samoyeds, and Siberian huskies really flourish when given this kind of physical-psychological challenge. They don't look at pulling as a chore—they look on it as the kind of challenge that makes them feel useful and brings out the best in them. Rob and Diane look forward to raising a family soon, and are hoping that Kane will be the most popular dog on their block, and that one day he'll be pulling their child and all his or her friends along on his cart.

Schutzhund Exercises

A fantastic way to channel the many brainy and brawny drives of the working breeds is through Schutzhund training. Originally developed specifically for German shepherd dogs, Schutzhund comes from the German word for *protection dog* and has evolved into a serious, competitive sport that tests and rates tracking, obedience, and guardian abilities in companion canines. For shepherds, Dobermans, Rottweilers, Malinois, boxers, and other agile working dogs with "fight drive," Schutzhund challenges both dog and handler in a physical-psychological, fresh-air form of skilled training. It is a misconception that Schutzhund training creates out-of-control killer dogs. In fact, dogs can't pass the various rigorous tests unless they are balanced, and will instantly stop any aggressive behavior at the sound of a handler's command. Done properly, these exercises cannot only be an excellent way to *channel* breed-related aggression into a controlled form, but they can also forge an even stronger bond between dog and handler.

In order to perform in Schutzhund, the dog must undergo a temperament test to make sure she's mentally sound, calm, and submissive. The first two parts of Schutzhund work concentrate on tracking and obedience. During the first two phases, the dog is asked to respond instantly to commands and to perform skilled feats, despite a number of distractions, including other dogs, strange people, and even a gunshot test! During the third, protection phase, the dog is required to track down a hidden human decoy and to guard that decoy until the handler approaches. If the decoy attempts to escape or attacks, the dog is expected to give chase and hold the "intruder" (wearing a padded arm) until its human "pack leader" arrives and orders her off. When given the order to stop, the dog must stop the attack instantly.

The third phase of this training is the same training that police, security, and military dogs go through, and if a working dog is properly exercised and fulfilled at home with rules, boundaries, and limitations, Schutzhund training is not supposed to turn her into a killer. Ideally, these activities provide a focused outlet for many of the dog's natural drives, and help to create a much more sensitive, balanced, and obedient animal. Similar exercises are used to train search-and-rescue dogs (also working dogs). Schutzhund "games" can also be enjoyed by other breeds with strong prey drives, though without a fight drive, these dogs won't be able to compete officially in the sport. Still, the exercises become a fun, energy-draining psychological challenge for them. Overall, many parts of the Schutzhund training can be adapted in creative, fun ways to challenge any dog.[1]

The Herding Group

The instinct to control the movements of other animals comes from the predator drive that is rooted in the wolf nature of domestic dogs. If you watch any of the canine pack hunters at work, you will notice how they coordinate their positions in order to weed out the weakest members of the herd they are preying on, and how effortlessly they seem to steer the animals they're chasing, to "corner" them, readying them for the kill. Over the centuries, humankind has taken that innate skill and created dogs that complete all these actions, right up until the final moment. These dogs, the members of the herding group, don't kill the animals they are corralling. They simply keep them grouped together for human benefit, following both their own judgment and their owner's commands. Some nip at the heels of livestock to keep them in order, others bark, others stalk and stare, and others simply use their motion and their energy. Popular herders include the German shepherd dog (considered by some to be both a herder and a working dog), the Shetland sheepdog or sheltie, the short-legged corgi breeds, the Old English sheepdog, the Australian shepherd, the blue heeler, the collie and Border collie, the Australian Cattle Dog, and the Bouvier des Flandres.

It takes a lot of stamina in order to guard and herd livestock, so herding dogs were intended to have high energy levels. If you have a high-energy herder, walking, Rollerblading or bike riding for thirty minutes to an hour at least once a day, and at least one shorter outing later on, are absolutely necessary to drain energy and achieve balance. These are not dogs that should be left to meander in the backyard with nothing to do. Remember, herding is a *job*, so being a worker is deep in the herding dog's genes. The dog is happiest and most fulfilled when using her energy toward a purpose. Giving her a challenge is your best bet for preventing or helping solve behavior problems that are caused by boredom or repressed energy.

Once you have completed your regular walk or run, there are dozens of different breed-fulfilling activities that herders enjoy. Of course, most of us can't bring cattle, goats, or sheep into our own backyard, but we can substitute other challenging activities. Due to their patience and agility, herders often make great Frisbee or "disc dogs"—an official dog sport since 1974. Of course, dogs of all kinds can play Frisbee—some world champions were mixed breeds rescued from shelters—but cattle dogs have really distinguished themselves in this field. The 2006 world champion is Captain Jack, an Australian cattle dog known as "the hardest working disc dog in the sport." If you are seriously interested in the sport, the International Disc Dog Handler's Association (www.iddha.com) can help you find a club in your area, but the great thing about Frisbee playing is that all it really requires is a flat, grassy area and the plastic disc you can pick up at any sport or big box store for well under ten dollars. Even if you're just playing in your own backyard, however, it's important for your dog that you make the exercise a challenge. You don't have to teach her fancy midair twists and leaps. But instead of simply throw and catch, throw and catch, make your dog wait between throws. Give her a set of simple behaviors to perform before you throw the disc, such as sitting down, lying down, or begging. The point is to create a psychological challenge in addition to the physical one. After all, that's what herding cattle is—a physical-psychological exercise.

Since they were designed to perform intricate "dances" around moving groups of livestock, the herding breeds often do well at agility competitions. Like Schutzhund, agility competitions and exercises are growing in popularity and are great activities to both redirect energy and strengthen the bond between human and dog. Dogs learn to jump hurdles, run through rings and tunnels, navigate their way through mazes, and complete increasingly complicated obstacle courses while racing against a clock, encouraged and directed by the handler. In America, the United States Dog Agility Association, based in Richardson, Texas (www.usdaa.com), has all the information you need to get started in the sport, but there is no reason you have to take the full-out competitive route. I often help clients create informal backyard games that challenge dogs in obedience and agility without the pressure of the real thing. An old tire, some hoops, a low goalpost, and a plank balanced on a couple of bricks, coupled with a treat reward at the end, can create the kind of focused challenge that gives even the highest-energy dog a stimulating job to do. And you, the owner, will find that the more you guide your dog through these activities, the closer you and your dog will become, and you will discover more and more of the pack leader inside you.

Flyball is another dog sport that is great for many breeds, but especially popular with cattle dogs. In the United States and Canada, the official branch of the sport is governed by the North American Flyball Association (www.flyball.org). It's a team sport for dogs—basically a dog relay race through an obstacle course, where the dog has to release a ball from a box at the end of the course, then return. Like human relay races, the next dog on the team can't begin until the first dog is back, so it requires an incredible amount of concentration, discipline, and respect for the handler. It also requires speed, intention, and consistency—all the factors present for livestock herding. If you have a high-energy herding dog at home, you don't have to watch her vent her frustrations on your furniture, your cat, or worse, the other dogs in the neighborhood. There are so many ways to find additional outlets for that extra "boost" the herding genes have given her.

Gus the Bouncing Bouvier

While participating in man-made sports is a wonderful way to bond with your herding dog while helping her connect with her "roots," there is one way that's best of all—the actual experience of herding real livestock! In the first season of *Dog Whisperer,* I visited Tedd Rosenfeld and Shellie Yaseen, two busy professionals who work in the TV business. Their year-old Bouvier des Flandres, Gus, had a habit of, well, bouncing. Of course, being a large dog with a lot of power and energy, Gus's bouncing was causing more and more trouble as he grew, to the point where he would actually knock over guests, and even his owner, the petite Shellie. The couple had not set up a regular walk routine for Gus, and they didn't know how to guide him properly through the neighborhood as pack leaders. In fact, Shellie was a little intimidated by Gus's strength and energy.

I worked with the couple on the basics of the walk, and of course, on improving their leadership skills. But after our first session, I scheduled another appointment, to take them to the All-Breed Herding facility in Long Beach, California, run by my friend Jerome Stewart, a decorated American Kennel Club (AKC) and American Herding Breed Association (AHBA) herding test and trial judge and a true expert when it comes to everything about herding dogs. Tedd and Shellie seemed a little hesitant when they first saw the flock of sheep at Jerry's ranch, and I'm sure they wondered if their city dog would know what on earth to do with them all. But as Jerry reassured them, biology and genetics had already implanted the herding program into Gus's brain. It would just take a matter of patience, practice, and some professional guidance to bring it out.

Watching Gus as he first approached the sheep was watching one of nature's own miracles unfold. First, Gus darted after the sheep in a haphazard manner, not knowing whether to listen to his prey drive ("kill the sheep") or herd drive ("organize the sheep"). With a couple of slight corrections from Jerry, he passed through the prey phase in the blink of an eye, and suddenly began to swing wider, guiding the slower, straying sheep back into the center of the herd. It was amazing, seeing this city slicker Bouvier return to his ranching roots, and I was jumping up and down and hollering with joy. Tedd was truly moved by the end of the day—"I don't think I've ever seen him so happy, or relaxed, before," he said afterward. Tedd and Shellie have continued to bring Gus back to herding class, and it's gone a long way toward managing his seemingly boundless energy.

All across America, herding clubs run by dedicated people like Jerry provide this activity to many breeds of working dog, and the American Kennel Club (www.akc.org) can put you in touch with facilities in your area. Recently, I even helped an antisocial Rottweiler by introducing him to Jerry's herding classes. Jerry has a saying that I think sums up the primal power of the herding experience for any cattle dog: "A dog with herding instinct and no training can make enough work for nine men to do. A trained herding dog can do the work of nine men. You need to decide which you would rather live with."

The Terrier Group

The word *terrier* comes from the Latin root *terra*, meaning earth—and that's an apt description of the earliest functions of the terrier breeds. Terriers excelled at hunting down and killing rodents, vermin, and small mammals, even digging deep into the earth to catch them. Later, the more muscular terriers such as the American Staffordshire terrier, the Staffordshire bull terrier, and the American pit bull terrier were bred to fight each other in public contests. Because of their convenient body size and perhaps also their incredible cuteness, terriers are popular dogs in America.

Despite their smaller size, it's important to remember that terriers have hunting and working in their bloodlines, so they can tend to be high-energy dogs—some, like many Jack Russells, can be ultra-high-energy dogs. If you have an opportunity to raise a terrier from a very young age, then socializing and familiarizing her with other dogs *and* other small animals is a must. With older or rescue dogs, often the habit of aggression toward other animals has already begun, so in addition to your calm-assertive leadership skills, you may need a professional to help you break it. Don't make the mistake so many of my clients do, simply saying, "Well, she doesn't like other dogs, it's just her personality." Dogs are born to be social with their own kind.

I've found that many people assume that because a dog is small, she will be content just to lounge around the house or, as terriers tend to do, simply chase squirrels around or dig in the backyard. As we've clearly seen, the more energy the dog has, the more primal exercise is needed to fulfill its inner animal, dog, and breed. Despite their short legs, terriers often need a lot of primal exercise, or else they will begin to engage in obsessive or neurotic behavior. I often have clients who need to constantly add challenges to their walks with their high-energy terriers, especially when they can't walk a full forty-five minutes to an hour. I advise them to add a backpack or Rollerblade, bike, or skateboard to help drain all their dogs' excess energy.

Many of the activities and exercises listed for herding dogs— disc dog, flyball, and agility games—are also great for high-energy terriers. And it's no accident that many of the canine stars of the large and small screen belong to this group. Remember Eddie, the Jack Russell terrier on the sitcom *Frasier*? He was played by the recently departed Moose, whose son Enzo now follows in his actor father's footsteps. Wishbone, the PBS star, is also a Jack Russell. Skippy, a wire fox terrier, was one of the busiest stars in Hollywood during the 1930s. He costarred with Cary Grant, Katharine Hepburn, and a leopard named Nissa in *Bringing Up Baby*, played Asta in the popular *Thin Man* detective series, and played Mr. Smith in *The Awful Truth*. Budweiser's notorious Spuds MacKenzie was a bull terrier, and the beloved Petey of *Little Rascals* fame was an American Staffordshire terrier. Once a terrier has been properly exercised, teaching her tricks and commands using positive reinforcement techniques such as clicker and/or food rewards is a satisfying way to redirect breed behaviors, for both human and dog.

A little something you may not know about pit bulls and other muscular terrier breeds whose excess energy can sometimes turn into jumping or aggression is that pulling activities can be as wonderful outlets for them as they are for working breeds. Criminal "dog men" who breed and train pit bulls to fight and kill each other in illegal underground contests often use pulling exercises to get their dogs in shape for the ring, but the same activity doesn't have to be used in such a dark, negative manner. When Daddy was younger, I used to challenge him constantly by having him pull logs, tires, and other weights up the hills of the Santa Monica Mountains. I love to think back on the image of him, trudging up those slopes, with a determined expression on his face and what always seemed to be a gleam in his bright green eyes. He was in his glory with such an important job to do, and it is exercises such as that one that helped him become the fulfilled, happy dog he is today.

The Toy Group

At an ancient burial ground near Bonn, Germany, archaeologists uncovered the skeletons of an early man and dog, buried together. The site dates to about fourteen thousand years ago. In Israel, a twelve-thousand-year-old skeleton of a woman was found buried with what appeared to be a puppy cupped in her hands. And in Alabama, remains of middle-archaic humans from about eight thousand years ago buried dogs in ways that were, in the words of archaeologist Carl F. Miller, "much more careful burial[s] than . . . man." All over the world, throughout human history, dogs have played not only a working role, but a very emotional role in our lives.

The dogs of the toy group are the lasting evidence of how deeply we are connected with our dogs. While some toy breeds served the purpose of hunting small vermin or flushing birds from brush, many of them have been bred throughout the centuries for no other reason than human emotional needs—as companions and for accessories. They didn't do any important jobs or help ensure human survival. We simply loved them. Many of these breeds are miniature versions of their larger relatives, but others have their origins so deep in our past that they have been forgotten.

Toy dogs have varied genetic pasts, so you can't really generalize about their behaviors. Some dogs were once bird dogs or ratters, like the King Charles and English toy spaniels, the toy Manchester, toy fox, Yorkshire and silky terriers, the papillon, the Maltese, the Pomeranian, the toy poodle, and the miniature pinscher. These dogs were selected for higher energy levels, and that can show up in their descendants. Pure lap dogs like Chihuahuas, Pekinese, pugs, and shih tzus were bred for looks, size, and, of course, for cuteness.

Unfortunately, the cuteness factor is where the trouble with most small breeds starts. Human beings are suckers for cuteness—anthropologists tell us it's actually a feature that's hardwired into us, so we'll be sure to take care of our babies. Because toy breeds are so adorable, we tend to let them get away with things that we'd never tolerate in other, larger breeds. For instance, most people don't let big dogs bark too long. It's simply too loud and bothersome to us. Plus, when a larger dog barks, we tend to take it more seriously. However, when a small dog barks to alert us of something, or simply to get our attention, we tend to allow it to go on as long as the dog wants it to. At first, we think it's cute: "Oh, he's telling me he wants his bone," so we give it to him, or "Oh, he's telling me he wants to play." After a while, the behavior becomes annoying, but by that time we have convinced ourselves that it's just the personality of the dog or the breed, so we don't do anything about it. An even worse behavior is biting. We would never allow a Rottweiler to use its teeth to manipulate or control us, but when little dogs bite, that's exactly what they are trying to do. The more we allow these behaviors, the more we teach our toy breeds that this is how they can get their way. Eventually, these dogs become so unstable that their behavior can escalate to attacking other animals or people.

The key is to remember that behind the big fluffy mane or the sweet little pug face, your toy breed is an animal-dog first. Remembering this, and the formula of exercise, discipline, and affection, fulfilling the needs of smaller dogs becomes no different than fulfilling those of large dogs. Toy dogs also need vigorous outdoor walks, though because they use more energy walking a shorter distance, they usually don't require an extended trek. Play activities should be performed in a controlled manner, with a set beginning, middle, and end. The secret is not to let little dogs store too much excess energy. When little dogs become compulsive chewers, biters, barkers, or end up antisocial, it's because they have found that these negative activities are ways to drain energy. No matter how small your dog is, she needs to replace destructive behaviors with alternatives—physical-psychological challenges that can be anything from a game of catch the tennis ball, to agility courses and flyball for higher-energy dogs. And all small dogs can profit from a variety of reward-oriented obedience exercises.

The Nonsporting Group

This final grouping contains basically the kitchen sink of leftover dog breeds that don't really fit into any of the other categories. Many of these breeds are among the most interesting and popular dogs in America, and include working dogs, herding dogs, terrier types, and miniatures. The 2006 American Kennel Club top ten most popular breeds in this group are (most popular first) the poodle, the bulldog, the Boston terrier, the bichon frise, the French bulldog, the Lhasa apso, the Shar-Pei, the Chow Chow, the Shiba Inu, and the Dalmatian. Depending on the breed, any of the many activities and exercises above can be used as add-ons to the walk for you and your nonsporting dog.

The Breed Is Only the Suit

After all is said and done, the many diverse strengths and weaknesses of this last group serve to point out the bottom line—that when it comes to any dog, "the breed is only the suit." In other words, the more purebred the dog, the more of a genetic "boost" she will have for the characteristics her ancestors were designed to have. However, by fulfilling her as an animal-dog through walking—the primal connection between human and dog—and through the three-part fulfillment formula, you will go a long way toward preventing any breed-related behavioral issues from cropping up. It's important to be aware of the needs and tendencies of certain breeds, but it's even more important to understand the basic psychology of all dogs—and to appreciate their direct link to the rest of the animal kingdom. I often notice that owners with mixed breeds treat their pets more like dogs generically, and the dogs sometimes get a better life out of it, no matter what their ancestral heritage may happen to be.

When people put too much weight on a dog's breed, what I call *breed prejudice* can arise. That's why, when I was a presenter for the Creative Arts Emmy Awards in 2006, I made a point to

Rollerblade onto the stage at the Shrine Auditorium with six pit bulls, all of whom had once suffered from aggression issues. There they were, under the bright lights in front of nearly 2,500 people, perfectly mellow and well-behaved—the ideal ambassadors for their entire breed. And of course, Daddy had to be the star performer. Off-leash, Daddy brought me the envelope with the winning name for television stunts in it. Remember, Daddy isn't a trained dog—he's just a balanced dog. My communication with him isn't based on commands or rewards or treats; it's based on a long-term bond of total trust and respect.

Pit bulls have been the latest victims of breed prejudice in this country. I define *breed prejudice* the same way I do racial prejudice—both are based on fear and ignorance. American history shows that the Native Americans, Irish, and Italians were some of the first groups that people in power demonized and blamed for problems, crime, and poverty. Then it became the African Americans who were responsible for all the problems. And now, it's all the Latinos who are to blame. Of course, all thinking people realize that it's not the race, because we have great people in every race. All Italians are not mafiosi, all Irish are not drunks, all African Americans are not criminals, and all Latinos are not lazy. But every decade or so, a new group of people come along for people to blame for their unhappiness. It's the same thing with dog breeds. In the seventies it was the German shepherds that were the vicious breed. In the eighties it was the Dobermans. In the nineties, everybody feared the Rottweiler, and since the nineties it's been the pit bulls that everyone blames. The more educated people become and the more owners of powerful breeds like pits and Rotties take their responsibilities seriously, the less likely we are going to blame the dogs.

That's why dogs are such great role models for us—they don't discriminate on the basis of breed. Yes, dogs sometimes gravitate to others of their own breed when it comes to certain behaviors or play—like in the example of Lotus and Molly. But energy plays a bigger role in attraction. Dogs are just dogs to each other. If you watch the news clips from Hurricane Katrina, when the abandoned dogs of New Orleans started coming out of their homes, they automatically began to take up with one another and form packs, for survival. In one photo of such a pack, I noticed a big old Rottweiler, a German shepherd, and some other big dogs. But they were being led by a beagle! Why did they choose to follow the beagle? Because the beagle had a better sense of direction, that's why. And she obviously had leadership energy. Animals know that if another animal shows the determination and takes the leadership role firmly, they should go with her. They don't say, "Look, you're a beagle. I'm a Rottweiler. I don't follow beagles. That's against my religion." The Rottweiler sensed that that beagle was in a calm-assertive state, and that's all she was looking for in a leader. Dogs show common sense. They aren't prejudiced against other dog breeds. And we shouldn't be, either.

PART TWO

BALANCING OURSELVES

What is man without the beasts? If all the beasts
were gone, man would die from a great loneliness
of spirit. For whatever happens to the beasts,
also happens to the man.
—*Chief Seattle*

You knew we'd get to this point eventually, right? All the people profiled in part 1 needed some practical information to conquer their canine problems. But like my friend Mr. Tycoon, they all also came to realize that their dogs were not the only source of their problems. It's time to open our eyes to how our own problems influence our dogs' behavior—and how to address the human side of the equation.

5

Dysfunction Junction

"If a dog will not come to you after having looked
you in the face, you should go home and
examine your conscience."—*Woodrow Wilson*

There it was again. That sound. That terrible hissing,
whirring, grating sound. It was coming from the garage,
and as usual, Lori knew exactly what was going to happen. She braced herself, and waited

Sure enough, Genoa, Lori's nine-year-old golden retriever,
came dashing from out of the bedroom where she'd been napping. Lori's usually sweet, docile dog started tearing around the

room in a panic, hiding behind furniture, whimpering. Lori went over to comfort her. "You hate that air compressor, don't you," Lori whispered in a low, soothing voice. But Lori's petting had absolutely no effect on the trembling dog. Lori sighed and shook her head. Genoa was having another of what her husband Dan called "panic attacks."

Unstable Owners, Unstable Dogs

When husband and wife Lori and Dan adopted Genoa, they found she was as near to perfect as any dog could get. She was the classic golden retriever, with a Hollywood-elegant coat and a loving loyalty that put Lassie to shame. Genoa was superaffectionate and obedient, and she even ran out in the morning to the curb and retrieved the morning newspaper. Lori and Dan had their dream dog, and they couldn't imagine their family without her. But there was just one thing.

For the past nine years, ever since the children had grown, Dan had developed a hobby of coming home from work, changing his clothes, then going into the garage to work on his cars and bikes. This usually involved turning on his air compressor. But all of a sudden, the couple noticed that Genoa had begun to grow more and more panicked at the sound. She would run in circles, whimper, and run into the back bathroom and huddle in the tub. Lori would often end up behind a piece of furniture, comforting this magnificent animal who had changed from a sweet, mellow companion to a trembling, neurotic wreck, as if someone had flicked a switch.

Lori and Dan sent in a home video of Genoa's behavior to our *Dog Whisperer* staff, who thought the behavior looked pretty extreme. Our producers pre-interviewed Lori and asked her the usual health questions. Had Genoa been checked by a vet for any physical or neurological problems that could explain the behavior? When they learned that Genoa was in perfect health, it looked to the staff that they'd be sending me out on a class "phobia" case. They—and the couple themselves—were in for a shock.

Four-legged Mirrors Never Lie

As we've discussed regarding the case of my friend the tycoon, there is no more accurate mirror of our inner lives than our dogs. Because they don't live in a world of thought, logic, past regrets, or future worries, dogs interact with each other and with us in the now, and on a purely instinctual level. Their interest in us centers on how our personal behavior and energy is going to affect the rest of the pack. And if something inside us is threatening to make the pack unstable, our dogs are going to reflect that right back—sometimes subtly, sometimes dramatically.

Earlier on in this book and in *Cesar's Way,* we looked at the different issues our dogs can develop and examined various ways of dealing with them. What we haven't faced full-on is the fact that 95 percent of the time, the cases I'm called in on have much more to do with an unstable human than an unstable dog. You can't even begin to correct your dog's behavior until you correct your own behavior. And in order to correct your own behavior, you have to be willing and able to see what needs fixing. We have big blind spots in our lives that make their homes in our prefrontal lobes and call themselves "rationalizations." That's where our dogs come in to save us! If you are having a problem with your dog, chances are, there's something in your own life that's out of sync. Unlike humans, dogs don't selfishly think about their needs all the time; they don't put priority on the protection of their own egos. Dogs think about the good of the pack. And if you the human don't have your ducks in a row, your dog will find himself living in an unstable pack—and will act accordingly.

There are many ways through which our dogs sense our emotional states. One way is through their incredibly powerful noses. Those noses are life savers in search-and-rescue operations, and dogs are even being used now by scientists to be able to scent out everything from rare species of endangered animals and plants to whale droppings on the high seas![1] Dogs today have new jobs, sniffing out cancer, diabetes, and other serious illnesses in people.[2] They seem to be able to sense nearly invisible changes in human bodies and human chemical composition. In his classic and important book *The Dog's Mind*, Dr. Bruce Fogle refers to studies from back in the 1970s showing that dogs can detect butyric acid—one of the components of human perspiration—at up to a million times' lower concentration than we can.[3] How do police lie detectors work? By electronically measuring increases in human perspiration. This is only one of the ways your dog is your "four-legged lie detector."

In *Emotional Intelligence*, Daniel Goleman reminds us that 90 percent or more of any emotional message is nonverbal.[4] We are constantly transmitting signals through our body language, faces, and body chemistry—signals that our dogs find relatively simple to read. Although we humans place the highest worth on what we say with our words, all animals communicate using nonverbal cues. Many of these messages we send are automatic—we don't even know we're doing it. And according to Allan and Barbara Pease in *The Definitive Book of Body Language*, human body language is almost impossible to fake, because the observer (animal or human) will instinctively notice that all the gestures won't be congruent, especially with what the subject pretends to be communicating. "For example, open palms are associated with honesty, but when the faker holds his palms out and smiles at you as he tells a lie, his microgestures give him away. His pupils may contract, one eyebrow may lift, or the corner of his mouth may twitch, and these signals contradict the Open-Palm gesture and the sincere smile. The result is the receivers, especially women, tend not to believe what they hear."[5] If you can't fool a person by faking your body language, how can you possibly expect to trick an animal?

Interestingly, animals can and do trick each other at times. Being able to deceive another animal has been selected across many species as a trait that greatly assists in survival. Harvard ethologist Marc D. Hauser gives many examples of deception in the animal kingdom in *Wild Minds,* such as birds in the rain forests of Peru that use "false alarms" to distract competitors away from food in order to claim it; mantis shrimp that pretend to be tough during their vulnerable molting periods; nesting plovers that fake injury in order to lure predators away from their nests.[6] Dogs—especially loud, little dogs—bluff each other all the time when they act overly aggressive but are really feeling fear. The question is, do animals "lie" intentionally, or are these simply survival techniques? Hauser writes that nature has evolved a built-in "honesty policy," where most of the time, what you see is what you get in the animal kingdom. But animals clearly read below each other's surfaces. In their book on body language, the Peases describe an experiment where researchers tried to trick dominant birds into believing submissive birds were also dominant: In many bird species, the more dominant a bird is, the darker its plumage will be. Darker-colored birds are the first in line for food and mates. The scientists dyed some weaker, more submissive birds darker, to see if they could visually lie to the real dominants. They couldn't, because the liars were still displaying the weak, submissive body language and energy. In a later test, the researchers injected the "liar birds" with testosterone, which made them display dominance in their body and actions. This time they completely fooled the real dominant birds.

Although most of my clients are not consciously trying to deceive their animals or the other humans in their lives, they often go about their lives totally unaware of their own true emotional states. Because we humans have the amazing power to rationalize, we can find excuses for all sorts of behavior that would be unacceptable in the natural world. The miracle of dogs is they are four-legged mirrors—and when it comes to us, they never lie. I try to teach my clients how to see their own dysfunction in the mirror of their dogs' behaviors.

Genoa's Nightmare

Lori and Dan turned out to be a fit, very youthful-looking couple in their forties. When I arrived at their cozy home, we sat down in their backyard and Genoa curled up at my feet. When they described to me her extreme behaviors and what they thought was her "phobia," I sensed an inconsistency there. Genoa's energy was perfectly calm, relaxed—in fact, she seemed totally balanced. The instability must have been coming from somewhere else. But where?

It came to me the moment I asked the couple about when the behaviors happen. Dan said, "It's only when I turn on the air compressor." At that moment, a fleeting expression passed across Lori's face. A little eye roll, a little dip of her mouth. Just like that. Talk about body language never lying! "Lately, it happens even if he just goes into the garage. And he's been going out there *a lot*, lately!" I laughed at the way Lori had said "a lot." That, to me, was a conversation Lori was trying to have with her husband. The conversation was internal, but to me it was crystal clear. To me it said, "I've been trying to tell you this for a long, long time. I totally hate it when you spend time in the garage." I am obviously not a human psychologist, and I am certainly not a marriage counselor, but as it happens, most of the time my work tends to involve starting with the humans and working backward to the dog. As politely as I could, I asked Lori how she felt when Dan went into the garage. She hesitated, because now she couldn't be passive-aggressive about it anymore. She had to be honest. She finally admitted that, yes, she resented it when Dan had been at work all day, then came home and spent more time in there than with her.

Wow. There it was in a nutshell. Lori was furious about her husband working in the garage every night. It was so simple. Her husband, who hadn't picked up the signals at all, began laughing nervously. But Lori got it right away. "You mean she's getting it from *me*?" She gasped. "That's right," I replied. It was a classic "triangle" situation. The wife was hiding her feelings of hurt, resentment, frustration, and anger. Her husband was ignoring her to go work with that bicycle, and every time she heard that compressor, it just intensified the feelings. The garage and the compressor had become Lori's rivals, competing for her husband's attention. She was having an angry conversation in her head every time the husband went into the garage—and Genoa was "listening" to that inner conversation. Lori was eventually going to explode, but for nine years she had managed to keep her feelings inside her. But the dog, which could only be honest about the feelings, had exploded a long time ago. The compressor was just the tipping point for Genoa, the trigger—the thing that came to signify the moment when all those angry, tense, negative emotions would surface in the house. And like a child whose parents are always fighting, poor Genoa was so overwhelmed by Lori's toxic feelings, she would have to run and hide.

Once we made that important breakthrough, solving Genoa's issue was simple. We went into the garage and Dan worked with his air compressor. Using peanut butter to calm Genoa's mind, I talked to Lori about pleasant things to distract her from her long-standing resentment of Dan's garage-related activities. But mostly I worked with Lori, trying to change her belief about the garage. Even though the verbal conversation was between Lori and me, Lori's changed energy went directly to Genoa. As we talked, I could feel Lori's tension beginning to melt away. She had finally gotten her terrible, angry secret off her chest, her husband was finally listening to her, and she was clearly very relieved. And at the moment Lori changed her feelings about the garage, Genoa changed—a perfect mirror. The whole exercise took only sixteen minutes before Genoa was completely relaxed. Then the three of us discussed ways Dan could reach out and incorporate Lori into his activities in the garage, to make it a pleasant place for *both* of them to enjoy.

Like Human, Like Dog

The story of Lori, Dan, and Genoa is a classic example of how our emotions affect our animals, and how our animals become the mirrors of our emotions. I would have to say that, in one way or another, the majority of my cases involve some element of that principle. Though the people I work with deeply love their dogs and truly want the best for them, time and time again, they end up blaming their pets for issues in their own lives that they are avoiding, or are unaware of. It's like a boss blaming his employees for being unsure of themselves, when at the same time, he's constantly finding fault with them. You can't have it both ways. Like Lori and Dan, we all need to look inside ourselves before we can fix our unstable dogs. And we can't do anything at all until we admit there's a problem.

Denial of Danger

The moment Danger saw Onyx from across the park, the hair on the back of his neck went up, his lips curled in a snarl, and he sprang forward on his leash, so hard that he pulled his owner, Danny, about five feet.* Even though Onyx was a good hundred feet away, Danger strained on his leash, trying to get at him. Onyx, who had been behaving well for the past hour, immediately returned the aggressive energy. Then, it happened. Danger redirected his aggression toward the human closest to him—one

*Names and details of this case have been changed for reasons of privacy.

of his owners. He turned around and sunk his teeth into the arm of Danny's wife, Heather. Heather, a delicate redhead in her late twenties, gasped, grabbed her arm, and started to cry.

It was a cool but sunny winter's day in L.A., and I was in a dog park helping a client, Barbara, with the dog-aggression of Onyx, her lab mix, when Danger, an enormous two-year-old Rottweiler, came into our lives. I had been working with Barbara and Onyx for several hours already, and they'd already progressed by leaps and bounds. But Danger was Onyx's archenemy. The two dogs hated each other so much that Barbara and Danny, Danger's owner, always checked with each other to make sure they wouldn't be in the park at the same time. Barbara had lost track of the time during our session, and had forgotten that Danny, Heather, and Danger might soon arrive. Barbara had mentioned Danger to me before, but she was more concerned with controlling her own dog's behavior and learning about how *she* was contributing to it. In this sense, Barbara was an excellent client. Yes, she had been doing a lot of things wrong when it came to Onyx, but she was willing to look at her own issues and was determined to make it work. Not all owners are willing to admit their dogs have a problem, let alone admit that they do. As long as they continue to deny, I can't help them or their dogs.

Danger's owners fell into the latter category. Of course, Danny, Heather, and Danger were not my clients, and they hadn't made the decision to ask for help, which is a vital first step. But when I saw Danger redirect his aggression toward Heather, I ran over to see if I could help. Fortunately, Heather had been wearing a thick jacket and Danger's bite, though fierce, hadn't broken her skin. Tears still in her eyes, Heather told me, "It's okay, I'm used to it. He's done it before." What? This was a

120-pound, dog-aggressive Rottweiler that was also biting his owner, and she was "used to it"? Nearby, instead of tending to his injured wife, Danny was in an even deeper state of denial. He had Danger's head in his lap and was stroking him. "That's okay, big guy. You're really a sweetie. You didn't mean it, did you?" He sheepishly assured me that Danger was a real softie back at the house.

I was immediately concerned. Danger was a large, aggressive dog belonging to one of the most powerful breeds there is, and his owners clearly weren't able to manage him. His very name said it all! And yet even though they were fully aware of his behavior, here they were, in a dog park—exposing this out-of-control dog to other dogs! Danny, a charismatic man in his mid-thirties who told me he had a stressful career as an agent, was clearly deeply attached to Danger, but he was powerfully rein-forcing with affection the fact that (a) Danger had been aggres-sive toward another dog, and (b) Danger had actually bitten his wife. After talking with Heather for a while, I learned that Danger had been kicked out of two other local dog parks for his aggres-sive behaviors, and that he'd not only bitten her, but had bitten their dog walker and several other dogs. Yet when I offered my help, Danny was outwardly willing, but I could tell he really didn't want to hear me. Heather was a little more open, but she was following Danny's lead. Danny showed me how he walked Danger. Danger was clearly the one in command. It was clear to me that there was something deep in Danny's ego that made him need to believe he could control this powerful dog, even though he really didn't have a clue how to do it. Danny was happily pad-dling down the river of denial, and even though I was able to give the couple some pointers before he, Heather, and Danger left the park, I was left with a sinking feeling. I couldn't help but worry that they might be heading for a disaster—or a lawsuit.

Denial is a powerful force in human lives. For some of us, our dogs become projections of our own egos, and we see them the way we *want* to see ourselves. Until we see ourselves as we really are, however, we can't help our dogs.

Babying Bandit

There haven't been any cases on *Dog Whisperer* where I thought I couldn't help the dog—but there have been a handful of cases where I believed I might not be able to help the owner. As we've seen, one of the hardest things for any human being to do is to admit his or her mistake and change. The case of Lori and Bandit was one I actually almost gave up on.

Lori had originally bought Bandit as a pet for her fourteen-year-old son, Tyler, so he could have his first experience of loving and bonding with a dog. Tyler had wanted a Chihuahua and picked Bandit out over the Internet because of the cute little mask-like pattern over his eyes, making him look kind of like Zorro, a little outlaw. But once Bandit arrived, mother and son soon discovered that instead of being from a licensed breeder as advertised, Bandit was actually the product of a puppy mill. Puppy mills (which the Humane Society of the United States has been battling ever since the early 1980s)[7] are breeding facilities that pump out brood after brood of puppies "in bulk," to be sold in pet stores or over the Internet. Because of frequent overbreeding and inbreeding, puppies from puppy mills often come into the dog population suffering from genetically transmitted diseases, which, if they continue to reproduce, they pass on to future generations. Bandit was one of those puppies, and soon after he arrived at Lori and Tyler's home, he had to have intensive veterinary care that cost thousands of dollars.

During these first two weeks, Lori bonded with Bandit, but Tyler never had a chance to. Bandit starting attacking everyone but Lori—especially Tyler. Bandit bit Tyler on the finger, arm, leg, cheek, ear, and lip. He even narrowly missed Tyler's eye. Bandit also turned his aggression on the outside world. He attacked Lori's husband, in-laws, neighbors, and friends, making it impossible for her to invite people over to her home. This one-pound dog, said Lori, "makes grown men in their forties scared." In turn, Tyler came to really dislike Bandit. "The only thing my son has learned from this dog is how not to trust dogs," Lori said. "He's learned anger and bitterness and jealousy. It's really sad."

The problem was, Lori was helping to *create* that nightmare, but she was not seeing it. She had started by feeling sorry for Bandit, and so her energy around him was always weak, and he had become the dominant one, her protector. She was the only one who could be around Bandit, because she never corrected him when he would attack people. Instead, she rewarded him with affection.

I sat down with Lori on the couch as she held Bandit on her lap. I wanted to observe her reaction when Bandit acted up, which he did right away, snarling and lunging at me. When I put up my arm simply to protect myself, he threw himself at it and madly started biting me. With no effort whatsoever (after all, Bandit barely weighed one pound soaking wet!), I nudged him away with the same elbow he was digging his teeth into. Bandit was totally shocked that someone he was actually biting wasn't backing away from him! Confused and frustrated, he growled, squealed, and jumped off the sofa. Lori was clearly very upset. "He's biting, I have to touch," I explained to Lori. "I'm not kicking, I'm not hitting, I just touch." "But he yelped!" Lori said, clearly in distress. "Okay," I told her, "you want me to yelp so it's even?" For Lori, it was okay for Bandit to bite or attack anyone, because in her mind, they were bigger than Bandit and could just move away. She didn't see that every time she encouraged someone to move away when Bandit attacked, the dog was growing more and more powerful. Lori had created a monster—and she didn't want to change herself in order to change the situation. She looked down at Bandit, wandering around the room, looking confused and avoiding eye contact with me. "Now he doesn't know what to do!" she said. "But that's good!" I replied. Bandit was now going to have to figure out other ways besides aggression to get what he wanted. But Lori started to cry. She couldn't bear to see her dog unhappy, even for a moment.

"This isn't going to work," I said. Suddenly, everyone in the room went quiet. The *Dog Whisperer* crew was stunned. They had never heard me say anything like that before. I was a little shocked at myself, too. But in the past, it's always been easier for me to give up on humans than on dogs. Without Lori stepping up to the plate, there was no way I could help either species. Lori had so invested all her nurturing instincts on this one little dog that she was even choosing him over her own son. This part of her behavior did not sit well with me. To say I love my dogs—all dogs—would be the understatement of the century. But I would never, ever choose any of them over my sons! I would never allow any animal or human to hurt my sons— even by accident—without stepping in and making a correc-

tion. Of course, Bandit didn't premeditate what he was doing—
he couldn't be blamed for his actions. But he was being allowed
and even encouraged (by Lori's constant protecting and petting
him) to continue the behavior. She was overprotecting Bandit,
but she was allowing her own son to be hurt. This was unacceptable to me.

Our Eternal Babies

I am frequently called in to help people—both men and
women—who cannot see their dogs as anything but eternal babies. Like Bandit, we make many of those dogs who could otherwise become happy, balanced animals, into the world's worst
spoiled brats. All throughout human history, the "cuteness" of
dogs has been a big part of why we love them. The term *neoteny*
is used to describe animals that maintain the physical appearance and behaviors of childhood, even after they are full grown.
In many ways, dogs are neotenized wolves, since all their lives
they retain the playfulness of wolf pups.[8] Of all animals, humans are the most susceptible to neoteny in other animals, perhaps because we care for our own young for such a long time
before they become independent. Ethologist James Serpell calls
this "the cute response," which allows the cutest, most youthful-
looking animals to have a better chance at survival. In *If You
Tame Me,* sociologist Leslie Irvine writes that in the shelter
where she spent 360 hours monitoring the interactions of humans and animals, animals that looked younger and cuter had
an easier time of finding homes than older-looking animals.[9] I
think a lot of people are trapped in the view that their dogs are
their eternal babies. I've personally observed a pattern among

my clients, both male and female, that when the nest begins to empty out—when children leave home or, as in Lori and Tyler's case, become teenagers needing less direct caring from parents—owners often redirect their nurturing instincts onto a dog. Now this can definitely be good therapy for humans and often inspires us to take care of needy dogs in the first place. But even Chihuahuas don't stay puppies forever. Think of it this way—if you always treat a full-grown human by fulfilling his every need like a baby, do you think you'll be creating a human with good social behavior?

Lori had to put aside the belief that Bandit was her son or her baby. She didn't have to get rid of it altogether, but she did have to put it in its place, get her priorities straight, and see things as they really were. She was absolutely not capable of simply telling Bandit no. She was actually afraid she would hurt his feelings. Since her own son, Tyler, was clearly growing up into a fine, well-mannered young man, I asked her if she'd raised Tyler like that. She told me that, of course not, with Tyler, she understood that sometimes she had to tell her son things he didn't like to hear, because "It's for his own good." She simply could not make the same connection with Bandit. Either consciously or unconsciously, she was choosing Bandit over her own son.

After I told everyone that this case would not work because the owner would not let go, Lori informed me that she was very, very afraid. Bandit's last vet had informed her that if Bandit jumped off something and hurt his leg, he'd have to be put down, and Lori admitted that she felt as if she had to handle him like glass. Once she acknowledged that fear, I thanked her for being honest with me, but I asked her if just for today, she could try to give it up. To just let go of it, hand it over. To my grateful surprise, she let out a sigh and said, "Okay. I give it up." She really wanted to try. At least now I felt there was a chance.

Once she let go, Lori was an amazing student. She was able to feel the difference between the soft energy she had been communicating with and the calm-assertive energy she saw me displaying, and she began showing me that she could correct Bandit in a nonemotional way. Once Lori had practiced being Bandit's pack leader and had seen him immediately respond, I brought Tyler into the mix. Tyler had built up a lot of resentment toward Bandit—after all, the dog had bitten him about a dozen times. I explained to Tyler that Bandit was not premeditating those bites. They were just reactions based on what position he felt he played in the household "pack." Tyler took on my challenge of turning his resentment against Bandit into calm-assertive energy. In fact, he was happy to change. He wanted to love Bandit—after all, Bandit was supposed to be his dog.

This case that I was about to give up on ended up having the happiest ending imaginable. Today, a year later, Lori and Tyler say that things with Bandit have just continued to get better. On November 30, 2006, Lori gave birth to a new baby boy named John Jr. After the baby came home, Bandit only required one correction before he submitted to John Jr. as a new pack leader. Bandit is still great around Tyler, who now takes charge and disciplines Bandit himself. Lori no longer treats Bandit like a baby. He shows no more vicious behavior and when he tries to test the boundaries, Tyler can just say "Tssst!" to redirect his attention. Bandit loves going on walks and has learned a new appreciation for people. I am so proud of both Lori and Tyler. Lori, you are now the new poster girl for calm-assertive energy, and I'm glad that neither of us gave up!

Retraining Ourselves

We cannot create balance without self-knowledge, and we can't achieve leadership without balance. And here is where our dogs are an amazing gift. They can teach us lessons about ourselves that we can't even begin to learn on our own.

Humans often seek out extra drama in their lives to complicate things. A balanced animal knows that life provides enough drama already. If you are having difficulties with your dog, the first thing you need to do is take a good, honest look within. We humans have our blind spots, however, and sometimes you need an outside observer to help you pinpoint what quality it is in you that needs retraining. Are you, like Genoa's owner, Lori, harboring a resentful emotion deep inside that your dog is picking up on? Are you, like Danger's owner, Danny, projecting your own ego onto your dog—using him as a status symbol or representing the "tough guy" you want to be? Or, like Bandit's owner, Lori, are you fulfilling a need within yourself that is preventing you from seeing that your well-meaning babying of your animal is hurting not only that animal, but your entire "pack"? These are difficult facts to admit, yet without exception, none of my clients who have changed their lives because of their dogs has regretted it. More often, it has made their lives considerably better—and not just when it came to their dogs!

But once you have recognized your own part in your dog's dysfunction, how do you go about changing it? Especially if what you're doing wrong is something subtle, like in the case of Genoa's owners. The answer is that you need to learn how to cultivate *calm-assertive energy*. It's the power deep within us that can make us not only the pack leaders of our dogs, but also, the pack leaders of our own destinies.

SUCCESS STORY
Kina, Whitey, Max, and Barkley

For Christmas, I bought my husband *Cesar's Way*. I've never known my husband Whitey to finish a book so quickly—a day and a half later, he was determined to "master the walk." Mastering the walk entails being able to walk your dog on a leash while never allowing the dog to walk ahead of you or pull on the leash. If you've ever met Barkley, you'd know that this is a virtually impossible task. While Barkley is a loving, kind, sweet dog, he's also the devil. Yes, Satan. He pulls so hard on a leash, it hurts. It hurts whomever is at the end of the leash, as well as his own *throat,* and sometimes he'd have a cough so bad after a walk that we'd feel guilty taking him again.

Whitey announced that we would be walking the dogs the next morning. Sure enough, as soon as we woke up, Whitey was getting the leashes ready and informing me of the rules. We must be calm before they were allowed to walk. We must leave the doorway before we allowed the dogs to. We must never allow the dogs to walk before us.

We must be crazy.

(Okay, the last one was not really a rule, but that's what I thought when he explained all of the rules.)

And yet, he was right.

I have never, never been able to walk Max our Rottweiler

on a leash with such ease. The dog practically asked me to guide him by the time we got home. And Barkley, while still a more difficult dog, had such a different demeanor that Whitey proclaimed him as "cured."

We now start our day by walking the dogs. Before anything else—breakfast, coffee, making the bed—our dogs are on a leash, and we walk for at least two miles minimum. What an amazing change we've seen.

Today, Max and I did three miles through neighborhoods around the northwest side of the city. He was amazing. He sits at every curb, ignores other dogs, and walks right at my side. Even when a huge St. Bernard lunged at a fence only feet away from us, he didn't react and just kept walking.

My Max is one of the best dogs I've ever known, now that I understand what's going on in his mind. Dogs are pack animals, and being his "doggie mom" was doing neither of us any good. Now that I am his pack leader, he is so affectionate, so submissive, and one of the most gentle dogs I've ever known.

As for Barkley, he's a very special dog, and incredibly headstrong. Previously, he would pull so hard on a leash that I was physically unable to walk him. He'd choke himself to the point where I thought it was cruel to walk him. We tried every leash imaginable: full-body harness, head lead, and traditional "roaming" leashes. Nothing worked. The change in him has been remarkable. He is not allowed to lead or pull on the leash, and any unwanted behavior is followed by having him sit until he's in a calm-submissive state. Then the walk continues.

Barkley has so much energy, we aren't able to walk him

enough! So we decided to teach him how to walk on the treadmill. I never thought it would work, as he fought us every time we got him on it. However, it only took us three days, trying a few times each day, to get him trotting at a comfortable pace. After just two weeks, Barkley is now up to a mile a day on the treadmill, and is a much more relaxed and stable dog.

I'm so very, very proud of my boys.

6

Transforming Energy into Action

The energy of the mind is the essence of life.

—*Aristotle*

fter *Cesar's Way* came out, I think I was asked the most questions about the chapter on the universal language of energy. In the book, I explained that energy is the way all animals communicate with one another, all the time—and that projecting the energy quality I call "calm-assertiveness" is the key to becoming a better dog owner and pack leader. Later in this book, I'll explain how the power of calm-assertive energy can change other aspects of your life for the better as well. Some critics called this concept too vague and "New Agey" to be of any use to help people with their dogs. On the more practical side, many readers simply wanted to better understand what I was trying to say, and wanted to know in more detail about how to put the concept of creating calm-assertive energy to use in their lives. Truly, understanding the energy we project is the cornerstone of creating better relationships with both our animals and each other. It's the energy that we share with our dogs that makes or breaks our effectiveness as pack leaders in their lives. Nothing else will be useful if our energy is not that of a calm-assertive pack leader.

Energy Level Versus Energy: Two Different Concepts

What is energy, anyway? In *Cesar's Way,* I talked about energy in two distinct ways. *Merriam-Webster's Collegiate Dictionary* has several definitions for it, but let's start by focusing on the simpler of two meanings it lists:

> **Energy 1a: dynamic quality** < narrative *energy*>
> **b : the capacity of acting or being active** < intellectual *energy*>.

These definitions describe the kind of energy I'm talking about when, as in chapter 2, I described the energy level that all animals are born with. Here's a human example. A family has two sons. From an early age, one is like an Eveready bunny, running around the house and destroying things. The other is quieter and likes to play by himself. Later on, the first becomes crazy about playing sports. The other is very focused and likes to read and play word games. We'd describe the first as having been born with high energy. The second would be described as a lower-energy person. Is one energy level better than the other? Of course not. They are simply different. As we discussed in chapter 2, we include energy level in what we call *personality*. In the dog world, energy is personality. I believe all dogs are born with a fixed state of energy. The possibilities for energy levels in a dog are:

- Very High Energy
- High Energy
- Medium Energy
- Low Energy

How Personality Translates into Energy

Let's look at some familiar human beings and translate their human personalities into "dog." Deepak Chopra is a pacifist. If Deepak Chopra were a dog, he'd be at medium-level energy, but a somewhat dominant type, because he does move forward and create things on his own. He's not simply a follower, but since he is a pacifist and is very spiritual, he understands how to be a follower and the concept of surrender. In the animal world, he will not be seen as spiritual leader or best-selling author. He will be seen as having medium-level energy with the capability to be both follower and leader. Of course, Oprah is always my best example of calm-assertive energy. I see her as a high-level-energy, dominant type, if she decides to be who she is on television. And Anthony Robbins would be a very high-level-energy, dominant-state-of-mind animal if he were a dog. I see myself as a high-level-energy, dominant type person—though with my pack at home, I am able to become a follower and act calm-submissive to my wife.

When choosing a dog, I always suggest that people try to select an energy level that is lesser than, or at the very most equal to, their own. Because people so often mistake a dog's excitement for what they see as "happiness," when going to a local shelter, they sometimes fall in love with a dog that's "happy" to see them, not realizing that the dog has a very high, excited energy that may not necessarily match theirs.

The Other Kind of Energy

Consider *Webster's* other definitions of *energy*:

> **c: a usually positive spiritual force < the *energy* flowing through all people> 2 : vigorous exertion of power : EFFORT <investing time and *energy*> 3: a fundamental entity of nature that is transferred between parts of a system in the production of physical change within the system and usually regarded as the capacity for doing work 4 : usable power (as heat or electricity); *also*: the resources for producing such power**

Chemists, quantum physicists, electricians, nutritionists, doctors, and athletes will all use different parts of these definitions, or have their own specific meanings for the word. In *Cesar's Way*, I defined *energy* as a language of emotions, the way that all animals read the feelings and states of mind of other animals. Reading energy is about *survival*. It's about animals experiencing and understanding every signal their environment is sending them *right now*. In the world of the animal kingdom, survival is not something to be taken lightly. Animals never say to themselves, "Well, I think this lion *may* be a predator, but I'm tired, so I'll just sleep on it tonight and worry about it in the morning." If two dogs meet each other and one bares his teeth at the other and goes into the attack position, the target dog doesn't think to himself, "He seems like he's going to try to kill me, but you know, he looks like a nice enough dog. Maybe he's just had a bad day." Survival for animals is about *right now,* about instant reaction. Is it safe? Is this other animal a friend or a foe? Should I fight, flee, avoid, or submit?

What we seem to forget as humans is that we project these signals, too. We are also reading them from other animals (including other humans) all the time, but since so many of us have lost (or simply stopped paying attention to) our instinctual sides, we don't always understand the signals our bodies are both sending and receiving. Gavin De Becker is a specialist in security issues, especially for governments, corporations, and celebrities. In his outstanding book *The Gift of Fear* (and its sequel, *Protecting the Gift*), he describes all the instantaneous processes that go on in our brains and our bodies *before* we feel the kind of warning "gut feelings" that we usually don't pay attention to. De Becker points out that those messages that we are getting (and usually, ignoring) are what we call *intuition*. "Intuition connects us to the natural world and to our nature," writes De Becker, "but we 'civilized' people ignore it at our own peril. Intuition is usually looked upon by us thoughtful Western beings with contempt. . . .

But it isn't just a feeling. It is a process more extraordinary and ultimately more logical in the natural order than the most fantastic computer calculation. It is our most complex cognitive process and at the same time, the simplest."[1]

Reading the energy in emotions and making life-or-death decisions on the messages we get from them isn't something farfetched or New Agey. It is hardwired into our very biology. We may call it a "sixth sense"—but it really has its basis in all our other senses put together. Our brains are constantly receiving huge amounts of information that we're not *consciously* processing. In his breakthrough best-seller *Emotional Intelligence,* Daniel Goleman writes, "In terms of biological design for the basic neural circuitry of emotion, what we are born with is what worked best for the last 50,000 human generations . . . the last 10,000 years—despite having witnessed the rapid rise of human civilization . . . have left little imprint on our biological template for emotional life."[2] In other words, we are the same primitive animals that our ancestors once were—except now we have cell phones and iPods to distract us from all the danger signs that helped our ancestors to survive.

"The brain is a good stagehand," writes author Diane Ackerman in *A Natural History of the Senses.* "It gets on with its work while we're busy acting out our scenes."[3] As an example of how all our senses are constantly working, sending messages to our brains about details all around us of which we're not consciously aware, Gavin De Becker describes a harrowing experience undergone by a man named Robert Thompson. Thompson, a pilot, walked into a convenience store to pick up some magazines, then suddenly became afraid, turned, and hurried out again. "I don't know what told me to leave, but later that day I heard about the shooting." Thompson first attributed his survival to "just a gut feeling." But after De Becker prodded him for details, the reasons for his flight became clear. Below his conscious awareness, Thompson later remembered that the store clerk had been focusing his attention on a customer in a heavy jacket, even though it was very hot out. He also had noticed two men sitting in a station wagon in the parking lot, with the engine running. His senses were busy inputting all that information into his brain, even though on the surface, he was totally unaware of the very details that would save his life. "What Robert Thompson and many others want to dismiss as a coincidence or a gut feeling is in fact a cognitive process, faster than we recognize and far different from the familiar step-by-step thinking we rely on so willingly. We think conscious thought is somehow better, when in fact intuition is soaring flight compared to the plodding of logic," De Becker explains. "Intuition is the journey from A to X without stopping at any other letter along the way. It is knowing without knowing why."[4] Animals, constant observers of every detail of life around them, are processing many of these hidden signals all the time. They have to, in order to survive.

We tend to think of feelings as things that just happen in our "hearts"—as things that are somehow not connected to the physical world. The truth is, very obvious chemical and physical changes happen in our bodies and our brains when our emotions change. When we're angry, our heart rate increases and our brains and bodies are flooded with hormones like adrenaline, to give us that extra boost to be able to fight. When we're afraid, blood flows to our biggest muscles such as our legs so we can be ready to flee, and other hormones put our body on alert, ready for action. Love creates the opposite responses to fear and anger, and makes us feel calm, content, safe, and relaxed. When we're sad, our body's metabolism slows, conserving our energy so that we can heal, both physically and psychologically. And finally, happiness increases the activity in our brain, blocking negative feelings and allowing us better access to our available energy.[5] In this regard, we feel and react to emotions in exactly the same way that our dogs do. With all these complex biological changes going on inside of us every time we have a feeling, is it any wonder that other animals can tell what we're feeling at any given moment? "The truth is that every thought is preceded by a perception, every impulse is preceded by a thought, every action is preceded by an impulse," writes Gavin De Becker, "and man is not so private a being that his behavior is unseen, his patterns undetectable."[6]

What Energy Are *You*, Right Now?

My goal is always to help people become more aware of and in control of the energy they are projecting at any given moment. After all, we are among the few species on the planet that has the amazing gift of self-awareness, right? But think about it. How many of you reading this are truly aware of how you are thinking and feeling when you are interacting with other beings— especially your dogs? The thing about energy is, talking or writing about it doesn't always cut it when it comes to truly "getting" how it applies to you and your everyday life. That's why dogs are such an amazing gift to us. As was the case with my friend the tycoon, mentioned in the beginning of the book, our dogs are our emotional mirrors. If we are unsure of how we are feeling or what energy we are projecting at any given moment, all we have to do is look to our dogs to figure it out. They will often understand us much more deeply than we understand ourselves.

When visitors come to my Dog Psychology Center, I am always very observant of the energy they are projecting, because they themselves are often clueless about it. But with a pack of forty dogs, any energy, good or bad, will be mirrored back to them forty times over. I have to evaluate people before they enter into my place. Obviously, some people feel overwhelmed, others feel very anxious. Until the latter feel more relaxed, I don't invite them in. Because when a human being is unstable, his energy can trigger a dog to nip or bite or bark or run away. Either reaction is probably going to be bad for the dog or bad for the human. When a dog runs away from him, the average person thinks, "Well, I didn't do anything!" But the reality is, he did do something, though he may not even know it. Something in his energy caused that dog to run away. Before he came, the dog was totally fine. The same goes for when a dog nips at somebody. For some reason, the dog feels a need to say, "Look, this is my turf. I run the show here and you've got to respect my rules."

It is important to learn to sense and read your dog's energy along with her body language. If you are waiting to hear your dog growling, barking, or whining to know how she feels, then you have already missed the most important part of the communication she is trying to share with you. The paradox is, before you can truly communicate with your dog using energy, you must learn to understand the energy that you are projecting.

A prime example of someone who intellectually understood the concept of how we project energy and emotion but wasn't always able to reflect that in her life was my cowriter Melissa. During the summer we wrote *Cesar's Way,* she would drive down from the Valley to South Los Angeles through traffic and usually arrive at the Dog Psychology Center tense. When she'd walk through my pack of forty dogs to get to the office area where we worked, she would be assertive but tense, and the dogs would react by swarming her and pushing up against her. They weren't going to hurt her, but they were obviously not happy about her tense energy and were letting her know with their bodies and their own energy. You'd think that, after more than three years of working with me on the television show and writing the book with me, she'd finally get it, right? Wrong. Although she totally understood the concept, and could sometimes correctly assess energy in *other* people and dogs, she was not always aware of the energy she herself was projecting. The same thing kept happening a year later, when we started this book! Well, one sizzling hot day this past summer, she arrived at the Dog Psychology Center frazzled after being stuck in traffic, loaded down with her notebooks and a stack of research books she wanted to share with me. Her energy was bouncing off the walls, and I decided it was about time that she learned this important lesson on an instinctive and emotional, not just an intellectual, level. I'll let her describe the experience from her point of view:

> It must have been at least 108 degrees out and I had been battling the smoggy, bumper-to-bumper traffic of downtown L.A. for over an hour. I was late, and that stressed me out because Cesar was shooting four days a week and doing seminars on the weekends and so far we'd had very little time together to do our writing work. Dogs may live in the mo-

ment, but people have deadlines—and I was incredibly anxious about ours. When I finally made it to the center, I was sweaty, thirsty, and my heart was racing. I slid open the gate to the front entry area (the place where Cesar always tells new visitors, "Remember the rules: no touch, no talk, no eye contact" before they enter the dogs' area) and I didn't miss a beat, starting to babble at the top of my voice about time and traffic and all the things that were stressing me out. Of course, the dogs started barking and going crazy. They all ran toward the fence and wouldn't stop barking, and it escalated when I moved forward to the gate to let myself into their area. There was Cesar right in the middle of them, sitting peacefully like a Buddha under an umbrella. "Just slow down," he said to me. "Take a deep breath. Take a minute and just relax." Oh. His comment stopped me short. I took a couple of deep breaths, a gulp of cool water, and centered myself. I quieted down, regulated my breathing, and closed my eyes. I felt the comforting warmth of the sun on my face and listened to the gentle splashing of water from the pool, where a couple of dogs were playing. When I opened my eyes barely a moment later, all the dogs had stopped barking and were calmly going about their business. "Do you see it?" asked Cesar. "Do you see how right away they change?" Of course, I'd been writing about this kind of thing with Cesar for a while now, but it wasn't until that moment that the lightbulb finally went on for me. It was miraculous. The dogs transformed the very moment I changed. The ripple effect throughout forty dogs was instantaneous. "Wow," was all I could say. Cesar just nodded. "Now you see why I always tell people to ask themselves, 'What energy am I being, at that moment?' " Finally, I did see.

Horses "Speak Energy," Too

Monty Roberts, the famous "horse whisperer," taught the use of energy to tame and manage the behavior of wild horses. Working through energy has been accepted by many in the horse community for decades. Brandon Carpenter, a horse trainer descended from generations of horse trainers, describes the techniques that his grandfather passed on to his father and in turn passed on to him: "I often see people having problems with their horse during clinics or lessons. I ask them how they feel about the relationship they have with the horse. Within a short time we drill down to the core issue, and find that the person is scared of the horse, or scared of putting the horse into certain situations. Some have even said they don't like what the horse's behavior is and over time have begun to dislike the horse. They are looking for ways to fix the horse. What those honest answers reveal is an underlying emotional 'state of being' on the rider's part. *Before they even approach the horse, they envision how the horse is going to react.* This thought process often takes place whenever they think of the horse and so becomes their dominant belief system. And what happens? The horse does exactly what the individual's emotional communications has told it to do."[7]

These uneasy riders are doing exactly what so many of my clients do, yet they are probably just as unaware of what they are doing. They are communicating through energy a very strong impression of what they *don't* want from their dogs—but never sending them the message of the behavior that they wish to achieve.

Calm-Assertive Energy

Animals in general respect a certain energy, and they relax around a type of energy that I call *calm-assertive energy*. They are programmed to respect and trust this energy. This is why I believe Mother Nature is perfect, because all animals except humans are attracted to certain frequencies and driven to make certain connections that are going to help them survive. We are the only animal that can be fooled by the "mask" of a certain energy, or can be attracted to an energy that is not calm and assertive, or in fact, is actually negative or bad for our survival.

If you wake up in the morning depressed, the energy you are projecting is considered weakness in the animal kingdom, and you're not going to perform at your highest potential. Every time you're feeling negative about yourself or doubt yourself—even if you don't realize it—you are still projecting that negative energy. Or you can wake up very happy and project a positive, excited energy. Your state of mind creates that energy. Any animal—your dog, cat, or bird—is going to sense that you're in a low level of energy state, and he's going to respond to you based on that energy. You will never have to tell your dog that you are sad, happy, angry, or relaxed. He already knows—usually long before you do.

In *The Gift of Fear*, Gavin De Becker tells a perfect story to illustrate this point. He had a friend who was interviewing contractors and decided against one because her dog, Ginger, growled at him. De Becker reminded his friend, "The irony is that it's far more likely Ginger is reacting to your signals than that you are reacting to hers. Ginger is an expert at reading you, and you are the expert at reading other people. Ginger, smart as she is, knows nothing about the ways a contractor might inflate the cost to his own profit, or about whether he is honest." The problem, De Becker suggests, is "that extra something you have that a dog doesn't is judgment, and that's what gets in the way of your perception and intuition. With judgment comes the ability to disregard your intuition unless you can explain it logically, the eagerness to judge and convict your feelings rather than honor them. Ginger is not distracted by the way things could be, used to be, or should be. She perceives only what is."[8]

Negative Energy—the Dark Power

I had a strange, uneasy feeling from the moment I stepped off the elevator of the upscale apartment building in an exclusive Atlanta neighborhood. When the door opened and I saw Warren—a handsome, stylishly dressed businessman, and his fiancée Tessa standing there, I knew something was very, very wrong—but I still wasn't sure what.* Working with animals, I am always aware and very respectful of my instinctual feelings. With aggressive animals, having that "sixth sense" and well-developed intuition can save your life. So, what were my "animal instincts" trying to say to me now?

Before I go on a consultation, I usually prefer not to have too much prior information about a case unless it's absolutely necessary. By the time I arrive, my wife Ilusion and, in the cases we do for the television show, the producers, have already met, interviewed, and learned as much as possible about the new clients

*The names and details of this case have been changed.

ahead of time, so they know whether or not I need to bring along a skateboard, a bike, some balanced dogs from my pack, or other special tools that the specific case might require. They have also already made sure the dogs in question have had thorough veterinary checkups and have no physical conditions that might be the cause of the bad behavior. Sometimes, they will give me some general information, such as in an ultra-aggressive case where someone has already been bitten. Still, my preference is to come in with an open mind and trust my own observations, experience, and instincts. Through these twenty years of working with dogs, my instincts have proven right for me nearly every time.

The consultation is an important part of my work, where I sit with the owners and let them tell me what they believe the problem is. My role in the consultation is to be quiet and nonjudgmental, and to listen. Often, the consultation reveals issues that the owners never even knew existed. Many times, those issues are very different from what the owners had earlier perceived. In this case, I didn't have a free moment between entering the apartment and sitting down with the couple to address my feelings of foreboding—but once we began talking, it became crystal clear. There was a powerful negative energy in the room—and it was coming directly from Warren.

How do you describe a "negative energy" to someone, without sounding superstitious or just plain vague? The bottom line is we've all recognized negative energies in our lives. I'm sure all of you have examples from your own daily routines. Whether it was a teacher you had years ago in elementary school or the banker who turned you down for a loan or the man who takes your tickets every morning on the train on the way to work, there's just something about this person that makes you want to get away from him or her. And sometimes we ourselves turn out to be the negative person. The problem with powerful negative energy is that no matter how positive or calm-assertive you may be; the feelings and emotions behind that negative person—be they anger, anxiety, frustration, disgust, scorn, deception, whatever— are so potent that sometimes they can even bring the cheeriest person down. Why is negative energy so powerful? I haven't found anyone yet who can answer that for me, although I do know that negative energy tends to be related to fear and anger—the two "fight and flight" emotions that are so tied up with survival. Maybe it's the survival aspect of negative energy that makes it such a potent force, and maybe that's why those of us who cultivate positive energy and positive people in our lives react so instantly to it, like an allergy. Because negativity is so strong, there are some rare people whose dark energy can over-power even the most secure among us, at least while we are in their presence.

Warren would turn out to be one of those people.

During the consultation, Warren wasn't too bad—he was simply not respectful. When I come to someone's house, I am there for two reasons—one, to help the dog, and two, to em-power the human. Usually, people are at least a little bit open and willing to take in what information I have to share with them, even if I'm telling them something they may not want to hear. Like many negative people, Warren knew how to act "open" on the surface and he knew how to say the right words, but it was clear by his subtle hints and body language that he really didn't respect what I was trying to do. I was supposed to be there to help the couple deal with their four-year-old female sheepdog, Rory, and her compulsive barking and aggression toward other dogs. Throughout our discussion, however, Warren would roll his eyes, whisper little comments to Tessa (who, as more of the "follower" in their relationship, seemed infected by his negative energy whenever she was near him), and laugh at Rory's bad behavior and constant barking. Now, I am all for laughing and trying to find the lighter side of every situation. After all, laughter is one of the greatest joys that dogs bring into our lives. But this was the kind of snickering laughter shared by two kids in the classroom who are passing notes about the teacher. Warren would avoid my eyes and look around the room. He was anxious, tense, angry, and projected energy even darker than the chic, all-black outfit he was wearing.

Once we were outside, Warren's dark side really came to the forefront. Rory had developed a habit of compulsively barking, pulling, and trying to get at other neighborhood dogs while on the leash. While Tessa was now relaxed and willing to learn, Warren was even more tense and started arguing with me about everything—about how Rory could never accept the leash I was using and would choke, about the fact that his dog had "never" not lunged at other dogs, about the fact that even if we could control Rory, we couldn't control the other dogs who might lash back at her. Rory was "his" dog, and he wanted to be in control—despite the fact that he had asked for my help for the very reason that he couldn't control his dog. When I looked him in the eye and told him that I believed what we were doing was best for Rory, he looked away, shrugged his shoulders, and said, "Fine. Okay. No problem." But of course, he was being passive-aggressive. He didn't really mean it. I knew it, but even worse, Rory knew it, too.

Warren was what *Emotional Intelligence* author Daniel Goleman might refer to as a "repressor" or an "unflappable"—a person who is able to very effectively and consistently block out emotional upsets from his conscious awareness.[9] This is a very workable strategy if you are a person with lots of stress who needs to appear "together" to other humans. But as I've pointed out above, it just doesn't work with animals! Why? Goleman sites a study done by Daniel Weinberger at Case Western University, where "repressors" were given word-based tests about stressful situations. The responses they gave on paper indicated that everything was fine, but their body responses always registered signs of stress and anxiety, such as fast-beating hearts, sweaty palms, and rising blood pressure.[10] There's a lesson in this: as adept as any of us humans believes we are in hiding our emotions, our bodies and our energies will almost always give away our true feelings to the ones that really have our numbers—our pets.

An example of this happened when I began an exercise in which I walked Rory next to one of the neighborhood dogs that had formerly provoked her. The exercise would be going along fine, and then Warren would interfere by walking beside me, way too close—pushing past the normal social boundaries we call "personal space." As soon as Warren started voicing his doubts— "But what if the dog snaps? What if you lose control? What if Rory pulls on the leash?"—Rory would begin to freak out again. I tried to point out to Warren that it was his energy creating the tense situation, and he would smile at the camera and say, "Okay, I see," and then keep right on creating the anxious behavior.

The truth was, I felt as if all my positive, calm-assertive energy was being drained into Warren's black hole of faceless, nameless anxiety. No matter how hard I tried, I simply could not get him to relax and just watch and listen. Finally, I called Tessa over and asked her to take Rory. Right away, Rory calmed down! Warren got upset, and actually began shouting. "But that's my dog! I should be handling her." I pointed out to him that Tessa had a calmer energy with Rory at that moment. "But Tessa has the same energy I do!" Warren whined. "Rory always does the same thing with Tessa that she does with me!" I turned around, looked him firmly in the eye, and said, "But she's not doing that right now."

I had to be a little more assertive with Warren than I usually am with clients, and I insisted that he stay back while I walked with Tessa, Rory, and the former "enemy dog." As soon as we were less than half a block away, the energy returned to normal. Tessa and I and the two dogs walked around the block together in peace, having a nice conversation. Tessa was amazed—she had bought into all of Warren's powerful negative predictions and was now seeing that there was a much better reality available to her. When we returned, Warren had also settled down a little bit. By this time, he was beginning to acknowledge how his own worry and negativity was creating a toxic effect on his dog. To this day, however, I'm not sure what the end result will be for Warren and Rory. As is true for so many negative personalities, it was clear that Warren had a lot of bottled-up pain and rage inside. But the problem didn't lie in anything Warren had been through in the past. It was absolutely due to his unwillingness— or his inability—to see himself objectively in the now.

Energy and Reality

Warren's energy was dark, and it was infectious. That doesn't mean he was a bad guy. In fact, I believe he was totally unaware of all the subtle ways in which he was sabotaging Rory's—and his own—progress. Psychologists share an inside joke. "Denial," they say, stands for "Don't Even Notice I Am Lying." Human beings are the only animals who are happily lied to by our own minds about what is actually happening around us. Our lying minds can protect us from things that can be damaging to our sensitive egos, but they can also make us vulnerable to terrible dangers—especially those from members of our own species—that would be obvious to any other animal. We're the only beings on the planet that get blaring signals from nature about threats to our very survival, but tell ourselves, "Never mind, it's probably nothing." But as far as science has proven, we are also the only species with the access to consciously *change* our mental or emotional states. I'm not talking about putting on a brave face when you're actually trembling inside—that is simply halfhearted acting. I'm talking about actually working *from the inside out* in order to change our state of being at that moment. To be able to do this gives us an amazing power over our world—a power we don't tap into often enough.

Eastern religions have long been champions of the idea that we create our own reality—that what goes on in our minds becomes manifested in our lives. Today, respected scientists—especially in the field of quantum physics—are coming to the same conclusions as the mystics of thousands of years ago. We live our lives under the illusion that we have no control, but the model of quantum physics says that what is happening within reflects what happens outside of us. What does any of this have to do with dog psychology and becoming a better pack leader? It means that you, with your more powerful consciousness, can do something your dog cannot. You have the ability to control your reality—and with it, the energy you project—in ways that you probably don't even think possible.

"Mind over matter" isn't just a saying anymore. At Cornell University, social psychologists David Dunning and Emily Balcetis wanted to find out if "wishful thinking" could actually influence what the brain perceives. They told volunteers that a computer would either assign them a letter or a number to determine whether they'd get to drink tasty orange juice or a bad-tasting smoothie. When the computer flashed an image that could be seen as either the letter *B* or the number 13, volunteers told that a letter would get them orange juice most often reported seeing a *B*. Those told that a number would get them the orange juice most often saw 13. Overwhelmingly, the volunteers saw what they wanted to see. Dunning says, "Before we even see the world, our brain has interpreted that world in such a way that it lines up with what we want to see and avoids what we don't want to see."[11] I'm not a scientist by any measure, but that sure sounds like an explanation of "denial" to me! Take Warren, for example. He was so invested in the fact that Rory couldn't be handled, that was all he was seeing, despite the fact that the opposite thing was happening, right in front of his eyes.

We as humans have the power to turn our perceptions around and use them to our advantage. Instead of seeing the negative things we are used to seeing, we can *choose* to see something different. Researchers have found that the brain can't tell the difference between what is real and what is imagined, because the same neural pathways are used when someone looks at a tree or is asked to visualize the tree. The processes in the brain are exactly the same.[12] When people who fear snakes are shown pictures of snakes, sensors on their skin will detect sweat breaking out and other signs of anxiety, even if the experiment subjects don't admit to feeling fear. The limbic system of the brain buys into the belief that the snakes are real, even if the conscious mind does not. Deepak Chopra describes another common thought experiment, where subjects are asked to imagine putting a lemon slice in their mouths, bite into it, and let the juice squirt into their mouths. "If you are like most people," Chopra writes, "just that quick thought led to a rush of saliva in your mouth, your body's way of saying it believes what your mind is telling it."[13] Centuries before science had the facts to back up those findings, holy men in India were using the power of their minds to walk across hot coals without being harmed. The power of their concentration left their feet unscratched, where other men's feet burned.

The Power of Intention

In order to achieve a calm-assertive state of mind, your emotions and your intentions have to line up in harmony. If you are "acting" tough, but inside still feeling terrified, your dog will know it instantly. Your boss might not, but your dog definitely will. When your insides and your outsides conflict, you are powerless in the animal world. But our human minds are incredibly powerful tools, and with the power of intention, we can actually change our feelings—not just on the surface, but from the inside out. If you can positively project the intention you desire through *real* strength and honesty, your dog will instantly react to that calm-assertive energy.

As animals, we can't change our instinctual feelings any more than our dogs can. As we've seen, our emotions have a purpose: to help us react to our environments and to keep us alive. But as humans, we *can* change our thoughts. That's where the *power of in-*

tention comes in. I first read about this concept many years ago, in Dr. Wayne W. Dyer's book *The Power of Intention: Learning to Cocreate Your World Your Way.* In it, Dyer defines *intention* as the force in the universe that allows the act of creation to take place; not something you do, but as an energy field of which you are a part. I can't stress enough how this concept changed and improved my life and helped me realize my dreams of being able to help unbalanced dogs. Some of the things Dyer said in the book resonated with me and confirmed so many of the observations I had made back in Mexico, before I had access to books like his. Recently, Deepak Chopra has explored the same topic. "Intent orchestrates all the creativity in the universe," he writes. "And we, as human beings, are capable of creating positive changes in our lives through intent."[14] Intent works in the same way that prayer works, according to both authors. The key, say the experts, is to be willing to get rid of our ego—the "I" that tries to oversee and shape the process from a selfish point of view. If someone who is trying to walk over hot coals suddenly lets her rational mind say to her, "This defies the laws of physics—what if it doesn't work and I get hurt?", in the middle of the process, she sabotages her intention and ends up burning her feet.

I'm not going to teach you how to walk on hot coals, or to find the answers to the questions of the quantum universe. But I do hope to help you become more aware of what energy you are projecting at every moment, and to be able to use the power of that energy to communicate a calm-assertive leadership with your dog. That is something that hundreds of my clients have already done, and something you will learn to do in the following chapter.

7

Leadership for Dogs . . . and for Humans

When the effective leader is finished with his work,
the people say it happened naturally. —*Lao Tse*

The lounge was elegantly furnished, the lighting dim, the chatter soft. My wife and I could not believe we had been invited here. We pinched ourselves to make sure we really weren't dreaming. Everywhere we looked, there was a headline, a *Time* magazine cover, a top story on the evening news. Sitting by the fire, the newly elected president of a Middle Eastern country was deep in debate with a former top official of the

U.S. government. Over at the bar, the CEO from one of the world's largest office-supply companies was having a drink with the CEO of America's fastest-growing airline. And there, staring out the window lost in his own thoughts, was probably the richest and most powerful media mogul in the entire world. Working the rest of the room were national and international policy makers, celebrities, media giants, and corporate magnates. There were presidents of universities and founders of political think tanks. There were millionaires and billionaires. There were Learjets and Rolls-Royces. This was a room full of the most successful pack leaders in the human world.

Amazingly, I had been invited to speak to this elite group about dogs and calm-assertive leadership. Who, me? Telling these major power brokers about leadership? What could I, a working-class kid from Mexico, possibly have to offer them? Much to my surprise, I had a lot to offer. Because among all these international leaders, not one of them could control his or her dogs!

Hail to the Dog

If you ever wonder where the American people came up with the idea that the dog should be out in front of the walk, take a look at a film, video, or photograph of any president of the United States getting off Air Force One. Who's the first one out of the plane? Who's the first one into the White House? Ronald Reagan, Bill Clinton, George W. Bush—all of them trail behind their dogs on the White House lawn. In the animal world, position means a lot. And in all of these images, the dogs are going first. In my lifetime, I haven't seen a powerful breed dog in the White House yet. I've seen Labradors. I've seen lots of terriers, a lot of the softer breeds.

But a Rottweiler? A pit bull? Not since JFK have you seen a German shepherd in the White House nor Rhodesian ridgebacks, or Belgian Malinois, or mastiffs. If you had a powerful breed in the White House, no one would ever get to meet with the president. Why? Because if presidents can't control their terriers or happy-go-lucky labs, how could they control a powerful breed? You'd have ten secret service agents trying to handle one dog, because it would be a dog without a pack leader. I got a lot of applause during one seminar when I suggested that everybody write letters to Congress and suggest that before anyone gets sworn in as president, he or she has to learn how to walk a powerful dog. Maybe even a pack of dogs! It would be a test they'd all have to pass. All world leaders of all countries should be able to do it. If that actually happened, then all of our human pack leaders would have to practice calm-assertive energy, because that's the only energy that dogs naturally follow. I believe we'd have a lot more balanced people running the world if they based their leadership on calm-assertive energy.

You see, animals don't follow unstable pack leaders; only humans promote, follow, and praise instability. Only humans have leaders who can lie and get away with it. Around the world, most of the pack leaders we follow today are not stable. Their followers may not know it, but Mother Nature is far too honest to be fooled by angry, frustrated, jealous, competitive, stubborn, or other negative energy—even if it is masked by a politician's smile. That's because all animals can evaluate and discern what balanced energy feels like. A dog cannot evaluate how intelligent a human is, or how rich, or how powerful or how popular. A dog doesn't care if a leader has a Ph.D. from Harvard or is a five-star general. But that dog can definitely tell a stable human from an unstable one. We humans continue to follow the unstable energy of our leaders—which is why we don't live in a peaceful, balanced world.

Unfortunately, there aren't a lot of people born to be pack leaders in the human world. But we all can be pack leaders in the animal world. We need to be, because like it or not, the human species has taken over the planet, and we have brought many animals into our civilized world with us. Domesticated animals don't have a choice anymore—they're here living with us— usually behind walls. Becoming pack leaders of our dogs is especially important when we bring them into environments with dangers that they don't understand, such as traffic, electricity, and toxic chemicals. How can we expect them to navigate those hazards without our guidance? We need to lead them for their own well-being and safety. We also must become good pack leaders for the sake of other humans. Remember, dogs are predators. They are social animals, but they are also social *carnivores*—and deep in their DNA is the wolf in them that wants to hunt and kill prey. We need to have control over those instincts if we are to live in harmony among other animals and humans.

Third-World Instincts

The world leader and captains of industry that I spoke to that day all had intelligence. They all clearly had fierce determination, ambition, and the ability to be pack leaders over other people. Many of them were very tough, very aggressive in the energy they projected. What they didn't have was *instinct*. They weren't very happy with me when I told them that, when it comes to Mother Nature, poor people in third-world countries were better pack leaders to their dogs than they were! In America, people are culturally conditioned to be intellectual and emotional. In third-world countries, many people are culturally conditioned to be instinctual and spiritual. Lower- to middle-income people (most of the people!) in third-world countries can control a dog without even thinking about it. I'm talking three-year-old kids with dogs following them and obeying them, no question. If you tell a three-year-old who lives on a farm anywhere in the world (including America), "Go get that horse," he'll go get the horse. And the horse will follow. My cowriter told me a story of when she was with a film crew in a rural oasis in the middle of the Egyptian desert. She and some other Americans on the crew were passing by a herd of camel, when all of a sudden a pregnant camel started to give birth. The camel was standing up and the baby camel was coming out of her—all hoofs and long legs. It looked as if the baby was stuck, and it couldn't have been very comfortable for the mother. While all the Americans debated among one another, wondering what to do and totally without a clue, a six- or seven-year-old boy from a nearby farm came running up to the camel and without hesitating, grabbed the hoofs of the baby and started to pull. In a few moments, there was a newborn camel in the world. The mother camel lay down and cleaned off her baby, while the little boy wiped his hands and headed back toward home. The film crew could only stare in amazement. To them, they had witnessed a miracle. To the little boy (and to the camel), this was an ordinary, everyday occurrence in the world of Mother Nature.

In a third-world country or on a farm anywhere in the world, you're more likely to be forced to rely on the instinctual side of yourself for survival. You're relating to Mother Nature every day, much the way our ancestors interacted with plants and animals. You're forced to be calm-assertive because you have to connect with Mother Nature *on her terms,* in order to survive.

In Southern California, there are a lot of legal and illegal Mexican immigrants. Many are from poor or rural backgrounds, with the same kind of instinctual-spiritual upbringing that I had. Wealthy Americans hire them to do work such as gardening, housekeeping, and groundskeeping. I also get hired by these wealthy people to help them with their dogs. If I see a bunch of guys from my country working in the yard, I might ask them their opinions on what's really happening with the dog problems in that household. Nine times out of ten, they'll tell me in Spanish, "Well, the owners just don't tell the dog what to do. They treat him like a baby." Simple as that. They get right to the point. They'll say of their employers, "When they leave, we tell the dog what to do. He listens to us. But they don't let us tell the dog anything when they're around, because they're afraid we're gonna hurt his feelings." The workers aren't people who are hurting the dog—I'll see right away that the dog likes and trusts them. Sometimes, it even seems the dog would rather be around the workers than the owner. When the owner comes home, that's when I'll see the dog's instability and anxiety come to the surface.

One point that I want to make: though I believe that, in general, third-world people are more instinctual and tuned in to Mother Nature than Americans are, I'm definitely *not* saying that third-world countries treat their animals better than people do in industrialized nations. In fact, the third world often treats animals very badly. Part of the reason I am here in America is that dogs are not valued in Mexico, except perhaps by the very rich. The career I dreamed of did not exist there at all. Because many third-world people don't exercise their intellectual-emotional side, they don't always feel bad when an animal is hurt, and they don't read books on dog psychology to learn about what makes dogs tick. In fact, in many third-world countries such as Mexico, the women are treated worse than all the dogs and cats in America. Until people in third-world countries learn how to value women, how can they even begin to see the dignity in animals? However, they do not have the difficulty *communicating* with animals that we do here. That's because they live interdependently with animals. In urban America, we don't need animals in our daily lives for survival. We have removed ourselves from our animal natures, blocking our connection with our illusions of intellectual and emotional superiority.

Dominance and Submission—Two New Definitions

Third-world people, homeless people, and farmers all relate to animals in terms of survival. They also aren't afraid to assert dominance with animals. In rural environments, the concept of dominance isn't politically incorrect. On a farm in America, the farmer knows that only he can create harmony among all the animals. In order to do that, someone has to be in control. The animal with the biggest brain, the one that can study and understand all the psychologies of all the others, gets that job. On a farm, even though animals are domesticated, they all work for food and water. And they all live together in harmony. The farmer created that harmony, with calm-assertive energy and leadership. Leadership, by definition, means some degree of authority. Of influence. Of dominance.

Unfortunately, *dominance* seems to have become a dirty word

in the United States. When I use this word in reference to our relationships with our dogs, it seems to make people feel very uncomfortable and bad about themselves, like I am asking them to
behave with their dogs like dictators of a banana republic. The
fact is, dominance is a natural phenomenon that cuts across social species. Mother Nature invented it to help organize animals
into orderly social groups, and to ensure their survival. *It does not
mean one animal becomes a tyrant over another!* In nature, dominance is not an "emotional" condition. There is no coercion, no
guilt, no hurt feelings involved. Any animal that wins the dominant status in a dog pack must earn his or her place at the top—
and just like being a leader of human beings is sometimes a
thankless job, recent studies seem to hint that being a pack leader
in nature isn't all wine and roses, either.

Wolves, and many other members of the canid family, are coop-
erative breeders—that is, the dominant pair get to do most if not
all of the mating and reproducing. In a 2001 study, research en-
docrinologists wanted to find out if being subordinate members
of a cooperative-breeding social pack caused the follower animals
to have more stress. After all, they lose most conflicts and don't get
to choose their mates. But studies of the stress hormones in
African wild dogs and dwarf mongooses (both social carnivores)
had a surprising result—the *dominant* animals actually had much
higher stress hormones, across the board! If these early studies
prove correct, researcher Scott Creel of Montana State University
writes that "being dominant" might not be "as beneficial as it
might first appear. Hidden physiological costs might accompany
the access to mates and resources that dominant individuals enjoy.
If so, this would help to explain why subordinates accept their status with perplexing readiness."[1] In other words, dominant animals

don't take on leadership roles for the cash and prizes involved. They are born with the energy to lead, and they naturally take up the baton. With dogs, it's all about the good of the pack. That's the same reason that dog owners need to learn pack leadership—and yes, that means expressing *dominance*—with their pets.

Being a pack leader is not about showing your dog "who's boss." It's about establishing a safe, consistent structure in your dog's life. Natural pack leaders do not control their followers by fear. They sometimes have to challenge or display their authority, but most of the time they are calm, benevolent leaders. In *Never Cry Wolf*, his famous account of living among the gray wolves of Alaska, naturalist Farley Mowat describes George, the dominant male wolf of the pack he observed for two years: "George had presence. His dignity was unassailable, yet he was by no means aloof. Conscientious to a fault, thoughtful of others, and affectionate within reasonable bounds, he was the kind of father whose idealized image appears in many wistful books of human family reminiscences, but whose real prototype has seldom paced the earth upon two legs. George was, in brief, the kind of father every son longs to acknowledge as his own."[2] Sure, Mowat is humanizing the wolf. That tendency helped make him a popular writer. But if you have misgivings about being your dog's pack leader, reread that beautiful description of George. Think about it. Wouldn't you love your dog to see you that way?

We've already established that dogs do not desire to live in a democracy. They also do not always equate submissiveness with weakness. I like to explain dog submission as open-mindedness. A submissive animal is open and willing to take direction from a more dominant one. In humans, open-mindedness creates the willingness and possibility to learn and take in new information.

You are usually calm-submissive when you are reading a book or seated quietly, watching a concert or a movie. Do you consider yourself "subservient" when you are in this state? Of course not! You are, however, relaxed and receptive. When I give seminars, most of my audience is in a calm-submissive state. They have come to be open, to hear and learn new information. When humans go to church, you can have all the races—white, Latino, black, Asian—sitting peacefully together in the spirit of prayer. The pack leader is the religious leader—or God—and everyone is calm-submissive. When the congregation goes to coffee hour afterward, everyone is in a good state of mind and able to get along together socially. It's only once they go out the door of the church that all the old issues and differences and prejudices come back to haunt them. We want to create such a world like the shelter of the church for our dogs, to make them feel safe, relaxed, and free to engage in social behavior. In order to produce that environment, we must become masters of projecting calm-assertive energy.

The Secrets of Primal Leadership

Calm-assertive leadership is the only leadership that works in the animal world. In our own world, human beings have followed leaders who have coerced us, bullied us, acted aggressive toward us, and filled us with fear in order to control us. But even among humans, research has shown that calm-assertive leadership—*primal* leadership—is really a better way to go. Daniel Goleman (author of *Emotional Intelligence*), Richard Boyatzis, and Annie McKee have spent decades researching the role the human brain plays in creating the most powerful and effective leadership behavior. Based on everything we have learned about how energy works in the animal kingdom, what they learned and recounted in their book *Primal Leadership* should not surprise us at all: "Great leadership works through emotions."[3] This, they tell us, is because the root of our emotions—the limbic system in the brain—is an "open-loop" system; that is, it depends on sources outside the body to manage itself. "In other words, we rely on connections with other people for our own emotional stability." In this way, we are exactly like other social animals—especially dogs. We mirror each other's emotional signals, "whereby one person transmits signals that can alter hormone levels, cardio-vascular function, sleep rhythms, and even immune function inside the body of another."[4]

Remember Warren, my client with the negative energy so powerful it was affecting his dog, his fiancée, and me? That energy we were feeling from him wasn't in our imagination. Not only can a person's negative mood or emotions affect us; the stress hormones secreted when they make us upset take hours to be reabsorbed into the body and to finally fade away. That's why it took me hours to come down from my encounter with Warren.[5] According to the authors of *Primal Leadership*, "Researchers have seen again and again how emotions spread irresistibly in this way whenever people are near one another, even when the contact is completely nonverbal. For example, when three strangers sit facing each other in silence for a minute or two, the one who is most emotionally expressive transmits his or her mood to the other two, without speaking a word."[6] The results of negative energy can literally have lethal consequences: Nurses in cardiac care units who were grumpy and depressed had a four times higher death rate among their patients than those in units where nurses' moods were more balanced.[7]

As we've learned, animals are even more attuned to these emotional-mood-energy signals than we are. They are called "emotional contagions," and they are the very reason that my "power of the pack" form of rehabilitation works so well for "impossible" dogs in cases where human intervention hasn't helped at all. Since the dogs are communicating with one another without words, using only energy and body language to have "conversations," inviting an unbalanced dog into a balanced pack can turn him around almost instantly—as long as he is in a calm-submissive state, which is an open-minded state—ready to learn and absorb the new energy. In a pack of dogs, instability is not allowed. It is targeted for some sort of group action—often, an attack. I talked earlier about how my coauthor experienced the way in which the ripple of emotional contagion passed through my pack in a split second, practically the very moment she changed her thoughts and state of mind. If you've witnessed any animal pack or herd in action, in person, or in a wildlife documentary, it is one of the most visual, dramatic examples of how emotions and energy work together to regulate all the social species of the animal kingdom.

In their studies, Goleman, Boyatzis, and McKee defined two types of leadership. The first they called *dissonant leadership,* and in American workplaces, it's responsible for 42 percent of workers reporting incidents of yelling, verbal abuse, and other unhappy behaviors. "Dissonant leadership," they write, "produces groups that feel emotionally discordant, in which people have a sense of being continually off-key."[8] Many movers and shakers still swear by this form of leadership, the argument being that it keeps people "on their toes." The documentary film *Enron: The Smartest Guys in the Room* depicted a company where dissonant leadership was absolutely the norm. If you can imagine a Wall Street trading floor where traders are constantly competing with each other and yelling at each other, blood pressures and tempers are high, and everyone is exhausted and jittery at the end of the day, wondering if they're going to make enough profit to keep their jobs—that's dissonant leadership.

Unfortunately, that is the kind of leadership my clients often exhibit with their dogs. They are emotional, easily upset and frustrated, panicky, weak, or angry. They are also inconsistent with the messages they send, so their dogs don't know what to expect from one minute to the next. Is my owner the pack leader? Am I the pack leader? A confused dog is an unhappy dog. Although it might still be the norm on Wall Street, dissonant leadership does not cut it in the animal kingdom.

The other kind of leadership the authors describe is *resonant leadership*: "One sign of resonant leadership is a group of followers who vibrate with the leader's upbeat and enthusiastic energy. A primal leadership dictum is that resonance amplifies and prolongs the emotional impact of leadership."[9] This is the kind of leadership that I call "calm-assertive leadership," which of course arises from calm-assertive energy.

Creating Calm-Assertive Energy

It is one thing to understand what calm-assertive energy is, but how do we create it—and how do we maintain it, whether we're with our dogs, our families, our bosses, or our coworkers? In *Emotional Intelligence,* Daniel Goleman tells a fascinating story of a firefight between American and Vietcong troops early in the Vietnam conflict. Suddenly, in the middle of the shooting a line of six monks appeared and starting walking along the rice paddies that separated the two sides—directly toward the line of fire. One of the American soldiers, David Busch, later described the amazing incident: "They didn't look right, they didn't look left. They walked straight through. It was really strange, because nobody shot at 'em. And suddenly the fight was out of me. I just didn't feel like I wanted to do this anymore, at least not that day. It must have been that way for everybody, because everybody quit. We just stopped fighting."[10]

What did the monks do to create this miraculous event? They sent powerful emotional signals—peaceful signals that apparently were more powerful than the hateful signals of the warring soldiers. Although this is a very extreme example, it gives you an idea of how the strength and intention of the energy we project can profoundly affect and change the others around us. Goleman describes this as "setting the emotional tone of an interaction," which is "a sign of dominance at a deep and intimate level; it means driving the emotional state of the other person."[11] What the more powerful person does to control the energy of the other is to actually "entrain" their biological rhythms so that they are working together, not separately: "The person who has the most forceful expressivity—or the most power—is typically the one whose emotions entrain the other. . . . Emotional entrainment is the heart of influence."

In order to gain this gift of emotional influence and become a resonant leader, a person must master the four domains of emotional intelligence. The first two involve mastery of *self-awareness* and *self-management*. These abilities are what make all humans able to be pack leaders in the natural world if they desire it. "Self-aware leaders are attuned to their inner signals. They recognize, for instance, how their feelings affect themselves and their job performances. Instead of letting anger build into an outburst, they spot it as it crescendos and can see both what's causing it and how to do something constructive about it."[12] This is an advantage you have over your dog, because humans are one of the only species on the planet able to accomplish this process. Your dog cannot reflect on how his feelings make him feel. He can only react. You, on the other hand, can recognize an emotion and redirect it before it becomes the energy you are spreading on to others. The self-management part of the equation means getting your own emotions in control before you act.

The other two domains of emotional intelligence as described by Daniel Goleman are social functions that your dogs practice among each other all the time. I call them *instinct. Social awareness,* or *empathy,* means being tuned in to the emotions and energy of the other animals around you. *Relationship management* involves the tools of leadership itself—managing the emotions and interactions of your followers. When a dominant dog gives eye contact to another dog that is moving toward his food dish and the other dog stops and turns away, that is relationship management. When a submissive dog responds to a dominance display by rolling on his back, that is relationship management. It's only humans who often use these tools to manipulate or hurt other people. With dogs, relationship management is done for the good of the pack—to preserve social harmony, reduce conflicts, and ensure survival.

Understanding and achieving skill in these four domains is the key to creating the right kind of energy to project with your dogs.

Techniques

Becoming a calm-assertive pack leader usually doesn't happen overnight. Many of us have been conditioned from a young age to doubt ourselves, to have low self-esteem, or to believe that being assertive is the same as being aggressive. We are often ruled by our emotions or are simply unaware of our moods and emotions. My clients all take their own, individual routes to nurturing this energy in themselves, and there is no easy step-by-step route to achieving it that I can give you. Calm-assertive energy comes from the inside out, however, which is why the following techniques can be helpful in cultivating it in your life.

Before the nineteenth century, most theater performances were very "external" things. Acting styles were large, emotional, and over-the-top. Actors' voices were loud and boisterous, which was necessary to project into large theaters and auditoriums. Most plays were written in exaggerated or lofty language. In twentieth-century Russia, however, actor and stage director Konstantin Stanislavski pioneered a new acting method. His revolutionary idea was for actors to go within themselves and act from the inside out. Acting would be a psychological and emotional experience, a truth-based experience, and the actor's objective was to be believed by the audience. Stanislavski and later American Lee Strasberg taught that the power of the imagination can be used to alter an actor's consciousness. Actors were trained in relaxation, concentration, and "sense-memory" techniques, so they could call up emotions from their pasts in order to bring the characters they are playing to life. Method acting, as it is now known, is more than just "pretending" to be angry, or happy, or grief-stricken; it's learning to call on deep, buried memories of the actual emotion and apply them to the dramatic scene you are playing. When you're watching really gifted actors perform a scene, you can actually feel the contagious energy of the emotion they're portraying.

This is why, when training my clients to harness the power of calm-assertive energy, I often suggest they use acting techniques. Long before I had even met an actor or knew what Method acting was, I would ask people to remember a time in their lives when they felt powerful, try to call up that feeling, and use it when they are walking their dogs. When I came to Los Angeles, I learned that what I was suggesting is a very simple form of the intensive training most professional actors go through. Many actors base the fictional characters they play on real people they have known. In *Cesar's Way,* I recommend imagining yourself as a person or a character who signifies leadership to you. For Sharon, an actress who was trained to use her imagination in this way, it was the role of Cleopatra that gave her confidence and helped her to feel in charge when she was walking her fearful dog Julius. For other clients, it's been everything from Superman to Bruce Springsteen to Oprah Winfrey . . . to their own mothers! In fact, I channel my own mother every time I use the sound "Tsssst!" There's nothing magical about that sound, it's just that it has a big significance for me, since that was the sound my mother made in order to get us kids to behave!

If you want to learn more about these techniques, there are many books about the basics of Method acting. You can take a beginning acting class, or if you know someone who is an actor, take her to coffee and ask her the tricks she uses to bring a character to life. It's not like you have to learn to perform Shakespeare. Remember, your dog is not a theater critic, but he has to believe your performance!

Much like acting exercises, *visualization techniques* are another behavior I suggest to clients who are struggling with the concept of calm-assertive leadership. Though some may find this approach simplistic, thousands of athletes, CEOs, world leaders, students, military officers, entertainers, and others would never even think of doing their jobs or even starting their days without visualization. Sometimes, visualization involves taking a moment before an event to play the whole thing out successfully in your mind, writing a story with a happy ending. If clients are having trouble with their dogs on the walk, for example, after correcting their physical techniques, I tell them to "script" their walks in their imaginations. As Tina Madden—NuNu's owner—tells us in her "success story" in chapter 1, when she was in the process of transforming NuNu (and her life), it was important for her to visualize passing by barking dogs and ignoring them. She had to do it over and over again, but when the real situation occurred, she was able to "switch over" in her mind to the visualization. Some people take visualization to its extreme, *self-hypnosis.* Much has been written about both visualization and self-hypnosis by psychologists, psychiatrists, and self-help gurus. They will all tell you that visualization takes practice to be truly effective. You will probably not get it right the first time you try it. But the mind becomes more and more powerful every time you do the exercises.

Inner dialogue is another powerful technique that can greatly improve the communication between you and your dog. So many of my clients talk to their dogs constantly. They talk in full sentences, on subjects ranging from what the dog wants for dinner to the state of international politics. This is good therapy for the human, of course, but it's not usually an effective way to get better behavior out of your best friend. Many times, when you are asking your dog to do something using words, you really should be talking to yourself. For instance, Brian and Henry, the owners of Elmer, a beagle with a chronic howling problem, were setting themselves up for trouble before they even left the house for their daily walks. Elmer would be excited and hyper before they even finished putting on the leash, then he would always try to get out the door in front of them. Since they had watched my show, they knew the owner is supposed to go out the door first. So what did they do? They *talked* to Elmer, nagging at him! "No, Elmer. Us first. Us first." All the time, they were letting Elmer try to push them aside! Of course, Elmer couldn't understand the words they were saying. He could, however, understand that the energy behind the words was a frustrated, helpless, weak, and uncertain energy. Their inner dialogue went like this: "Oh my God, Elmer's going out first again, we're not the pack leaders! We have to stop him!" Who was in control? Elmer, of course. His energy and intention was much stronger than theirs, even though intellectually, they knew they *should* be the ones in front.

When calling up the calm-assertive pack leader inside, some people are more emotional, some more visual, and some more verbal. The verbal types often prefer to use words first, before they can access their emotions or senses. That's why I suggest that these clients have a conversation with *themselves* any time they find themselves wanting to have a verbal conversation with their dogs. Dogs often respond better when there's less sound involved, and you are strengthening your energy by turning your thoughts inward. When claiming a piece of furniture, for instance, focus your mind, and then tell yourself, "This is *my* sofa." Use your body to claim it, repeating that thought in your mind over and over again. By talking to yourself, you are gradually changing your brain, your body, your emotions, and in turn, your energy. It is your energy that speaks to your dog. In other words, talking to yourself is a much faster way to communicate your energy to your dog than trying to use human language to reason with him—no matter how persuasive you are, or how loudly you yell, or how nicely you ask.

There are other powerful methods that champions in many walks of life use to help themselves feel more confident and powerful. Some of them listen to *motivational tapes,* like those by Anthony Robbins. Some repeat *positive affirmations,* or write them on pieces of paper and leave them in places all around their house, like on the bathroom mirror, on the refrigerator door—or above the hook where they hang their dog leashes. Others read *motivational quotations* and books with *daily inspirations* in them. *Music* is one of the most potent sources that can trigger emotional responses. My coauthor makes different compilations of music on her iPod based on her mood—some that she plays before business meetings or stressful situations to motivate herself; some to calm her down when she's anxious, or to cheer her up if she's blue. Clients have told me they do *yoga, meditation,* and *tai chi,* and read *spiritual texts* such as the Bible to connect with their spiritual sides and call up their intuitive inner strength. When, at eight years old, I started developing frustration and aggression at home in our city apartment in Mazatlán, my parents

SOME TECHNIQUES FOR ATTAINING CALM-ASSERTIVE ENERGY

- Clear and positive *intention*
- Method acting techniques
- Visualization
- Self-hypnosis
- Inner dialogue
- Motivational recordings
- Positive affirmations, written or verbal
- Motivational quotes or readings
- Music
- Yoga, tai chi
- Martial arts
- Meditation or prayer

wisely sent to me to *martial arts training,* where I first learned to focus my energy and turn negative energy into positive. Brandon Carpenter, the renowned horse trainer with similar views to mine about the human-animal connection, also studied centuries-old martial arts techniques where he learned to control his emotion, energy, and body all at the same time.

And *prayer,* of course, is the most powerful force of inner dialogue and *intention* on earth. Even modern science is becoming open to research that shows that prayer, meditation, and faith can influence events in ways most "realists" never dreamed of.

These are all means to access the calm-assertive side of you—the leader within. With calm-assertive energy in your life, you have not only the power to change your dog's life, but if you so desire, your own as well. As for the movers and the shakers I addressed at the conference, some of them will learn to become calm-assertive pack leaders to their dogs. Perhaps it will inspire them to share more calm-assertive energy with the people who work for them and the rest of the world. Others, of course, will keep doing things the way they have always done them. President Theodore Roosevelt once said, "People ask the difference between a leader and a boss. . . . The leader works in the open, and the boss in covert. The leader leads, and the boss drives." In order for your dog to follow, you cannot be just a boss. You must be a guide, an inspiration, a true leader, from the inside out.

SUCCESS STORY
CJ and Signal Bear

I was working as a contractor in a fenced maintenance yard (about the size of a city block) when a supervisor came into our office and told us, "We can escort you to your cars for lunch. There is a wild, pregnant Chow dog loose in the lot that is terrorizing everyone. We just called Animal Control to come and get her." I thought, *Ahh gee, a Chow, pregnant and wild? They will put her down for sure,* as that was the policy of the local animal control people regarding feral dogs. I felt compelled to go take a look at this poor victim of a certain death sentence. When I got to the lot, however, I saw a male dog who was scared out of his mind! He was in a panic, barking, snarling, and running around. As an environmental safety and health risk manager with thirty-five years experience, my first thought was, *Can I safely help this dog without endangering myself, the other workers, or even the dog himself, if he escapes from this secure yard and runs out into the street?*

I had recently been watching the new *Dog Whisperer* show with Cesar Millan. Working with rescue and show dogs all my life, I thought I was capable of safely trying some of the techniques he had talked about on the program. I specifically remembered two things Cesar had said: "Depression and aggression are often really frustration" and "Discharge the energy first; let the dog wear himself out." That's just what the dog did, finally hiding between the storage shed and concrete wall, changing his energy from aggressive confrontation to fearful retreat. Next, I followed steps I had seen Cesar take in his red-zone cases—even though I knew the show tells people not to try these things at home. *Take control of the space.* (I blocked the dog's way out, sat down in the entry, claimed the space.) *No touch, no talk, no eye contact.* (I sat sideways blocking his exit, in 105-degree heat for two hours.) Finally the dog came up to me. I ignored him. He bumped me with his nose—his energy had shifted to calm-submissive, quiet, balanced energy. Without looking at him, I reach my hand out to massage his shoulder and finally pulled him to me, then carried him to the car to introduce him to my pack of four dogs at home: I did it Cesar's way.

Signal Bear, as I came to call him, was the first dog in my "pack" to be raised "Cesar's way" from his first moments with me. I have been astonished at how much easier it has been simply working with a dog using Cesar's techniques, than with all my other dogs that I had humanized for the past ten years. Since that time, I have become inspired to facilitate a *Dog Whisperer* fans and friends e-mail list on Yahoo! and have rescued, rehabilitated, and placed four other dogs (so far!) who were about to be put down for supposedly "incurable" behavior problems, but all of whom changed with the consistent application of Cesar's formula of "rules, boundaries, and limitations.".

Cesar's philosophy and techniques have not only given us a better life with our dogs, but have actually helped both my husband and me in our workplaces. I had a client who had been a raging emotional tyrant for years. Recently, when he was unjustly blaming something on me, I decided to change my approach. Instead of feeling and acting like a victim, I mentally let go of my long past history and usual emotional/fearful reaction to this man. I took a deep breath to calm myself, then did an energy distraction technique that I have seen Cesar do while walking dogs. Though I couldn't exactly say "Tsssst!" to a client, I used the same energy that Cesar uses, and simply said the man's name while firmly touching his arm. He stopped cold—his rage stopped—and he actually *looked* at me. I then continued addressing the project decisions. My client simply followed along calmly. I had made him part of the team (pack) again!

8

Our Four-legged Healers

Come forward into the light of things,
Let Nature be your teacher.
—*William Wordsworth*

A bbie Jaye ("AJ" to her large network of loving friends) had just gone through five solid years of personal hell. Her beloved German shepherd–Lab mix, Scooby, had just passed away. Then her father and mother died, one shortly after the other. Desperately trying to have a baby with her husband, Charles, Abbie suffered a total of four miscarriages in a row—each one more heartbreaking than the last. If it's true, as they say, that "God doesn't give us anything we can't handle," then He was certainly putting AJ to the test—a test that, for a while there, AJ was certain she was failing. "Imagine a punching bag," she explained, pushing back the emotion. "When you punch it down, it comes back up. Well, I never had time to recover from one loss before I was hit again."

The result of all these tragedies, one after the other, was that AJ began to suffer a psychological reaction to severe stress that is known as panic disorder. Everything you have just learned about how your dog experiences unreleased energy applies to all animals—especially humans. When people undergo the kind of traumas that AJ suffered and are not able to experience relief from all the grief, sadness, and frustration, that negative energy has to go somewhere. Panic attacks are one way in which negative energy is released. Over four million Americans—about 5 percent of the adult population—suffer from panic attacks, according to the National Institute of Mental Health. People who have undergone panic attacks describe them as devastating nightmares. They are both physical and emotional traumas—a sense of doom lying just around the corner, a feeling that they are about to have a heart attack, a sense that they are about to suffocate, or all of these feelings at once. Their hearts race hard and they hyperventilate, their arms and legs tingle and go numb, and they feel as if they are going crazy. Some people get dizzy and actually pass out. Before they are diagnosed, many panic attack victims end up in emergency rooms. The worst thing about panic attacks is that they don't always come on for any obvious reason. Sufferers describe them as coming "out of the blue." That leaves panic attack victims in a terrible, helpless, depressed place, even after the attack is over. They don't know when or where another attack will strike them, and what will happen to them if it does.

AJ became one of the millions of people with panic attacks who so feared having unexpected spells in public that she began to withdraw to her home. This was devastating for AJ, because she had been an outgoing, active, energetic person before the attacks began. She had always played the caretaker role, not the role of the one needing care. In addition to her job as an activity director at a retirement home, AJ was constantly giving back to society as a volunteer; in fact, for fifteen years, she certified her dogs as therapy dogs and brought them to visit people in need.

Therapy dogs are pets trained to come into hospitals, retirement homes, nursing homes, mental institutions, and schools to provide love and comfort to patients and residents. Calm-submissive dogs can often help where humans can't. When we see an ill person hooked up to a machine, we can't help but feel sad or sorry for them. Dogs don't see that. That's why a lot of people in a hospital would rather have a visit from a therapy dog than from a human. Doctors and nurses are trained to be more impartial, but often their energy isn't nurturing. They come using a purely intellectual energy. But a dog is always in an instinctual state of mind. If you bring a calm-submissive, balanced dog into a ward where people are suffering, the dog will immediately go after the weakest person in the room, get her into a better energy, and work the room until he brings everybody to that same state of mind. Research on the healing power of animals has only scratched the surface of the magical secrets of the human-animal bond. So far, it has shown that pets lower our blood pressure, triglycerides, and bad cholesterol levels.[1] If you happen to have a heart attack, you have an eight times better chance of surviving one year if you own a dog. If you have surgery, you will recover much faster with animal therapy. Chemical testing has shown that within minutes of petting a dog, both human and animal alike release a flood of beneficial hormones such as prolactin, oxytocin, and phenyl ethylamine. Therapy dogs are now being used for improving focus and stimulating memory in Alzheimer's and depression patients, aiding communication in those who have trouble with speech, such as psychiatric patients and stroke victims, and simply offering comfort and a sense of peace to those in stressful situations.[2] AJ, Scooby, and her other dog, a three-year-old boxer-Lab mix named Ginger, had performed these tasks until Scooby's death. Then a scrappy little one-year-old terrier named Sparky took over Scooby's functions.

But Sparky turned out to have a special talent all his own. Both Abbie and her husband, Charles, noticed that when she was with Sparky, she had fewer panic attacks, and when she did have them, she recovered much faster. Sparky brought her a sense of peace and comfort that no medicine could; in fact, the parade of drugs that had been prescribed to help AJ with her panic attacks either caused terrible side effects or had no effect at all. Marty Becker, veterinarian and coauthor of the book *Healing Power of Pets,* has said, "I believe having a pet has all the benefits of an antidepressant drug, and more—but without a single side effect," and that's exactly the way AJ described Sparky. "If I could bottle what I feel when I'm with him and drop it over the Middle East, there would be peace. Because that's what he gives me is a deep sense of peace and calm."

It seemed clear to AJ that if she wanted her life back, she'd have to get Sparky certified as a service dog, which is a much bigger responsibility than simply being a therapy dog. We mostly think of service dogs as the guide dogs for the blind and the dogs that help people in wheelchairs. But service dogs are now trained to help kids with autism and other developmental disabilities, to become the "ears" for the deaf, to assist people with problems of balance, and even to remind those with chronic illnesses to take their medication on time! And there's a whole new movement promoting psychiatric service dogs—dogs that help people with psychiatric disabilities.[3] Psychiatric service dogs are trained to help people with psychiatric problems in such ways as snuggling with them when they're feeling sad or hopeless, waking them up if they have "hypersomnia" or excessive sleeping, and reminding them to take their medication if they have problems with focusing or memory loss. Because, as we've seen, dogs are so completely tuned into our feelings, emotions, and even barely perceptible physical and chemical changes in our bodies and brains, they are much more intuitive than even the most expensive Park Avenue psychiatrist, and can sometimes act much faster than paramedics to save us in emergencies.

Sparky was already acting as Abbie's guide and comforter. But in order for him to be able to be with her at all times, he'd have to be professionally certified as a service dog, so he could wear the special vest and have the "credentials" to go with her into stores and restaurants, on airplanes, and other public places. Sparky easily passed all the basic tests, such as answering to commands and riding in a car, but there was one area in which he really was a dismal failure. He was unpredictable in public situations, often becoming distracted by passing people, cars, or trucks, and worse, he could be aggressive to other dogs. Without passing this "public access test," AJ wouldn't be able to make use of the best medicine she had available to her—her dog. That's when she called me in to help.

I had never seen a service or therapy dog before I came to

America, and the minute I did, I was fascinated by them. It all made perfect sense to me. After all, since ancient times, the human race developed dog breeds to help us to survive. In today's modern world, we often face more mental hurdles than we do physical ones, so why not employ dogs to help us overcome those burdens as well? Becoming service or therapy dogs are jobs that are open to dogs of any breed, as long as they have the right temperament for it. Some dogs—like Sparky—just naturally shine at the task. Giving a dog a job and an important task to accomplish is the best thing you can do for him. It's in his genes to want to work for his food and water, and to feel like he has a mission in life. AJ and Sparky already had the kind of bond that many humans have to work a long time toward achieving with their therapy dogs. But could Sparky overcome his issues in order to make the grade?

My consultation with AJ and her husband was a very revealing one. I saw that AJ was a very, very strong person—a survivor—who had just hit the limit of her capacity for getting past traumatic events. What happened to her could happen to anyone—and it was clear by the tears in her eyes that Abbie was desperate to get over this obstacle and get on with her life. But although she was suffering from a very disabling psychiatric problem, I sensed a positive energy underneath. But that energy was being smothered by her fear, and with her being such a powerful person, that fear was becoming contagious to her husband and her two dogs. I wasn't surprised at all when she told me that both Ginger and Sparky had problems with fearful aggression. They were getting it right from their owner!

I worked on reducing Sparky and Ginger's aggression in the house, and from early in the session, I could see on AJ's face that the lightbulb was beginning to go on. She immediately clued in to the fact that her own instability was being reflected in her dog's behavior. This is a very important moment for my clients. Some people, like Danny or Warren, mentioned in previous chapters, never catch on to this vital concept. Sometimes, the most unlikely clients—the tycoon, for example—eventually get the message after I work with them for a long time. But AJ was catching on like wildfire. She is a person with a very quick mind, but she was also highly motivated. Unlike some people who seem to dwell on their misfortunes, AJ desperately wanted out of hers. The moment she began to see a possibility, she went barreling toward it. She said to me, "If only you could teach me to be calm and assertive, I wouldn't have panic disorder or need a service dog." I told her, "I'm not going to teach you how to be calm-assertive." I pointed to Sparky. "*He* is."

Calm-Assertive Healing

What I wanted Abbie to understand was the concept that the clearest way to see your own energy reflected back is to look at the behavior of the animals around you. My own pack keeps me a centered human being because they always show me who I am really being at that moment. If we can learn to read the energy of the animals around us, we *all* can become better human beings— and we can even heal some of our deepest wounds as well.

Earlier in the session, AJ had shared with me that she had a great fear of "dogs that are in the news"—Akitas, Rottweilers, German shepherds, and especially pit bulls. No wonder her dogs were afraid of strange dogs—they were picking it up from AJ! Well, she was in luck. For anyone who is afraid of pit bulls, I have the perfect cure, just waiting for them at the Dog Psychology

Center. I immediately invited AJ and Sparky down to the center to meet the "pack." At that time, there were forty-seven dogs there, including twelve pit bulls. I wanted AJ to meet them face-to-face. You see, I believe that the only way fear can leave any human or animal is if they can live through a worst-case scenario and conquer it. That is the way I learned to overcome my fear of flying— by getting on a plane and just experiencing my sensations. So far, no plane I have been on has crashed, so I have reinforced flying for myself as a neutral—if not exactly positive!—experience. Some people who share my same fear take tranquilizers or drink alcohol on flights to relax—then they wonder why their fear never goes away. That's because they are simply avoiding the fear, not facing it. The more they use artificial substances to block their anxiety instead of letting themselves pass through it, the more they are reinforcing themselves to be afraid.

I also happen to believe—and have seen from hundreds of experiences with dogs—that many animals can overcome phobias by facing their own fears. That's the way that I helped Kane the Great Dane in season one of *Dog Whisperer* overcome his fear of shiny floors. By using Kane's own momentum to bring him onto the same shiny floor no power of man or beast had been able to get him on for a year, I simple waited with my calm-assertive energy as Kane became accustomed to this new situation. With me providing a feeling of leadership he could trust, his common sense was able to kick in, saying to him, "Hey, there's nothing to be afraid of here!" In less than fifteen minutes, Kane was freed of an unnecessary phobia that had been causing him and his owners extreme stress for over a year. Today, four years later, he's still 100 percent phobia free. Some psychologists and animal behaviorists refer to this as *flooding*, and some of my critics have attacked me for it. I asked my friend, psychologist Dr. Alice Clearman, to explain the way flooding works in the brain. She informed me that *exposure* is the current term for the practice, and that it is the best treatment for phobias in humans. She explained how it works:

Exposure is all about reinforcement in the brain. Whenever we engage in a habitual behavior in response to something we fear, we reinforce that fear. If we are afraid of spiders and back away from them, we reinforce that fear. Imagine a great fear of spiders. You see one in your bedroom. You run out of the bedroom and get someone else to kill it. Or you spray half a can of pesticide in your room. Or you call a pest control company. I've known one person who refused to sleep in her bedroom for three months after seeing a spider there!

The way it works is that they become more and more anxious as they approach the feared object or situation. In the case of spiders, if I'm afraid of them and I have to kill one, I become more and more afraid as I approach it. Maybe I have a shoe in my hand, poised to smash the creature. My heart is pounding, my pulse is racing, I'm almost hyperventilating. I'm terrified! I get closer and closer, sweating bullets. I suddenly decide that I can't handle it! I turn heel and flee from the room, calling my neighbor and asking her to come over and kill the thing. The moment I run away, how am I feeling? Relieved! My pulse slows and my breathing returns to normal. I wipe my brow with a shaking hand. Whew! That was close!

Look at what I did to my brain. I had increasing anxiety as I drew closer and closer to the spider. Then I decided I couldn't do it. I fled the scene and I had an enormous sense of relief. That relief—that feeling—was a reward. I rewarded myself for fleeing from the spider. I've taught myself, quite literally my brain, that spiders are indeed very dangerous creatures. I know this because of the feeling of relief I had when I left. The result is that I actually increase my fear. I have made myself a little bit more afraid of spiders every time I exit.

The difference between dogs and humans when it comes to phobias, says Dr. Clearman, is that humans attach thought, imagination, memory, and anticipation to their fears. Dogs do not do these things; they live in the moment, giving them a huge advantage over us in overcoming fears and phobias. But for humans, even with our complexities of thought and memory, the best treatment is still exposure. Dr. Clearman tells me that the treatment for spider phobias is to have the client have a spider on his skin until he is no longer afraid. The fearful person starts by talking with a therapist who can assess the degree of fear, but the treatment is always the same. It can be done in short stints over a longer period of time, or in just one session. Exposure has been used by psychologists for about thirty years. Dr. Clearman explained that the mountains of research that have been done on it continue to prove it is very, very effective.[4]

A powerful benefit of exposure is that it is quick. With humans and dogs alike, exposure eliminates the phobia in a very short period of time. What's the harm in letting someone just live with a phobia for the rest of her life? Plenty. Phobias produce stress hormones that shorten our lives by damaging our hearts, brains, and immune systems. Dogs are harmed by these hormones in the same way that we are. Helping eliminate these stresses *quickly* is the best thing we can do for anxious or fearful dogs. Some critics say that my use of exposure is "cruel." Of course, if a terrifying experience is suddenly *forced* onto a person or animal without a knowledgeable guide (a therapist or experienced animal professional) or helper, it can do more harm than good. But with the right information and calm-assertive energy, helping dogs eliminate phobias gives them the opportunity to relax and have a better quality of life. If you know you can stop the experience of fear or anxiety swiftly and safely, the kindest thing to do for anyone you love is to do exactly that. Why would anyone drag out the suffering? In my opinion, it's best to eliminate it quickly.

Another benefit of exposure is something Dr. Clearman calls "self-efficacy"—that is, feeling effective in your own life. It is important for both humans and dogs to have confidence and self-esteem. When they overcome a phobia, they are greatly empowered. This affects other areas of their lives and they feel stronger, more comfortable, and happier. This is what I wanted to help accomplish for AJ, by exposing her to my pack of pit bulls. I hoped for her not only to overcome her phobia of big powerful dogs, but to help her feel more empowered as a pack leader with Sparky—and in the rest of her life, where she desperately needed it. AJ's life at that moment was like a file cabinet with two drawers, except the drawer full of bad experiences was overflowing, while the other drawer for good experiences was nearly empty. It was my goal to help her fill up that side of the file cabinet. And my pack was going to help me.

The Mouth of the Crocodile

When AJ came to the center, I gave her the usual rules: no touch, no talk, no eye contact. I could see that she was hesitant, but she was definitely curious, and she had a very positive attitude. What was really remarkable was the moment I opened the gate, one of my pit bulls, Popeye, came running out to welcome her. AJ was afraid of pit bulls, yet it was Popeye who came out as the ambassador to invite her into the pack. Immediately I saw her anxiety begin to drain away. It was like there was an immediate bond between her and Popeye. Already, she was feeling the healing power of dogs.

AJ walked among the forty-seven dogs and was remarkably calm. She described it as an "out-of-body experience." I think she really couldn't get over the fact that she was actually doing it! She went out into the dirt park with me and threw the tennis ball for the dogs. With every moment, she grew more and more confident. In fact, I felt she was feeling strong enough for me to invite several pits into an enclosed area with us and give her a private "pit bull party." This was a little harder for her to do, but she trusted me and followed my lead. I let her see what happens when the pits have a conflict among one another—and how I stop the excitement before it escalates. And I showed her how to wait until a dog's mind is relaxed before sharing affection. This, of course, encourages a dog to relax. What was beautiful was that Popeye lay down in front of us and stayed close by AJ, almost guarding her. And nearby, Sparky watched the whole event unfold. By watching AJ's discomfort with the big dogs dissolve, Sparky's own dog aggression could take a step toward being cured.

A really important moment came when AJ and I took a walk through the neighborhood of the Dog Psychology Center, which is an industrial area filled with warehouses and a lot of off-leash dogs. Near a used car lot, we came across a pregnant female Lab mix, who started to bark at us aggressively. AJ remained calm throughout the encounter, so Sparky did also. Another lightbulb went off for AJ—it was a moment of hard evidence that indeed she *was* Sparky's energy source! I showed AJ how to hold her ground, remain calm and assertive, and just repeat in her inner dialogue, "I mean you no harm, but this is my space." I challenged her to take a step forward toward the aggressive dog, and AJ watched the aggressive dog walk away in submission. "That's it," I said. "You won." Abbie was elated. She was about to win a whole lot more.

About two weeks later, I invited AJ and her husband, Charles, to bring Sparky and Ginger back to the center. This visit would be about strengthening the whole pack, but it would also be about making sure AJ cemented her learning from the first visit. It was amazing to see the change in AJ. Her eyes were brighter, she was walking taller, and I could tell she just couldn't wait to get inside with all the dogs again! To test what she had learned, I asked her to share with Charles the same rules I had first given her during the earlier visit. She confidently launched into the "No touch, no talk, no eye contact" rules as if she'd been coming there a thousand times. Professional educators know that whenever a person shares her knowledge or teaches a skill to someone new, she strengthens her own learning of the material.[5] Simply teaching Charles all the things she had learned two weeks before gave AJ another boost of confidence.

Inside the center, AJ was calm and assertive at least 90 percent of the time. Her body postures and facial muscles were relaxed, and when she walked, her shoulders were up and her eyes remained focused rather than darting around scanning for danger on the ground. When one of the pits jumped up on her, she calmly and assertively asked him to get down, and instantly he sat in front of her, calm-submissive. Each time she accomplished a new skill with the dogs, her confidence grew. As she left the center that day, she told our director thoughtfully, "If I do what Cesar says all the time, if I'm able to do that, I not only won't have panic attacks, but I won't need a service dog in the first place."

As it turns out, Sparky needed a lot less rehabilitation than AJ did. When he passed his service test with flying colors, I was so excited, I couldn't stop jumping up and down and cheering. I felt like we'd won the Academy Award. AJ presented me with a drawing she'd done of Popeye, her friend from the center who first changed her mind about pit bulls. But the real success story of this case wasn't Sparky, it was AJ. Learning to master calm-assertive energy with dogs—and especially with pits!—set her on a path to self-discovery that just keeps growing and growing. She went back to work as an organic raw chef and started volunteering as a teacher for the blind at the Braille Institute. And her panic disorder continues to improve at the same time. She says,

> Cesar helped me to realize that if I don't start facing my fears, they will consume me. Not facing one's fears does not make them go away. Facing them actually can. Working with Cesar has really helped me change my fearful energy into a more assertive energy. I still get afraid—very afraid, at times—but now I am willing, as they say, to "feel the fear and do it anyway." With panic disorder one has a tendency not to fight or flee—simply to freeze. I have now become a fighter and I really have Cesar to thank for that.

The truth is, AJ taught me a lesson as valuable as the one I gave to her. I admitted to her that while I would never give up on dogs, I would sometimes give up on people and their ability to change. AJ had a very real, very serious affliction that some people suffer from all their lives. But because she had such a positive attitude, and such determination, she wasn't going to give up on herself. AJ taught me to never give up on people. And when people have dogs in their lives as teachers, there are no limits to how far they can grow.

The story of AJ and Sparky is a beautiful lesson about the healing power of dogs—and also about how mastering calm-assertive leadership can create amazing changes in all areas of our lives. The wonderful thing about our dogs is that they can often motivate us to change when nothing else can.

If a dog could choose which human he was able to live with, he would not put an ad in the personals that said "Seeking One Dog Lover for Affection, Affection, Affection!" That's because a dog *lover* doesn't create balance. A dog lover can create instability. In *Cesar's Way,* I told the story of Emily the pit bull. Born with a heart-shaped spot on her back, she was loved and adored from the moment her owner, Jessica, adopted her. Jessica showered her with affection every day. But Emily became a very vicious little girl. If a dog has to live with a human, she would choose a *knowledgeable* dog owner over simply a dog *lover.*

Most animals, if given the choice, would rather live among their own kind than with beings of another species. An animal that can't relate to his own kind is living in limbo, like a man without a country. Remember Keiko the killer whale from the movie *Free Willy*? Raised in captivity, trained, and loved by his handlers, he was set free again and again, but couldn't relate to the killer whales in the wild. He tried to, but they just wouldn't accept him. He didn't have the social skills, and humans couldn't teach him. Sadly, Keiko died never having known what it felt like just to be a killer whale, never having felt proud of himself for being a killer whale. I believe the same thing goes for dogs. I think they find themselves complete only when they can interact and relate to their own kind. Can they adapt themselves to live with a different species? Absolutely; it's part of our greater survival mechanism that animals can coexist with other animals, as long as we're not being attacked. But would a dog rather be a dog than a human? Back on my grandfather's farm in Mexico, we had "goat dogs" for herding goats. In order to become working dogs, they were weaned at an early age and the goat mother would raise the dog, so the dog would become part of her herd. But eventually, as the dog developed, he would no longer engage in goat behaviors; he'd behave in more doglike ways. Now, the goats are his pack—as far as he's concerned, a goat raised him; that's his family. But he'd still do dog activities. Eventually he would meet other dogs, find a mate, and detach himself from his goat family. He'd still spend his days with the goat herd—but it now would become a job to him, not his whole identity. He'd feel good about himself—good about being a dog.

Honoring Our Inner Human

In a way, the story of the goat-herding dog is a metaphor for my own life. When I was a boy in Mexico, I couldn't identify with people. I felt different from them. Instead of trying to find closeness, I gravitated toward dogs. I felt free with them, I wasn't judged by them, and I could become a very important part of their group. This became part of my identity, and I became extremely antisocial. I stopped trusting people. I shut them out. I totally gave up on them. For a long time, I lived this way, pouring all of my emotional, spiritual, and instinctual energies into dogs. I figured that was just my fate. The truth was, I was feeling rejected by people, but I really was rejecting myself. You can't turn your back on your own kind without in some way turning on yourself. You blame others for your misery, and you never look in the mirror. Things never change—you just exist. You may feel okay, but you are not growing.

Then I met my wife Ilusion. She is a very emotionally open person, despite the fact that she has suffered a lot from human beings all through her life. She never stopped loving humans and trying to see the best qualities in them. My wife turned on the lights for me. She reminded me how important it is to have relationships with humans. It was then that I realized I was not complete. The way I was living had become a habit, a way of existence, but in the back of my mind, I never felt totally whole or happy to be who I was.

I was like Mowgli, the wild boy in Rudyard Kipling's *The Jungle Book*. I remained in love with and devoted to my dogs, but in the end, I had to find a balance between my dogs and my own "pack"—my human family. If I hadn't accomplished that, I'd never be able to do the work I do today. As a boy, I dreamed of working with dogs as a way to get away from humans. Today, I help rehabilitate dogs, but the bulk of my efforts goes into "training" humans.

We all want unconditional love in our lives, but too often, we give up doing the hard work it takes to earn it among our own kind. Instead, we adopt animals and expect them to do it for us. Animals do have the capability to accept us for who we are, and I think everyone in the world should accomplish loving an animal—it makes us better humans and brings us closer to nature. But when we only think about our needs, it becomes a selfish way of having a relationship with someone. We feel that we have finally found somebody, our animal soul mate—and it is a wonderful therapy, an amazing opportunity to experience the feeling of someone loving us simply for ourselves. And that's a good first step. But that's still not the end of the journey, of finding our identity within our own species—connecting with the person or the "pack" of people who will also accept us for who we are in the way that only other humans can. We can't do this by blaming others for our failures. We need to look at our own mirrors and honestly face our fears.

When it comes to our dogs, our mission should be to fulfill their needs first. The most therapeutic thing, the most empowering thing you can do in your life is to fulfill another living being's needs. If you can watch your dog go from an insecure, anxious, and aggressive dog to a balanced, peaceful dog, that is an amazing kind of therapy. It builds your leadership; it builds your self-esteem. When you focus on what's best for animals, then you automatically get the benefit of learning from their balance, their natural way of living. They want very simple things from life—but for them, that has the same meaning as three billion dollars would to my friend the tycoon.

If you can accomplish calm-assertive energy and leadership with your dog, you can accomplish it in any other area of your life. Let your dog be your trusting follower, your mirror—and ultimately, your guide, on your journey to becoming the very best person you can be.

Epilogue

Humans and Dogs: The Long Walk Home

We are alone, absolutely alone on this chance planet:
and, amid all the forms of life that surround us,
not one, excepting the dog, has made an alliance
with us. —Maurice Maeterlinck

I've said before that two dog trainers can't seem to agree on anything except the fact that a third dog trainer is completely wrong. In the same way, scientists seeking the answers to how and when the dog became domesticated are constantly battling each other over the answer to one of time's greatest mysteries. I am no scientist, archeologist, or historian. But for a moment, please humor me—turn on that powerful imagination located in the front of your big human brain to visualize this possible scene:

It's around twelve thousand years ago—the height of the Ice Age. On a frigid subzero day, there's a sign of life on the land bridge that has formed across the Bering Strait, linking the Asian continents to the New World. In search of better hunting grounds, a small group of early humans slog their way across the frozen plain, fighting their way against the snow and wind. A pack of wolflike canids—the earliest ancestors of the modern dog—trudge along behind the ragtag band. Perhaps the four-legged animals are scavenging for the litter and scraps that the migrating humans leave behind. Perhaps they have been drafted to pull large items on a sled. But maybe— just maybe—they are keeping these humans alive by helping them to hunt. With their sensitive noses, they are able to smell potential prey from miles away. With their wolf DNA, they are naturally superior stalkers and trackers. They are faster than the humans, and more in tune with the rest of the animals around them. Perhaps without the presence of these animals, this little band of humans would not have survived the crossing.

What if early dog did not learn from humans, as much as early humans learned from dog?

This is only a fantasy, of course—my own private Hollywood movie that I like to play and replay in my imagination. But there is one truth in the image of which I'm totally certain: whatever we did to make it here, from our ancient pasts to the twenty-first century, there is absolutely no doubt that humans and dogs have made most of that journey *together*. I always say that walking with dogs—migrating with them—is our most powerful form of communication with them—because it re-creates these ancient, primal journeys. Side by side, we became two very different species on the planet, forming an alliance for survival. Both of us are social species; both of us live in "packs." We must have identified very strongly with each other from the beginning—so strongly, in fact, that the rest of our histories would always intertwine. We fell in love with dogs, giving them the same careful burials that we gave our own dead; painting murals of them on our palace walls; fashioning our ancient gods in their image. And for whatever reason, they must have loved us back. Dogs are the only nonprimate animals that instinctively respond to our gestures. They are the only nonprimates that search our facial expressions for clues to our intent. They are the only animals that automatically look to us for guidance in this strange, complex world that we have fashioned out of what used to be a simple planet.

These noble animals—so different from us in so many ways, so much like us in others—are our closest link with the instinctual selves we have left behind. When we look into their trusting eyes, we see both our strengths and our weaknesses perfectly mirrored back at us. There are endless lessons to be learned there, if we are willing and courageous enough to go seeking them.

I hope that this book has helped you see your beloved dogs in an even more meaningful light, and that you will always remain conscious of and grateful for the deep and everlasting bond we share together.

Appendix

Meeting a Dog for the First Time

1. Do not approach the dog. Remember, pack leaders never approach followers; followers come to leaders. This is very difficult for some people who see an adorable dog and simply must go and pet it. However, no matter how cute a dog is, please remember she is a living being with dignity and deserves as much respect as any human.

2. Normal dogs will be curious about your scent. So it's important that you allow them to come to you and smell you. When you go to a person's house for the first time, his dog will respond much better to you if you ignore her first, and allow her to find out about you on her own. Because most humans are not schooled in proper dog etiquette, many dogs are used to humans approaching them uninvited and have built up defense mechanisms, including shyness, fear,

and sometimes even aggression. Allowing a dog to explore you before you explore her gives her space to develop both respect and trust for you.

3. Remember my three rules: *no touch, no talk, and no eye contact* while the dog's nose is busy analyzing our energy and all the different scents in our body. This sniffing can last from three seconds to a minute. It's important not to interrupt the dog while she's intent on accomplishing this ritual. You wouldn't walk away in the middle of a handshake, would you?

4. When the dog is finished learning about you, she is going to give you a sign whether she wants to fight with you, wants to run away from you, wants to ignore you, or wants to give you "respect," which is another way of saying "submission." The last choice will be a very friendly vibe and sometimes she'll rub her against you in a gentle way. That will be a signal that you can now touch or share affection with the dog.

5. Many people pursue or force attention on a dog that would rather ignore them. In the dog world, that is rude behavior. Imagine if you had just shaken hands with someone formally, turned to go about your business, and that person just wouldn't leave you alone? If a dog wants to ignore you, she'll simply turn, face the other way, and either look at the floor or at something else that grabs her attention. She may wander away. She's basically saying, "Thanks, but no thanks." The best thing to do is to ignore her back.

6. If a dog displays any signs of dominance or aggressiveness toward you, however, ignoring her could be seen as a weakness. This could be a stare from her, a raised lip, or simply a more aggressive physicality—such as bumping up against

you forcefully or walking on your feet. In this case, you should stand your ground—don't give strong eye contact, as this will instantly be perceived as a challenge. Your goal isn't to argue with the dog or to force her to see you as "the boss"—it's just to ask that you be treated with at least the same degree of respect that you have given the dog. Simply use your body and your calming "inner dialogue" in order to own your space. In their own world, dogs "dialogue" over space all the time—and most dogs will give you yours once you claim it.

7. If the aggression continues, you should ask as calmly and firmly as possible for the owner to please remove the dog, because you're not feeling comfortable. Do this right away, because if you allow your own emotions to escalate into nervousness or fear, you can be setting yourself up for a long-term problem relationship with that dog. Of course, it's important that the owner remove the dog in a calm-assertive way. The most vital thing at this point is that nobody behaves excitedly at that moment.

Introducing Your Dog to a New Person (Especially a Child)

1. If you are walking down a street and a child or stranger wants to pet your dog, the most important thing to remember is that you are the pack leader and you must remain in control of the situation.

2. First, never let the child make the first move. You must observe the child or stranger and note how he behaves, paying special attention to body language and eye contact. If the

person is excited, this can be seen by the dog as a form of disrespect, and the dog might try to correct her by pushing him with her head, with her body, or with her feet. Remember, you cannot simply say to your dog, "Don't worry, this is my friend's son." Your dog is not going to see the child that way, or care if he is a person who "loves dogs." Your dog is going to make a judgment based on the intensity of the energy, the speed, and where the child is touching and how he's touching.

3. If you know and trust your dog with strangers (and if your dog has been exercised and is not in an anxious or frustrated state of mind), I recommend you say to the child, "Why don't you let her get to know you first? I have three rules—no touch, no talk, and no eye contact for two minutes." Then observe your dog's reaction. If you deem it is safe, allow the child to pet. But make sure you guide how the child gives affection to your dog—only you, the owner, will likely know if your dog doesn't like to be touched in certain places or in certain ways.

4. If the person's energy doesn't seem right to you, or you feel your dog is not in the mood to meet a child safely, the proper response to a petting request is to simply say, "I'm sorry, but my dog is in training right now." It's far better to be safe than sorry—especially when it comes to a child's welfare.

Introducing a New Person into Your Home

When a guest arrives at your door, most dogs will bark. This is normal and it's part of a dog's warning system. It's among the many reasons why early humans brought dogs into their lives—

to alert them to strangers or possible dangers. The difficulty comes when we want to be able to control our dogs' barking, but still want to use their common sense in helping us decide whether or not the person at the door should be trusted. We want an alarm system that we can turn on and off, but a dog is a living being with a mind of his own. This is where preparation, repetition, and your pack leadership skills come in.

1. It's wise to condition your dog that only a certain number of barks are expected. The more the dog barks, the more she will stay in that guarding-alert mode, which is not a calm-submissive mode. Three to five barks should be enough to alert any person on the other side of the door that there's a dog inside. And the dog is doing a job for you—alerting the pack to a new arrival.

2. Before you open the door, if your dog is going to be in the room, it's best for her to be in a calm-submissive mode. I like to create an invisible boundary around the entry area that belongs to me, not the dog. The dog can wait quietly outside the area, but she cannot crowd the newcomer until I give permission for them to meet. This can take a lot of practice that involves you, the pack leader, "owning" the space, and conditioning the dog, through corrections reinforced with treats and affection, to patiently wait for your go-ahead instead of rushing forward.

3. Now that you have a safe space, open the door. If the person is a newcomer to your home, respectfully ask him to follow the no touch, no talk, and no eye contact rule until the dog gets to know him. Give the dog the okay and allow her to go through her ritual. No, that doesn't involve excited jumping.

Once the ritual is completed, then you can continue with the human way of greeting.

4. As soon as the dog has become used to this visitor, you will no longer need to follow these rules so strictly. Once the dog is relaxed around the person and understands that the person is another human in a leadership role, she doesn't need to worry about where the person is going to fit into the "pack." Remember, your dog doesn't know that this is your oldest friend in the world, coming over to eat Thanksgiving dinner. She only wants to know, *What role is this new person going to play in my world?* It's up to you, the pack leader, to make sure both dog and guest understand this role.

Some dog owners—especially those with more than one dog—prefer to send the dogs out of the room when a visitor first arrives. Conditioning a dog with treats to leave the room when the doorbell rings can lessen the tension of a first meeting and get the dog to associate new people with something good, like snacks. However, it's important that you, the pack leader, still insist on and supervise a polite meeting once the guest has settled in—from both human and dog terms of etiquette.

Mastering the Walk

1. The ideal time for a walk is when you're not in a rush. Allow a full hour minimum—not necessarily for the walk itself, but including the entire ritual. Remember, this should be a meaningful, enjoyable experience for both you and your dog, not something you're just getting out of the way before

you get on to your "real" day. If that's how you feel most of the time, your dog will pick up on that and it will eventually weaken the bond between you.

2. Daytime is the best time to walk. Dogs are diurnal animals and walking them during the day is in sync with their biological clocks. Of course, dogs can become adapted to a nighttime activity just as we humans can, but biologically speaking, both species tend to do their best work during daytime hours.

3. To follow the principals of dog psychology, you must understand that you don't want to create overexcitement about the walk. Remember, your dog has got your number, and for her, the ritual starts the moment you first *think* about going out for a walk! The dog will become excited just at the presence of a leash. Don't call your dog in a high, excited voice, or allow jumping and other hysteric behaviors. It's important to wait until the mind is calm, even to put the leash on.

4. It's really important that you understand the ritual of a pack leader. A pack leader has a mission or an intention—which is why dogs instinctively know to follow him. A pack leader knows what he's doing—so at least pretend that you do! Remember your inner dialogue: strong, calm, and assertive.

5. After you successfully put the leash on and your dog's mind is calm-submissive, open the door. Is the dog *still* calm-submissive? If not, wait until she is. You move outside first, and then ask your dog to follow. You do not allow your dog to dart in front of you. After you are outside, ask your dog to sit, settle down, and relax—then close the door and lock it. Whatever you have to do, try not to do it in a rush. That's

why you're giving yourself a window of time. Believe it or not, the most important part of this ritual is the *beginning*. It sets the tone for the rest of the experience.

6. If you have the opposite situation and your dog is uneasy about the leash, try not to use sound, but remove any furniture if your animal tries to hide behind it. Then wait for the dog to come to you and put the leash on. This is a good time for treats, if necessary. Make sure you do everything slowly, with the highest level of calm-assertive energy. With this kind of dog, however, don't immediately go outside. Walk a little bit with the leash around your own environment until you create a flow of energy where slowly you come to the door and open it. Wait until the dog is calm-submissive before going out and closing the door. If she tries to flee, wait until she calms down before doing anything, so you are never rewarding an unstable mind. If you open the door when the mind is unstable, you are rewarding.

7. Walk with your dog next to you or behind you, never in front of you. If you haven't experienced the thrill of a dog (or more than one dog!) walking next to you, totally in sync with your energy and your movements, then in my opinion, you haven't lived! If you have only been pulled on a leash by a dog tugging you from way in front, then you haven't enjoyed the true beauty and bonding that comes with correctly walking with a dog. Once you've done it right, trust me, you'll never want to go back to the old way!

8. If your dog has maintained her wonderful state of mind during this time, you can reward her by letting her relieve

herself. If you have a dog that automatically relieves herself the moment you get outside, this is fine, as long as the dog is in a calm and not excited state. The next step is what people ask me the most. "When do I let my dog sniff?" I recommend allowing no more than five minutes or so for your dog to have "her time" during this "bathroom break."

9. Next, it's time for the migration ritual—the ritual of moving forward together. The challenge should be to not allow her to sniff the ground, look around, or be distracted by dogs barking behind fences. It's "I'm the pack leader, practice following me." Then after you have fifteen minutes or so of successful migration, you can reward her again by allowing her to go ahead of you and sniff the ground for two to five minutes tops. The reward time should always be much less than the challenge time, because you really want her to see you more as a pack leader than as a friend who walks behind her. Every time the dog walks in front of you without permission, it makes her believe that she's leading the walk.

10. Never try to meet a dog that is not in the same state of mind as your dog. Never experiment. If a dog is excited and your dog is calm-submissive, it's not a healthy thing to put them together. If you want this dog to be part of your dog's life, make sure you walk together as a pack before you allow them to go into a playful state.

11. Vary your route as much as you can. Dogs like routine—but they also like adventure! Experiencing new places, new scenery, and new smells is part of the psychological challenge for them.

12. Don't forget to pick up the poop!

One more note about walks—if the weather is too bad to walk outside, don't just leave your dog in the house without "telling" her why you're not walking today. Bring your dog out on the doorstep so she can sense the rain, the snow, the sandstorm—whatever. If your dog can get her own "weather report" instinctually, it will make perfect sense to her that you aren't going on your daily pilgrimage together.

Returning from the Walk

1. When do you come back from a walk? When you know your dog and you understand her physical and psychological needs, then you can determine the amount of time you will devote every morning and afternoon to walking with her. For smaller or lower-energy dogs, I recommend a minimum thirty to forty-five minutes. For all other dogs, except older dogs or dogs with disabilities, I recommend a minimum of forty-five minutes. If you add a backpack or devote time during the day to treadmill work or other vigorous energy, you can shorten the time. You will get to know her limits, and learn when she is beginning to tire and is ready to go back home.

2. Coming home, follow the same principles as you did when going out. Many of my clients master the first part of the walk, then "punch out" the moment they open the door to go back in, so almost everything they've accomplished just goes down the drain. You, the pack leader, should open the doors and go inside *your* territory first, then *you* determine right away what the dog's going to do after she arrives.

3. Have a plan for the moment you arrive. It's still very important to a dog to know what position she is going to play once she comes back home. You need to know ahead of time what activity you would like her to do. Perhaps there is a place where you would like your dog to sit and wait while you put away the leash, coat, or walking shoes, or take a bathroom break. A psychological challenge will extend the benefits of the walk and reestablish your leadership inside the house.

4. After the walk is the best time to share food and water with your dog. This way, you are imitating as best you can the experience she would have in nature—going out and moving forward, finding prey, then eating it. However, sometimes it's best for a dog to have some time to cool down and rest before eating. Providing water, then allowing a short rest while you shower and dress may be what your dog prefers after a long walk. At the Dog Psychology Center, it takes me some time to prepare the food after we come back from our morning exercise, during which time the dogs have their water and a short rest.

The Feeding Ritual

1. Personally, it's important for me to mix up my dogs' food with my hands. You can't buy love in a can, and I want to put both my scent and my energy into the meal. I want to give them more than just nourishment. I want to feed them as I was fed by my mom, with a lot of love in every meal she prepared for us. This is a personal ritual that I do—it's not something that's mandatory, of course, but I believe

becoming a good pack leader means always finding new ways to build that natural sense of connectedness between you and your dogs.

2. It's very, very important for your dog's psychological health, his whole entire being—if you want to call it his "soul"—that he *earn* the food he receives. Earning food for him feeds his self-esteem; it's an inner pride, a gold medal. When we just plop a food dish down in front of our dogs, we deny them this very basic animal need.

3. It's typical for a dog to become excited and interested when food is being prepared or when somebody's opening a can. The sounds and scents of food create very happy associations for him, so of course he's going to perk up right away. But it's also natural for him to go back into the state of mind that he was in the second before you opened the can. If you recognize that he's getting overly excited or interested, those are the first symptoms before the behavior escalates into something else. You have to address that behavior right away—send him back to a "waiting" mode and don't give him food until he changes from that obsessive or overexcited state of mind.

4. Creating a calm-submissive waiting behavior before feeding is an important psychological challenge for a dog. It's a very difficult thing for her to accomplish, because in the wild, it's excitement and dominance that allows her to eat. In the natural world, the most active, the fastest and boldest, are the ones who eat first. But because dogs are domesticated, we can create a totally different state where they don't have to be excited, where they don't have to be dominant for them to get their meal. *This is especially important*

if you have two or more dogs! You can ask your dog to be calm while you take your time in meal preparation. Providing a dog with a challenging moment, a focused activity like this creates focus and attentiveness, and builds confidence, too. It's always better to give your dog the challenge than to have her always challenging you.

5. At the Dog Psychology Center, I create another challenge at mealtime: I ask the dogs to look at *me,* not at the food dish, before I give the meal to them. This accomplishes two goals—one is to keep them from becoming obsessive about the food. The second is that I create an "appreciation" ritual between me and the pack. In other words, the food comes from me, the pack leader. I am the source of everything they have. If they stay focused on me, I can feed soothing energy through my eyes so that I can keep them relaxed. The conversation of the eye contact is *not* to dominate them! Instead, it's to further the bonding ritual—to create an extended conversation: "Yes, I'm going give you this food. I'm happy to be sharing food with you. And I'm very proud of you for being in the calm state that I wanted you to be in." As the "conversation" continues, we become the mirrors of each other's energy that I have described in this book. When both humans and dogs are feeding each other the same energy and we are in the same state, it creates a deeper bond among us all.

Managing Food Aggression

It's natural for all carnivores to be somewhat territorial over their food—it's those ancient survival instincts kicking in. I'm sure you know some people who refuse to share even one French fry off their plates! However, food possessiveness or obsession by a dog should never be allowed in a domestic situation. If the aggression is mild, it can be managed with some of the steps listed below. If it is more serious, this is not a process to be attempted by someone who is not experienced in dealing with aggression. A professional can begin the process of removing the food obsession, and then give you the "homework" to continue the rehabilitation. But take food aggression seriously, even in a puppy—it's not a "cute" behavior, and it's pretty good evidence that you are not a true pack leader.

1. Watch for telltale signs of aggression at the food bowl. If you are coming toward your dog and he is developing possessiveness over his food, you will see him lowering his head toward the food, covering it as if to block you from it. You may also see his hair stand up on his neck—making him appear bigger, like a blowfish. You will see tension in the body and the tail becoming rigid, even if it's moving. All those signs are intended as a conversation with you or another dog: "This is mine; stay away!"

2. If you have more than one dog and the aggression is directed at another dog, not at you, the situation is somewhat simpler to resolve. In my "pack," we never feed the excited dog or the dominant dog first. We always reward the dog in the most calm-submissive state. And that calm-submissive state is going to be the role model for the rest of the pack. So if you have more than one dog, you should never feed the one who is the pushiest, or the one who is older, or the

one who is your favorite. Many people will say, "I have to feed my more excited dog first, because he has to be the alpha." This is a misconception—it only creates competition, and ultimately more dominance. It can also create a fight and a lot of unhappy mealtimes.

3. At the center, I will ask the guy who normally is aggressive to be in the same state as the calmest submissive dog, and will take my time before feeding him until he goes into that state. If he is very aggressive, I will keep him on a leash or even behind a fence so he can watch the ritual being performed. By the time it's his turn, he's going to know that the other dogs are not moving toward the food anymore, so that alleviates a lot of his tension. By that time, those dogs that have just finished eating are satisfied, they're relaxed, so that's the energy that they're going to project. And that eventually helps all of them to realize that this is their ritual of eating. It's not about competition; it's really about waiting.

4. When a dog is exhibiting food aggression toward you, you must be very cautious when you go to redirect. Since food and mating are the two strongest drives in all animals, a dog with food aggression can cause serious harm to a human who interrupts her, and I caution anyone with this problem to immediately call in a professional.

5. *Do not* give a food-obsessive dog affection in order to stop her behavior. You will only reinforce it, and depending on the intensity of her aggression, you may also risk a bite.

6. The ritual of waiting can help prevent food aggression from happening, or stop it before it goes too far. When a

dog can manipulate you into feeding her by barking or jumping on you, she is telling you that she owns both you and the food. Watch for this warning sign.

Facing an Aggressive Dog

1. First of all, don't be automatically intimidated by "aggressive" barking. A lot of times what may look like aggression on the surface could just be a statement of dominance, or a way to say, "This is my territory!"

2. When a dog is charging you and she's territorial, she usually just wants you to go away. In this case, the best response is to simply stop, remain calm, and claim your *own* space. Face the energy that is coming toward you and project back your own calm-assertive energy. Use your "inner dialogue" techniques to project the understanding that "I mean no harm but I'm not backing away. I just want *my* space—not yours." That should block the aggression and slow down a dog that is simply territorial, and begin to create respect for you.

3. Once there is respect, you are providing an energy that blocks the dog. The dog becomes calmer and can analyze you better. If this is occurring, you will immediately see the body language change. The posture will relax, the head will lower somewhat, and the dog will avoid eye contact. The hair-trigger survival impulse is calmed.

4. If this is a place you have to pass by on a regular basis, it is vital that you "win" this first psychological battle. The battle is purely psychological—not physical. This is your energy versus her energy. The way you know you have won is

that the dog's body language changes as described above and she retreats.

5. Once she begins to retreat, you can step forward or use sound to accelerate the retreating—clapping your hand, for instance, or shaking pebbles in a plastic bottle. By doing this, you are conditioning her mind to associate this sound with moving away from you. This is something you can call on again, if the situation repeats itself with this same dog.

6. Remember not to use sound when a dog is moving toward you—unless, of course, you know she has been trained to respond to a certain command, and that the command will work for you. It's best to start by staying very calm and quiet, but being focused and assertive. Many times, people panic and scream, or yell "Go away!" if a dog approaches them. Unless the energy behind the sound is 100 percent calm-assertive, it probably won't work and may even escalate the dog's aggression. Remember, if she's aggressive, you don't want to *add* energy. You want to remove it.

7. Never turn away or continue walking until the dog retreats. Even if the dog is behind a fence, you are handing her victory, and you will have to go through this process again and again if you pass by the same place. It may even be more difficult, because now you will have empowered her—she knows she has beaten you once already. If there is no fence, turning away, walking, or running away can turn you into prey. It can trigger the dog to chase after you.

8. If you must walk through a neighborhood on a regular basis, you can walk with a walking stick to make yourself feel bigger. Kings and emperors of days gone by would

always have walking sticks and staffs—to make themselves more powerful psychologically, to look bigger, and to own more space. Use this psychology with dogs—the more space you can own confidently, the stronger and more dominant you appear. Don't wear headphones and space out or retreat into your own little world—be aware of your environment and own your space with every step you take.

9. Carrying a stick, cane, umbrella, or pile of books—even having a can of mace or pepper spray in your pocket—can help you feel more protected psychologically. The idea isn't to use the spray on the dog, and certainly not to *hit* the dog with a stick. If you hit the dog with a stick, she's more likely going to react by "hitting" you back—and in a physical match against a powerful dog such as a Rottweiler, a shepherd, or a pit bull, you are definitely going to be outmatched. The point is, you're not out there looking for a fight. But if feeling safer and more prepared gives you more of a calm-assertive demeanor, then it will make you *less* of a target—not only for aggressive dogs, but for aggressive humans as well.

10. If a dog seems to have backed off from her aggressive stance and is coming toward you to smell you, this is an important time to reassess the situation. Is her body language now totally relaxed, or is she sneaking up on you, getting ready to pounce? If you know this dog to be a generally peaceful dog, that's one thing. But if this is a dog you don't know, keep claiming your space and take a step toward her. The important thing is, never let a dog go behind you. That's a classic "ambush" move. Again, do not walk away until the dog has turned *her* back on *you*.

11. If there is more than one dog, do not let either one get behind you! A classic strategy of a "pack attack" is for one dog to face the prey and the other to circle around and attack from the rear. I recently did a session with a group of mail carriers from Atlanta where that very situation had happened to several of them. If you find yourself in this situation, *stay calm and claim your space even more assertively.* Place your stick, your cart, or your purse firmly out in front of you, spread your legs, and put your hands on your hips to make yourself bigger. If you stand your ground and use the power of your energy, you can fend off the attack.

Claiming Your Space

1. Claiming space is a very basic concept in the animal kingdom. Animals are constantly having "conversations" with each other about space all the time—projecting energies back and forth that say, for example, "That is my couch; I can share, but it's my couch first." If you have more than one dog, or even a dog and a cat, and there is an area of the house or a toy that one of them likes to claim, sit quietly some time and observe how their body language, energy, and eye contact interact to create a very clear communication. You can even learn to *feel* the energy of the conversation. We have to develop the ability to have the same kinds of communications with our dogs that they do with each other.

2. Knowing how to claim space from your dog is vital if you want to be able to control unwanted behaviors. It is not about being a bully or "showing your dog who's boss."

Again, it's a very basic communication skill that will allow
you to be able to disagree with a dog's behavior without
ever having to resort to anger or frustration. You are claiming a small part of space, not the whole universe! A couch is
a space. A bed is a space. A room can be a space. Your dog
will accept the rules of how to behave in that space if you
claim it. If it's in the house, is it you or your dog signing
those mortgage checks? Then don't feel bad about setting
the rules for how to behave in it.

3. Claiming space means using your body, your mind, and
   your energy to "own" what you would like to control. For
   instance, if a dog rushes at people who come to the door,
   you can keep her from coming too close by standing firm,
   putting your hands on your hips, and claiming the door.
   You create a circle of space around "your door" and between you and the dog. The way I claim an area like a door
   is the same strategy a sheep-herding dog would use to
   claim space away from a sheep that is straying from the
   flock. I move forward, and then I go *around* the dog, looking at her at the same time, telling her in my mind to move
   away from what belongs to me. If I go and *pull* her away
   from the door, I only intensify her need to claim it. Pulling
   a dog back makes her brain go forward. I recommend you
   watch a videotape of a herding dog. As she goes around a
   herd of huge cattle, communicating where she wants the
   cows to go while never touching the cows, she is saying,
   "Stay out of this space—go into that space." Everything she
   does is psychological. The cow, sheep, or goat are completely different species, but they all understand exactly

what the dog wants them to do. We are animals, too—we just let words and our big brains get in the way of this instinctual form of communication.

4. When you project an invisible line that your dog is not allowed to cross without your say-so, if you do the exercise with 100 percent focus and commitment, you will be shocked at how quickly your dog comes to understand exactly where that line is. If a dog barks at the window, you can get her to stop barking if you firmly claim the window. What you are saying is, "This window belongs to me, and I disagree with you barking at it." If I yell at the dog and say, "No, Sally, stop it! Be quiet!" I'm expressing weak, frustrated energy and not claiming that space. Once again, I'm wasting my energy trying to control a behavior with human language and rationality, when I can simply take a page from Mother Nature's time-tested playbook and do what animals do with each other.

5. When you pull things away from a dog, you're either inviting her to compete for it or you're inviting her to play. If your intention is to play, then fine. But if your intention is to stop the game before play behavior leads to possessiveness, you must firmly claim the toy so the animal will let it go. When you claim *objects,* your dog will give them to you if you are providing the right energy. You cannot be hesitant and you must be totally clear about your intention. You can't be "negotiating" with your dog—"Baby, please give me the toy?"—either mentally or verbally. Your dog will not take it personally. She doesn't have a problem giving you what she now knows belongs to you.

Many people worry that their dogs will resent them, or they will break their dog's "spirit" by not letting them have their favorite toy any time they want it. But letting your dog have and keep anything she wants can lead to obsessiveness, and obsessiveness is not healthy. Part of your job as a leader is to set rules, boundaries, and limitations for your dog to keep any frustration she might have from being channeled into obsession.

Dealing with Obsessive and Fixated Behaviors

For dogs, obsessions and fixations can become as seriously harmful as addictions are for humans. When we laugh at a dog that is fanatically mad over a toy, a bone, a shaft of light, a game of fetch, or the neighbor's cat, it's like laughing at someone who is falling-down drunk. Sure, his behavior looks comical at the moment, but the truth is, he's truly got no physical or psychological control over himself. Someday, he may really hurt himself and those around him. That's exactly what obsessive behavior is to a dog—an addiction. An interesting fact is that the term *addiction* derives from the Latin word *addicere,* to sentence. When we allow our dogs' habits to progress to the point of obsession and/or addiction, we are actually "sentencing" them to a very frustrated, unhappy existence.

Identifying Obsession

1. A normal dog plays well with others—you, your kids, and other dogs. Balanced dogs can like one toy or game more than another, but it's still a *game;* it's not a life-or-death situation. An obsessive dog will take such games very seriously. Her playing will have a whole different level of intensity to it.

2. When a dog is becoming obsessive, her face and her body language will visibly change. Her body will stiffen. A glaze will form over her eyes—her pupils become fixated and you can't distract her gaze. It appears almost as if she's in a trance. She's entered a zone in which there is no lightheartedness, no relaxation, and no joy in play. Think of a gambling addict at a slot machine, mechanically pulling the one-armed bandit over and over again, fixated on it but clearly not having fun. Obsession is not a happy place to be. It's a zone in which an animal is blind to everything around her that *should* make her happy.

Preventing Obsession

1. One step to preventing obsessive behavior is to monitor the intensity of your dog's play. I try to supervise the intensity of my own kids' play—because between them, one of them is going to be faster, or one is going to be physically stronger. If I can keep them at an intensity level that is mild, they can't hurt each other physically or emotionally. But they can still enjoy themselves. The point is, your dog must understand that there are limits to any game—whether it be playing with a favorite toy, or stalking the squirrels in the backyard. Those limits are determined by you, not by her.

Correcting Obsession

1. Make sure your dog is properly exercised and is not living with pent-up energy. Most of the time an obsession is something that a dog has discovered can work as an outlet for anxiety, frustration, or suppressed energy.

2. Correct obsessive/possessive behavior immediately: This is where the importance of *knowing your dog* comes in. You

must learn to recognize the physical cues and energy signs that your dog is getting into an obsessive state, and stop her at level one before she escalates to level ten. Your job should be at that very moment to correct the dog, to bring her to the highest level of submission, keeping the toy or object of obsession (if that's what it is) next to her until she moves away from it voluntarily. Most people will snatch a toy away and say, "No!" By doing this, they can escalate the obsessiveness into a higher level—making the object prey, and making *you* a potential target. Your dog may not want to bite a family member, but she's in a state now where she can't stop on her own. Remember, dogs don't rationalize.

Managing Stress at the Vet

1. Get to know your vet first! Remember, your dog is not an appliance you are taking to the repair shop; she is a sensitive, *feeling* being, but without the cognitive skills to understand exactly what the role is of the businesslike person in the white coat. Vets are wonderful, dedicated people—but they are also human beings doing a job. They have many clients and see many animals on a given day. If the vet is having a bad day or has too much stress and the dog doesn't know him, the dog will pick up on his energy and mirror it right back. That's why I advise a "consultation" meeting with your vet when it's not time for a medical procedure or emergency, so your dog can get to know him in another context. The dog won't be just a patient before she meets this person, but will begin to develop a friendship and trust. I believe the foundation of any successful visit to

the vet rests on trust—first of all, your dog trusting you, and second, your dog trusting the vet. It really isn't the vet's job to establish that trust, but you can take certain steps to try to make it happen.

2. At the vet's, the dog is going to be touched in various ways that may seem foreign to her. I advise clients to "play doctor" at home a few times—with the white coats, instruments, alcohol smells, and so on. Along with the medical stuff come treats—rewarding the dog, giving massages, praising—helping the dog to associate all these strange sights, smells, and objects either with something pleasant or with relaxation. Any time you can prepare a dog for a new experience in a pleasant way, you are making life easier for her, and embracing the role of pack leader to the fullest.

3. Besides preparing your dog for the examination part of the vet visit, make sure she is comfortable with traveling to the environment where the vet's office is. If your dog hates to get in the car and it becomes an anxious, traumatic experience for you both, then that obstacle needs to be tackled first. If your dog has never been to a city, or a mall, or wherever the vet's office is located, make sure you've done that first—don't pull too many surprises on her at once! I also suggest bringing your dog to sit in the receptionist's area of the veterinary office for no special reason except to socialize—it's a great way for both of you not to have the vet's visit be a "big deal."

4. Exercise, exercise, exercise! A tired dog is much less likely to be an anxious dog. After a good, vigorous forty-five-minute walk, your dog will be much more likely to be okay lying still on an examination table for ten minutes. I always like

to bring my Rollerblades, park a few blocks away, and run the dogs on their leashes next to me as I Rollerblade for a half hour to really wear out my higher-energy dogs. Then, when I bring the dogs inside the office, I ask the reception-ist or one of the technicians to provide them with a bowl of water and a cookie. *I* don't give the water and cookie, but one of the employees at the office does, to create a warmer connection between the dog and this new person who works there. That's a much different experience for the dog than just being given a cookie because she's bored. There's an appreciation and a "conversation" that happens when a person actually fulfills a dog's primal needs such as hunger or thirst. It's a more natural approach to bonding, rather than the artificial approach of "bribing" a dog with a cookie just so she will sit in the waiting room a little while longer.

5. It's most important to make sure that *you* are also calm and relaxed before, during, and after the vet visit! Most of the time, owners are nervous about the vet; they feel bad about bringing their dog there; they can't stand the image of their dog having to get a shot or have blood drawn; or they are very worried about their dog's health. Your dog picks up every single one of those signals—remember, you are your dog's energy source! Using your tools to create calm-assertive energy, prepare yourself mentally for the experi-ence. Play upbeat music in the car on the way to the office, and radiate positivity to your dog. So much of the experi-ence for your dog will be what *you* make it to be.

6. Even after accomplishing all these steps, your dog may still have anxiety at the veterinarian's office. Why? First of all, the waiting room will be filled with people who haven't

read this book! They'll be projecting all the same feelings of tension or foreboding that you've been working so hard to banish. Their dogs will therefore be very anxious. Your dog will be sensing all of this. Plus, the scents in the vet's office will tell your dog that there is fear and pain going on inside. When a dog becomes afraid, her anal glands open up and release. And every dog knows what that scent means. "Why is it so concentrated here? And why are we coming here, when my instinct tells me to run away from a place where this scent is so strong?" Your own attitude must be extra positive to counter all these natural signals the dog is getting.

7. If your dog is going to go through a procedure that's painful, it's natural for her to want to bite. It's a reflex. In this case, a muzzle is an excellent tool. Of course, you must have conditioned your dog to experience the muzzle long before any accident happens. In fact, you can use the muzzle as a psychological sedative if you condition your dog correctly. If you follow the guidelines in chapter 3 and create a pleasant, calming experience every time you put the muzzle on, you can use it as a back-up device so that the dog automatically associates it with relaxation. This can help her to reject fear—especially if she suffers a sudden injury or accident.

8. If your dog does have an accident and you must rush her to emergency, you will naturally be filled with all sorts of emotions—fear, panic, worry, hysteria. If you project this to your dog, however, you will increase her fear, which will increase her heart rate, which can worsen any life-or-death situation. If you find yourself in this situation, imagine you are a paramedic. Paramedics never rush up to an accident

site and say, "Oh my God, you're bleeding, oh my God, we'd better rush or you'll die!" These life-saving professionals always remain in the classic calm-assertive state and, in doing so, soothe and relax the frightened victim and help to save his life. You must brainwash yourself to remember, "When my dog is under stress, I can't go into a dog owner's state of mind. I have to be a paramedic." Try to prepare for this before it happens. You don't want to test yourself when it's already happening. Try to practice it so if it happens, you'll know exactly what to do.

Going to the Dog Park

1. Just as when you go for a walk, your dog will be on to all your behavioral cues. If you have a routine before going to the dog park—putting on a certain pair of shoes, getting the car keys—your dog will catch on right away and get excited. So many of my clients get into their high-pitched voice: "Hey Smoky, wanna go to the dog park?" Pay attention to all these details. Make sure your dog is calm-submissive while you go through *all* these rituals. Healthy excitement is natural—but it should be triggered by you, not by her. If your dog gets overexcited before you've even gone out the door, you are one step closer to having an out-of-control dog at the dog park.

2. Once you have accomplished leaving the house in a relatively calm, orderly manner, then you face the next obstacle where excitement tends to crop up—the car. Once again, your dog should not be catapulting past you to get into the car the moment you get the door open. I see people driving

down the street toward the dog park with the dog in the back seat jumping around, putting her paws on the window, breathing so heavily all the windows are totally fogged up! Of course, in addition to not being good for the dog, that can lead you, the driver, into an accident. If you are taking your dog anywhere—especially to a place where she needs to be in a calm state, not an overly-excited state— you need to have a routine for traveling in the car where the driving experience does not become a free-for-all.

3. Dogs are always aware of their environments through sights and sounds, but of course, mostly through scent. Therefore, a lot of times dogs get very excited two, three blocks before you pull up at the park. If your dog does this, stop the car and practice obedience until he calms down.

4. If everyone walked their dogs before coming to the dog park, the result would be a lot more happy dogs and owners and a lot more safe and pleasant places for dogs to play. Many people see the dog park as a physical activity—even a substitute for the walk. *It is not.* The dog park should be a psychological and social activity. Sure, your dog can play hard and be tired out at the end of the visit, but you need to drain physical energy in a primal way before you bring a dog among other dogs, so they don't have to deal with a dog with frustration and pent-up physical energy. If you live within walking distance of the dog park, then go there together on foot, and add a backpack for higher-energy dogs. If you must drive to find your nearest park, then park three blocks away and take a brisk walk or run to the park itself, then make sure to cool down so that your dog is calm-submissive again by the time she goes inside. If you

do this, you can become a role model for the other dog owners and help create a better experience for everybody.

5. Now it's time to go inside the park. I know that a lot of people are looking for this to be a time when a dog can run around and do whatever she wants. But once again, your dog will respond much more positively if you create a structure for the experience. Move calmly toward the park entrance, and make sure your dog is sitting in a calm-submissive state before you open the door. Make sure there aren't a lot of other dogs—especially overly excited dogs—crowded around the fence waiting for your girl to arrive. A way to influence this is to insist your dog's attention is on you, and keep her back turned to the dogs in the park until they lose interest and wander away. And once they move, it's safer to bring your dog inside, because the existence of eye contact can lead your dog to be attacked or attack others.

6. You can't let your dog pull you inside the park. Just like any other doorway experience, you open the gate and then invite your dog in.

7. Many of my clients admit to me that they tend to see the dog park as a break for themselves—the dogs get to go and play with friends, and they can punch out for a while. This isn't a responsible way to look at it. When I was a dog walker, I often took groups of dogs to dog parks. I never went in and right away plopped myself down on a bench. I would introduce the dogs to the park, then observe and study what kind of energies were in the park and which would be good or bad for my dogs. Remember, energy is more important than breed. If you study a dog park, you'll see that the dogs naturally find their own energies—the

playful ones will play with the other playful ones; the rough ones will stay with the rough ones; the shy ones will socialize with the shy ones. Just like a playground full of kids. So be sure to study the situation, then ask your dog to follow you around as if you're going to introduce her to the kids you think will be a good influence on her.

8. After that, let the dog do whatever she wants for ten or fifteen minutes, then ask her to follow you again. This way, the dog will get the freedom that people tend to want their dogs to have at dog parks, but will also never lose sight of the fact that the pack leader is in control. This is important, because if a fight develops in any part of the dog park, you will want to be able to command your dog to get away from it right away, and have your dog obey you in that environment.

People always say to me, "But I want to be able to catch up with my friends when I'm at the dog park!" Of course, that is another great benefit of a dog park—it brings humans out of their isolation and helps bring them together! Once you have accomplished the steps I have outlined, that's the time to go sit down, have your coffee, make phone calls, or have conversations with friends. But always, out of the corner of your eye, you should look out to make sure your dog is okay. As long as the structure and the leadership are there, you and your dog will have a much more relaxed time at the park.

Choosing a Dog with the Right Energy

1. First of all, please look inside yourself and examine the reasons why you are getting a dog. Are you going to get a dog

because you are in a very low emotional state? Are you very, very lonely and your dog will be your only spiritual soul mate? Are you just attracted to the look of a certain type of dog—certain markings, certain shapes or forms? These are all red flags, and although they mean well, people who go in with these attitudes often end up with big problems between themselves and their dogs. First, be honest with yourself. What is your energy? What is your state of mind? You absolutely must identify those things before you set out to choose a dog.

2. All dogs need a human who can love them, who can be affectionate with them, and even who can become a "soul mate." Dogs are looking for those things, too. But what they really need before all that is a human who can be a solid pack leader for them; who will have good instinctual common sense; who will offer adequate exercise and discipline before affection; and who can set rules, boundaries, and limitations that give them a secure structure for their lives.

3. After reading this book, you should now know how to recognize as a human what your emotional state is, what kind of energy level you have, and what kind of lifestyle you are able to provide for a dog. Ideally, you should be looking for a dog based on energy. Your dog's energy level should either be the same as yours or less than yours.

4. Many people today choose their dogs from shelters or rescue organizations, which I support 100 percent. There are way too many dogs out there that are being euthanized needlessly just because they have no home to go to. But when you go to a shelter, you have to be aware that 90 percent of those dogs are going to have some sort of baggage,

some sort of "issues." I believe with the right leadership, 99 percent of them can be totally rehabilitated. But you need to be vigilant about their energy levels and be honest about what you can handle. If you see a dog that has beautiful eyes and reminds you of a dog you had when you were a child, this might blind you to the fact that there are other signposts with that dog that indicate you might not be able to handle her behavior.

5. Recognizing energy levels in a shelter is not an easy task. I am often asked to come with clients to shelters because my eye is experienced at being able to tell if a dog is truly hyperactive when she is jumping up and down in her cage, or if she simply has too much pent-up energy because she has been in there too long. All dogs that are kept in cages will show frustration in some way unless they are resting. They might bark, they might pace, they might chew on a bone. If you can afford it, it is a wise idea to take a professional with you—or someone who is an experienced dog owner whose dogs' behavior you admire. They will be coming at the situation with a less emotional perspective than you will.

6. Even if you do have a professional or friends with you, I always recommend you get as much insight as you can from the shelter workers about what their day-to-day experiences with the dog have been. Does the dog pace consistently—or is she relaxed for a while after she's been taken outside? How does she normally act when visitors come by and when people she knows come by? How does she act at feeding time? When she's out with the other dogs?

7. If it's possible and the shelter allows it, see if you can take the dog you're interested in out for a walk. Will they let you

walk the dog around the building, the yard, or the block a few times? This will give you a better idea of the dog's temperament after you've drained a little bit of the frustrated energy. It will also help you to sense if this dog is able to bond with you as a pack leader.

8. Being in a shelter is a very emotional and sometimes heartbreaking experience. You get to be face-to-face with all these beautiful creatures and see up close how we humans are consistently letting Mother Nature down. Sometimes, you will know that some of the dogs will be put down if they don't find homes. But if you rely solely on these emotions as reasons to adopt a certain dog, you are coming into that dog's life as a weak energy. You are not doing a dog a favor if you adopt her just because you feel sorry for her. Think about it. Would you like someone to hire you for a job, or date you, or marry you simply because they felt sorry for you? That would put you in a permanently weak, insecure state, wouldn't it? The same thing applies to dogs. Try to balance your emotions with your common sense, and realize that if you end up bringing the dog back because you can't handle her, she is much more likely to meet an unhappy end.

Introducing a Dog to a House for the First Time

1. If you live alone and you are bringing your dog home, by this time you understand responsibility. And you've made a commitment—you're going to give this dog your 110 percent and you are in it for the long haul.

2. When you bring a dog from a kennel, or even someone else's house, you don't want to bring her from behind one set of

walls and put her behind another set of walls. No matter how beautiful your home is, or how big and beautiful your yard, you are really just moving the dog from one kennel to another. What you need to do first thing is to migrate together. After you park your car, don't bring the dog inside—give her water, then take her on a vigorous walk through the neighborhood, which will get her comfortable with her new territory, and start the bonding process with you as a pack leader.

3. Once you are home, remember that you are bringing a dog into your environment. You enter first. You invite the dog in. Then, instead of just letting her loose to "investigate" on her own, you will take her to the area that is going to be her den. You are going to set the limits on her resting place and where she will be allowed in the environment. Gradually, you will ease her into the rest of the house. But it's important to start with a strict structure. Remember, many rescued dogs have suffered all their lives with no structure whatsoever, which is exactly what made them unstable in the first place. You are going to be the pack leader who changes that!

4. Once your new dog is tired out—perhaps after you have fed her—it may be a good time to give her a relaxing warm bath or shower. You might want to take one yourself and change the clothes you wore to the shelter. As you know, scents are very important to your dog, and she may associate the scents of the shelter with anxiety or frustration. You want her to associate your home with relaxation and safety.

5. The next day, you can begin to guide your dog through investigating the rest of the house. Remember, you are not *depriving* her of enjoying her new house; you are simply giving her a chance to do it in steps. This keeps her from getting

overly excited or overwhelmed, and makes the job a pleasant, relaxing experience. When you have an overnight guest, do you simply invite him to find his own way around your house? No. You take him room to room on a tour—this is my kitchen, this is my den, this is my dining room, and so on. This is all you have to do with your dog. You invite her into every room where you want her to be allowed, taking her on a little "tour." I think it's a psychological challenge to give your dog a whole week to get to know each room. She will be very respectful at the end of the challenge, and will have a clear understanding of what the kitchen means, what the living room means, what the balcony means, what the hallway means. She will feel that she's going to live in a place that has meaning. It has the same meaning everywhere— very respectful, very trustworthy. This goes a long way toward preventing the experience of, "Oh no! My dog peed on the couch! Oh no, I can't have her in the kitchen!" which is something that can begin to damage the trust that you are just beginning to build. So that's why it's important to break it down for a dog, step by step. And your dog isn't going to feel bad or be angry at you if you don't introduce her to the whole house right off the bat. She doesn't feel that you are being mean about it. A lot of times people think, "My dog is going to feel sad because I'm in the room and she's over there." No, she won't. She is just going to learn how to live that way until you tell her otherwise.

6. If you already have a dog at home, hopefully you have a dog that is balanced, or is close to balanced. It's vital not to bring a dog into your house that's got a higher level energy than the dog you already have. If you do, you can see un-

wanted behavior in your old dog that he never displayed before; in order for him to deal with the new dog, he has to adapt his way of being. If the new dog has a lower energy, however, then your first dog becomes the role model for the new dog. It's important, of course, to have drained as much energy as you can from the new dog before you bring her into the house. You don't want your old dog to have to deal with a frustrated dog. And you must go through the same steps as outlined above with the new dog. The first full day in the new surroundings, walk the two dogs together as a pack—one on either side of you until they get used to each other. After that, your first dog will help teach his new friend all your rules, boundaries, and limitations.

7. If there are other family members, it's important that everybody is on the same page in regard to what the rules of the house are. If some people enforce the rules and others don't, it creates confusion. In a natural pack of dogs, they're all reinforcing the same behavior with each other. We have to provide the same consistency that a balanced pack provides. And not just behaviors, but the energy that everyone sends the dog should be consistent. Your family should not act as if they feel sorry for the dog. Feeling sorry for her will not do her any good—it will only put you in a lower level of energy, and you will lose some of your ability to be a good influence on her. Get everyone together, discuss the rules, and agree you're going to adopt an optimistic, positive attitude when it comes to your new "pack member." And of course, everybody should understand the importance of exercise, discipline, affection—as well as patience, because a rescued dog isn't going to be perfect right away.

NOTES

Mirror, Mirror?

1. American Animal Hospital Association, 2004 Pet Study. Used by permission. Cyber-Pet, "National Pet Owner Survey Finds People Prefer Pet Companionship Over Humans," http://www.cyberpet.com/cyberdog/articles/general/crawford.htm.

2. Marian R. Banks and William A. Banks, "The Effects of Group and Individual Animal-assisted Therapy on Loneliness in Residents of Long-term Care Facilities." *Anthrozoos* 18, no. 4 (2005): 396–408.

Chapter 2: Discipline, Rewards, and Punishment

1. Bruce Fogle, *The Dog's Mind* (New York: Macmillan): 1990, 26–27.

Chapter 3: The Best Tool in the World

1. Kenneth A. Gershman, Jeffrey J. Sacks, and John C. Wright, "Which Dogs Bite? A Case-Control Study of Risk Factors." *Pediatrics* 93, no. 6 (1994): 913–17.

2. http://www.freepatentsonline.com/6047664.html; http://www.gundogs online.com/ArticleServer.asp?strArticleID=CC9C3CA9-813B-11D6-9BF8-00D0B74D6C6A.

3. S.V. Juarbe-Diaz and K.A. Houpt, "Comparison of Two Antibarking Collars for Treatment of Nuisance Barking." *Journal of the American Animal Hospital Association* (May-June 1996): 231–35.

4. P.J. Darlington, "Group Selection, Altruism, Reinforcement, and Throwing in Human Evolution." *Proceedings of the National Academy of Sciences of the United States of America* 72, no. 9 (1975): 3748–52.

Chapter 4: Fulfilling Breed

1. More information on Schutzhund training and exercises for all breeds is available at DVG (Deutscher Verband der Gebrauchshundsportvereine) America, http://www.dvgamerica.com, the oldest Schutzhund organization in the world.

2. Interestingly, the Russian neurophysicist I. P. Pavlov also believed the dogs he worked with in his famous (or infamous) experiments were born with different levels of energy: "strong excitatory," "lively," "calm imperturbable," and "weak inhibitory" (William Salters Sargent, *Battle for the Mind*, 3rd ed. [Cambridge, MA: Malor Books, 1997], 4–5). These types correspond to my categories: "very high," "high," "medium," and "low" energy dogs.

Chapter 5: Dysfunction Junction

1. Linda Kerley, "Scent Dog Monitoring of Amur Tiger," *A Final Report to Save the Tiger Fund* (2003-0087-018) March 1, 2003–March 1, 2004; D. Smith, K. Ralls, B. Davenport, B. Adams, and J.E. Maldonado, "Canine Assistants for Conservationists," *Science* (2001): 291–435; R. Rolland, P. Hamilton, S. Kraus, B. Davenport, R. Gillett, and S. Wasser, "Faecal Sampling Using Detection Dogs to Study Reproduction and Health in North Atlantic Right Whales (Eubalaena glacialis)." *Journal of Cetacean Research and Management* 8, no. 2 (2006): 121–125.

2. Donald G. McNeil, "Dogs Excel on Smell Test to Find Cancer," *New York Times*, 17 January 2006. Published online; Sam Whiting, "Guide Dog Flunkies

Earn Kudos in Their Second Life as Diabetes Coma Alarms." *San Francisco Chronicle* 5 Nov. 2006: CM-6.

3. Bruce Fogle, *The Dog's Mind* (New York: Macmillan, 1990): 65.

4. Daniel Goleman, *Emotional Intelligence: Why It Can Matter More Than IQ.* (New York: Bantam Books, 1995): 103.

5. Allan Pease and Barbara Pease, *The Definitive Book of Body Language.* (New York: Bantam Dell, 2006): 27.

6. Marc D. Hauser, *Wild Minds: What Animals Really Think.* (New York: Henry Holt, 2000): 139–172.

7. http://www.hsus.org/pets/issues-affecting-our-pets/get-the-facts-on-puppy-mills/index.html.

8. Lyudmila N. Trut, "Early Canid Domestication: The Farm-Fox Experiment." *American Scientist* 87, no. 2 (1991): 160–169.

9. Leslie Irvine, *If You Tame Me: Understanding Our Connection with Animals* (Philadelphia: Temple University Press, 2004): 93–94.

Chapter 6: Transforming Energy into Action

1. Gavin De Becker, *The Gift of Fear: Survival Signs That Protect Us from Violence* (New York: Dell, 1997): 12–13.

2. Goleman, *Emotional Intelligence,* 6.

3. Ackerman, as quoted in De Becker, 26.

4. De Becker, 25.

5. Ibid., 5–7.

6. Ibid., 17.

7. Brandon Carpenter, "Energetic Training," *The Gaited Horse* (Summer 2004): 29–33.

8. De Becker, 32–33.

9. Goleman, *Emotional Intelligence,* 75–77.

10. Ibid., 75.

11. E. Balcetis and D. Dunning, "See What You Want to See: Motivational Influences on Visual Perception." *Journal of Personality and Social Psychology* 91 (2006): 612–25.

12. http://www.discover.com/web-exclusives/wishfulseeing/.

13. Deepak Chopra, *The Spontaneous Fulfillment of Desire: Harnessing the Infinite Power of Coincidence* (New York: Harmony Books, 2003), 88.

14. Ibid., 114–15.

Chapter 7: Leadership for Dogs ... and for Humans

1. Scott Creel, "Social Dominance and Stress Hormones," *Trends in Ecology and Evolution* 16, no. 9 (September, 2001): 491–97.

2. Farley Mowat, *Never Cry Wolf.* (Boston, Back Bay Books, 1963)

3. Daniel Goleman, Richard Boyatziz, and Annie McKee, *Primal Leadership: Learning to Lead with Emotional Intelligence* (Boston: Harvard Business School Press, 2002): 3.

4. Ibid., 7.

5. Ibid., 13.

6. Ibid., 7.

7. Ibid., 16.

8. Ibid., 20.

9. Ibid., 19.

10. Daniel Goleman, *Emotional Intelligence,* 114.

11. Ibid., 119.

12. Daniel Goleman, Richard Boyatziz, and Annie McKee, *Primal Leadership,* 30–31.

Chapter 8: Our Four-legged Healers

1. Chris Duke, "Pets Are Good for Physical, Mental Well-being." *Knight Ridder/Tribune News Service* (September 11, 2003).

2. PAWSitive Interactive, "A Scientific Look at the Human-Animal Bond" (2002). http://www.pawsitiveinteraction.com/background.html

3. T. Fields-Meyer, and S. Mandel, "Healing Hounds: Can Dogs Help People with Mental-health Problems Get Better?" (*People,* July 17, 2006): 101–102. For more information visit www.psychdog.org.

4. J. Wolpe, *Psychotherapy by Reciprocal Inhibition* (Palo Alto: Stanford University Press, 1958); K. Hellstrom, J. Fellenius, and L.G. Ost. "One Versus Five

Sessions of Applied Tension in the Treatment of Blood Phobia," *Behavioral Research and Therapy* 34, no. 2 (1996): 101–12; L.G. Ost, K. Hellstrom, and J. Fellenius, "One-session Therapist-directed Exposure vs. Self-exposure in the Treatment of Spider Phobia," *Behavioral Research and Therapy* 22 (1991): 407–22. K. Hellstrom and L.G. Ost, "One-session Therapist-directed Exposure vs. Two Forms of Manual-directed Self-exposure in the Treatment of Spider Phobia," *Behavioral Research and Therapy* 33, no. 8 (1995): 959–65. L.G. Ost, "One-session Treatment for Specific Phobias," *Behavioral Research and Therapy* 27, no. 1 (1989): 1–7. L.G. Ost, M. Brandburg, and T. Alm. "One Versus Five Sessions of Exposure in the Treatment of Flying Phobia," *Behavioral Research and Therapy* 35, no. 11 (1997): 987–96.

5. Angela W. Little, "Learning and Teaching in Multigrade Settings." *UNESCO EFA Monitoring Report,* 2005.

BIBLIOGRAPHY

AND

RECOMMENDATIONS FOR FURTHER READING

Chopra, Deepak. *The Spontaneous Fulfillment of Desire: Harnessing the Infinite Power of Coincidence.* New York: Harmony Books, 2003.

De Becker, Gavin. *The Gift of Fear: Survival Signs That Protect Us from Violence.* New York: Dell, 1997.

Dyer, Wayne W. *The Power of Intention.* Carlsbad: Hay House, 2004.

Fogle, Bruce. *The Dog's Mind.* New York: Macmillan, 1990.

Goleman, Daniel. *Emotional Intelligence: Why It Can Matter More Than IQ.* New York: Bantam Books, 1995.

Goleman, Daniel, Richard Boyatziz, and Annie McKee. *Primal Leadership: Learning to Lead with Emotional Intelligence.* Boston: Harvard Business School Press, 2002.

Hauser, Marc D. *Wild Minds: What Animals Really Think.* New York: Henry Holt, 2000.

Pease, Allan, and Barbara Pease. *The Definitive Book of Body Language.* New York: Bantam Dell, 2006.

ORGANIZATIONS
TO TURN TO

BATTERSEA DOGS HOME
Battersea Dogs and Cats Home
4 Battersea Park Rd
Battersea
London SW8 4AA
t: 020 7622 3626
f: 020 7622 6451

MISSING PETS BUREAU
Missing Pets Bureau
Freepost SEA999
Primrose Lane, Croydon,
Surrey CR9 8WZ
t: 0870 1 999 000 24hr Main Number
f: 0870 1 999 011

RSPCA
Enquiries service
RSPCA
Wilberforce Way

Southwater
Horsham
West Sussex
RH13 9RS
t: 0870 55 55 999 (24 hour national
cruelty and advice line)

BLUE CROSS HEAD OFFICE
Shilton Road
Burford
Oxon OX18 4PF
t: 01993 822651
f: 01993 823083
Email: info@bluecross.org.uk

DOGS TRUST
17 Wakely Street
London EC1V 7RQ
t: 020 7837 0006

Dogs Lost
PO BOX 227
WORKSHOP
NOTTS S81 8WU
t: 01909 733366
Email: admin@doglost.co.uk
www.doglost.co.uk

INTERNATIONAL ANIMAL RESCUE
Lime House
Regency Close
Uckfield
East Sussex TN22 1DS
General Enquiries
t: 01825 767 688
f: 01825 768 012
Email: info@iar.org.uk

Ireland
DOGS AID ANIMAL SANCTUARY
St Margaret's
Co Dublin
t: 003531 8347134
Email: dogsaid@eircom.net

Wales
ALL CREATURES GREAT AND SMALL
Church Farm
Llanfrechfa
Cwmbran
South Wales NP44 8AD
t: 01633 866144 (2–5pm)
Email: info@acgas.org.uk

Scotland
DAWGS (DOGS ACTION WORKING
GROUP SCOTLAND)
6 Whitemyres Holdings
Lang Stracht
Kingswell

Aberdeen AB15 6NB
t: 01224 208989
f: 01224 313877
Email: dawgsabdn@hotmail.com
www.dawgs.co.uk

SPCA
Animal Helpline
t: 0870 73 77722
www.scottishspca.org

Vets
PDSA (PEOPLE'S DISPENSARY FOR
SICK ANIMALS)
Head Office
Whitechapel Way
Priorslee
Telford
ShropshireTF2 9PQ
t: 01952 290999
f: 01952 291035

ROYAL COLLEGE OF VETERINARY
SURGEONS
Belgravia House
62–64 Horseferry Road
London SW1P 2AF
t: 0 207222 2001
f: 0 207222 2004
Email: admin@rcvs.org.uk

Trade Organizations
BRITISH INSTITUTE OF
PROFESSIONAL DOG TRAINERS
B.I.P.D.T
Bowstone Gate
Nr. Disley
Cheshire SK12 2AW
t: 01663 762 772
www.bipdt.net

ILLUSTRATION CREDITS

MPH Entertainment—Emery/Sumner Productions, Nicholas Ellingsworth: Cesar Rollerblading with his pack, p. iii; Cesar and Popeye, p. 1; Cesar with the Grogan family, p. 23; Wilshire at Firehouse 29, p. 43; Cesar and Booker, p. 75; with Charles, Sparky, and AJ at the Center, p. 239.

MPH Entertainment—Emery/Sumner Productions, Bill Parks: Tina Madden and NuNu, p. 40.

CMI, George Gomez: "The claw" hand position, p. 49; Labrador Rex wearing Illusion Collar (front and back), p. 93; all color-insert photographs.

MPH Entertainment—Emery/Sumner Productions: Wilshire on "his" treadmill, p. 59; Wilshire doing "stop, drop, and roll," p. 65; Center dogs with rattlesnake, p. 109; scared Genoa, p. 169.

Jen Hughes: Sid the bulldog on his 35-cent leash, p. 84.

MPH Entertainment—Emery/Sumner Productions, Todd Henderson: Calvin with choke chain, p. 309; Lila with prong collar, p. 101; Daddy, p. 121.

CMI, Christine Lochman: Illustration of three parts of a dog's neck, p. 93.

Missy Lemoi: Hope Lock Heirex, MH or "Hawkeye" retrieving a bumber, p. 134.

INDEX

Page numbers in *italic* refer to illustrations

Also by Cesar Millan with Melissa Jo Peltier

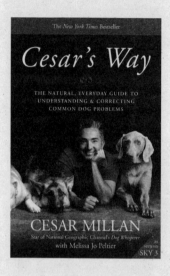

Now in paperback

Learn what goes on inside your dog's mind and develop a positive, fulfilling relationship with your best friend. In *Cesar's Way*, Cesar Millan helps you see the world through the eyes of your dog so you can finally eliminate problem behaviours.

£7.99 paperback

ISBN: 978 0 340 93330 5